# From Grids to Service and Pervasive Computing

T0181759

# From Grids to Service and Pervasive Computing

*Edited by*

Thierry Priol
*IRISA/INRIA*
*Rennes, France*

Marco Vanneschi
*University of Pisa*
*Pisa, Italy*

 Springer

*Editors:*
Thierry Priol
IRISA / INRIA Rennes
Campus de Beaulieu
35042 Rennes CX
France
thierry.priol@irisa.fr

Marco Vanneschi
Università di Pisa
Dipto. Informatica
Largo Bruno Pontecorvo,3
56127 Pisa, Italy
vannesch@di.unipi.it

ISBN-13: 978-1-4419-3481-9     e-ISBN-13: 978-0-387-09455-7

# Contents

# Foreword

The symposium was organised by the Network of Excellence CoreGRID funded by the European Commission under the sixth Framework Programme IST-2003-2.3.2.8 starting September 1st, 2004 for a duration of four years. CoreGRID aims at strengthening and advancing scientific and technological excellence in the area of Grid and Peer-to-Peer technologies. To achieve this objective, the network brings together a critical mass of well-established researchers (155 permanent researchers and 168 PhD students) from forty six institutions who have constructed an ambitious joint programme of activities.

The CoreGRID Symposium, organized jointly with the Euro-Par 2008 conference, aims at being the premiere European event on Grid Computing for the dissemination of the results from the European and member states initiatives, as well as other international projects in Grid research and technologies. The 2007 Symposium reported important research results about next generation Grids, P2P and other types of distributed technologies. The 2008 Symposium emphasizes the evolution of such technologies towards advanced solutions that favour the exploitation of Service and Pervasive Computing, in particular solutions for programming environments and application development frameworks, models for autonomic and self-organizing/managing components, complex resource management and scheduling strategies, SLA-based approaches, as well as performance and cost models for significant application fields.

The final programme has been organized into four sessions:

1. Component Programming
2. Resource Management and Scheduling
3. Service Level Agreement and Self-*
4. Grid Middleware

In the first session, the *component programming* paradigm is investigated from the viewpoints of both its semantics and its utilization in application development platforms. (Basso, Bolotov, Getov) propose a formal automata model for the specification of component-based Grid environments. (Ejdys,

Herman-Izycka, Lal, Kielmann, Tejedor, Badia) discuss how the Grid Component Model (GCM) of CoreGRID can be used to build mediator component-
based platforms. The autonomic features of the component paradigm are investigated in two papers: (Aldinucci, Tuosto) present a formal semantics to
model the dynamic evolution and non-functional issues, (Aldinucci, Danelutto,
Kilpatrick, Zoppi) introduce rule-based autonomic managers and apply such a
model to GCM-like skeletons, showing how this approach simplifies the design
of complex managers.

In the *Resource Management and Scheduling* session, the paper by (Nadeem,
Prodan, Fahringer) presents new metrics for resource availability comparison and an availability predictor based on pattern matching. (Tchernykh,
Schwiegelshohn, Yahyapour, Kuzjurin) address the non-preemptive on-line parallel job scheduling according to a two-stage model. (Röblitz) extends previous
works on multiple co-reservations scheduling by developing a mixed integer linear programming model. (Bustos-Jimenez, Caromel, Leyton, Piquer) deal with
the management of communication-intensive parallel applications and compare several load information sharing policies through experiments. The paper
by (Bertolli, Gabarro, Meneghin) presents a Markov model for predicting the
execution time of task parallel computation that adopt fault-tolerance Grid techniques.

In the third session, *SLA and self-\**, two papers deal with the exploitation of
SLA-based techniques in security related issues: (Naqvi, Mouton, Massonet,
Cosmin Silaghi, Battré, Hovestadt, Djemame) show how SLA-based information exchange can favour a sabotage-tolerant system design, while (Ziegler, Li,
Wäldrich) discuss SLA-based software licences and licence management, referring to two models developed in BEinGRID and SmartLM European projects.
Self management approaches to application development are investigated in the
papers by (Al-Shishtawy, Hoglund, Popov, Parlavantzas, Vlassov, Brand) and
by (Pasquali, Dazzi, Panciatici, Baraglia): the former presents a component-
based framework with self-management features, the latter proposes a design
pattern for self-optimizing classification systems and validates the proposal in
a complex application.

The *Grid Middleware* session comprises research results aiming at the definition and realization of Grid tools and/or frameworks. (Ostermann, Prodan, Fahringer, Iosup, Epema) present a method and a tool for analyzing
workflow-based workload traces from the Austrian Grid, identifying some performance features of typical workflow classes. (Chacin, León, Brunner, Freitag,
Navarro) present the Grid Market Middleware framework for the development
of market-based Grid systems. (Lucchese, Barbalace, Mastroianni, Orlando,
Talia) present a novel framework for the decomposition of a class of data mining
problems into independent task with intensive data-sharing. (Rycerz, Bubak,
Sloot) present a component-based framework for distributed multiscale simu-

lation according to the HLA approach, dealing with the problems of definition and setting of connections in a simulation federation.

The Programme Committee who made the selection of papers included:

Arenas, A., STFC-RAL, UK
Badia, R., Barcelona Supercomputing Center, Spain
Bal, H., Vrije Universiteit, Amsterdam, The Netherlands
Banâtre, J-P., University of Rennes 1 / INRIA, France
Bubak, M., Inst. of Comp. Sci. and Cyfronet, Poland
Corcho, O. University of Manchester, UK
Cunha, J., New University of Lisbon, Portugal
Danelutto, M., University of Pisa, Italy
Desprez, F., INRIA, France
Fahringer, T., University of Innsbruck, Austria
Fragopoulou, V., Forth, Greece
Getov, V., University of Westminster, UK
Gorlatch, S., University of Muenster, Germany
Guisset, P., CETIC, Belgium
Kacsuk, P., SZTAKI, Hungary
Kranzlmueller, D., Joh. Kepler University Linz, Austria
Laforenza, D., ISTI-CNR, Italy
Laure, E., CERN, Switzerland
Lee, C., The Aerospace Corp., USA
Lee, J., KISTI, Korea
Lengauer, C., University of Passau, Germany
Luque, E., UAB, Spain
Matyska, L., Masaryk University, Czech Republic
Meyer, N., Poznan Supercomputing Center, Poland
Moreau, L., Univ. of Southampton, UK
Pasin, M., Universidade Federal de Santa Maria, Brasil
Perez, C., IRISA/INRIA, France
Perrott, R., Queen's University of Belfast, UK
Piquer, J-M, University of Chile, Chile
Priol, T., IRISA/INRIA, France
Reinefeld, A., ZIB Berlin, Germany
Snelling, D., Fujitsu Laboratories of Europe, UK
Schwiegelshohn, U., University of Dortmund, Germany
Talia, D., Universita' della Calabria, Italy
Varvarigou, T., NTUA, Greece
Yahyapour, R., University of Dortmund, Germany
Ziegler, W., Fraunhofer-Institute for Algorithms and Scientific Computing, Germany

The Symposium Organising Committee included:

O. Vasselin, INRIA, Rennes, France
T. Priol, IRISA/INRIA, Rennes, France

All papers in this volume were additionally reviewed by the following external reviewers whose help we gratefully acknowledge:

Eduardo Argollo
Enric Tejedor
Jan Duennweber
Marek Wieczorek
Mikael Högqvist
Simon Ostermann
Thomas Roeblitz
Yvon Jégou

Special thanks are due to the authors of all submitted papers, the members of the Programme Committee and the Organising Committee, and to all reviewers, for their contribution to the success of this event.

Las Palmas de Gran Canaria, Spain, August 2008

> Dr. Thierry Priol and Prof. Marco Vanneschi (Symposium Chairs)

# Contributing Authors

**Ahmad Al-Shishtawy** Royal Institute of Technology, SE

**Marco Aldinucci** University of Pisa, IT

**Rosa M. Badia** Universitat Politècnica de Catalunya, ES

**Ranieri Baraglia** ISTI/CNR - Pisa , IT

**Alessandro Basso** University of Westminster, UK

**Dominic Battré** Technische Universität Berlin, DE

**Carlo Bertolli** University of Pisa, IT

**Alexander Bolotov** University of Westminster, UK

**Per Brand** Swedish Institute of Computer Science, SE

**Rene Brunner** Technical University of Catalonia, ES

**Marian Bubak** Institute of Computer Science, AGH, PL Academic Computer Centre - CYFRONET, PL

**Denis Caromel** INRIA, FR

**Pablo Chacin** Technical University of Catalonia, ES

**Gheorghe Cosmin Silaghi** Babes.-Bolyai University of Cluj-Napoca, RO

**Marco Danelutto** University of Pisa, IT

**Patrizio Dazzi** IMT (Lucca Institute for Advanced Studies), IT ISTI/CNR - Pisa, IT

**Karim Djemame** University of Leeds, UK

**Michal Ejdys** Vrije Universiteit, Amsterdam, NL

**Dick Epema** Delft University of Technology, NL

**Thomas Fahringer** University of Innsbruck, AT

**Felix Freitag** Technical University of Catalonia, ES

**Joaquim Gabarro** Universitat Politècnica de Catalunya,, ES

**Vladimir Getov** University of Westminster, UK

**Ula Herman-Izycka** Vrije Universiteit, Amsterdam, NL

**Matthias Hovestadt** Technische Universität Berlin, DE

**Joel Höglund** Swedish Institute of Computer Science (SICS), SE

**Alexandru Iosup** Delft University of Technology, NL

**Javier Bustos Jimenez** Universidad Diego Portales, CL

**Vincent Keller** Ecole Polytechnique Federale de Lausanne, LIN-STI, CH

**Thilo Kielmann** Vrije Universiteit, Amsterdam, NL

**Peter Kilpatrick** Queen's University Belfast, UK

**Nikolai Kuzjurin** Institute of System Programming RAS, RU

**Namita Lal** Vrije Universiteit, Amsterdam, NL

**Xavier Leon** Technical University of Catalonia, ES

**Mario Leyton** INRIA, FR

**Jiadao Li** Fraunhofer Institute SCAI, DE

**Philippe Massonet** Centre of Excellence in Information and Communication Technologies, BE

**Massimiliano Meneghin** University of Pisa, IT

**Stephane Mouton** Centre of Excellence in Information and Communication Technologies, BE

**Farrukh Nadeem** University of Innsbruck, AT

**Syed Naqvi** Centre of Excellence in Information and Communication Technologies, BE

**Leandro Navarro** Technical University of Catalonia, ES

**Simon Ostermann** University of Innsbruck, AT

**Antonio Panciatici** Engineering PhD School "Leonardo da Vinci" - Pisa, IT

**Nikos Parlavantzas** INRIA, FR

**Marco Pasquali** IMT (Lucca Institute for Advanced Studies), IT ISTI/CNR - Pisa, IT

**Jose Miguel Piquer** Universidad de Chile, CL

**Konstantin Popov** Swedish Institute of Computer Science, SE

**Radu Prodan** University of Innsbruck, AT

**Katarzyna Rycerz** Institute of Computer Science, AGH, PL

**Thomas Röblitz** Zuse Institute Berlin, DE

**Uwe Schwiegelshohn** Technische Universität Dortmund, DE

**Peter M.A. Sloot** University of Amsterdam, NL

**Andrei Tchernykh** CICESE Research Center, MX

**Enric Tejedor** Univ. Politècnica de Catalunya, ES

**Emilio Tuosto** University of Leicester, UK

**Vladimir Vlassov** Royal Institute of Technology, SE

**Oliver Wäldrich** Fraunhofer Institute SCAI, DE

**Ramin Yahyapour** Technische Universitäat Dortmund, DE

**Wolfgang Ziegler** Fraunhofer Institute SCAI, DE

**Giorgio Zoppi** University of Pisa, IT

I

# COMPONENT PROGRAMMING

# ADVANCES IN AUTONOMIC COMPONENTS & SERVICES*

Marco Aldinucci, Marco Danelutto, Giorgio Zoppi
*Dept. Computer Science – Univ. Pisa*
{aldinuc,marcod,zoppi}@di.unipi.it


Peter Kilpatrick
*Dept. Computer Science – Queen's Univ. Belfast*
p.kilpatrick@qub.ac.uk

**Abstract**     Hierarchical autonomic management of structured grid applications can be efficiently implemented using production rule engines. Rules of the form "precondition → action" can be used to model the behaviour of autonomic managers in such a way that the autonomic control and the application management strategy are kept separate. This simplifies the manager design as well as user customization of autonomic manager policies.

We briefly introduce rule-based autonomic managers. Then we discuss an implementation of a GCM-like behavioural skeleton – a composite component modelling a standard parallelism exploitation pattern with its own autonomic controller – in SCA/Tuscany. The implementation uses the JBoss rules engine to provide an autonomic behavioural skeleton component and services to expose the component functionality to the standard service framework. Performance results are discussed and finally similarities and differences with respect to the ProActive-based reference GCM implementation are discussed briefly.

**Keywords:**     Behavioural skeletons, autonomic computing, Service Component Architecture, task farm.

*This research is carried out under the FP6 Network of Excellence CoreGRID and the FP6 GridCOMP project funded by the European Commission (Contract IST-2002-004265 and FP6-034442).

## 1.    Introduction

Autonomic management is increasingly attracting attention as a means of handling the non-functional aspects of grid applications. Several research groups are investigating various ways to associate adaptive behaviour with distributed/grid programs [15, 19, 10, 18, 9].

Within the CoreGRID Programming Model Institute a component based grid programming model is being developed (the Grid Component Model, GCM) [12] which introduces the possibility of associating autonomic managers with grid application components. GCM allows hierarchical composition of components. This means that composite components can be perceived by the users as normal, primitive components. Thus GCM system designers can capitalize on composition to provide grid application programmers with composite components that encapsulate common Grid programming patterns such as pipes, farms, etc. [13]. Then, application programmers can simply use appropriately parameterized instances of these composite components to implement complete, efficient grid applications that exploit these patterns or nested arrangements of them.

Autonomic managers have been introduced into GCM to take care of performance concerns of composite components without requiring explicit/significant application programmer involvement [12]. The combination of well-known grid/distributed programming patterns together with an autonomic manager taking care of the pattern performance is represented by the concept of a *behavioural skeleton* [4–5].

Autonomic management of typical grid programming patterns is a complex activity *per se*. It requires the ability to monitor composite pattern execution, suitable policies capable of handling "irregular" executions as perceived via the monitoring activity and, last but not least, suitable mechanisms to implement the corrective actions described within the policies and triggered in response to monitoring of irregular execution activity.

Further complexity arises when the autonomic manager activities are not considered in isolation but as a part of more global autonomic management activities as happens when composite patterns are nested to model increasingly complex grid applications. In this latter case, complex autonomic management policies and strategies have to be identified that allow combination of the actions performed by the single autonomic managers in the application in such a way as to implement a more general, application-wide autonomic strategy.

In this work we build on previous work concerning behavioural skeletons and hierarchical autonomic management in grid applications [6] and we define a general principle that allows combination of autonomic behaviour of different, nested behavioural skeletons in a single grid application (Sec. 2). Then we discuss a prototype implementation *de facto* demonstrating the feasibility of the approach. The prototype implementation is built on top of the Tuscany/SCA (Service Component Architecture) [8] infrastructure rather than on top of the existing reference implementation of GCM under development within the Grid-COMP STREP project (Sec. 3). Finally, we outline how the whole methodology based on autonomic management within behavioural skeletons can be exported to plain service users. The result is a seamless integration of GCM behavioural skeleton concepts into the SOA/WS framework (Sec. 4).

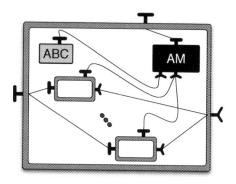

**Figure 1:** Sample behavioural skeleton structure.

## 2. Autonomic management using rules

We introduced autonomic managers enforcing user provided performance contracts within a single behavioural skeleton in [4–5]. The performance contracts enforced by behavioural skeletons currently include only service time (basically the inverse of throughput) and constant parallelism degree (i.e. the ability to keep constant the number of resources used to implement the application, in the presence of (temporary or permanent) resource faults).

In this section we discuss *hierarchical* management of grid applications. In particular, we make the assumptions used in [6] to discuss autonomic management of grid applications, that is:

- We assume that grid applications are developed using GCM components.

- We assume that behavioural skeletons modelling common parallel patterns are available. A behavioural skeleton is a parametric composite component modelling a commonly useful, efficient parallel grid pattern under the control of an internal autonomic manager responsible for guaranteeing a user-provided performance contract. Figure 1 outlines the structure of a behavioural skeleton. In the behavioural skeleton ABC is the *Autonomic Behavioural Controller*, the passive component responsible for providing probes for inspecting the status of a behavioural skeleton and mechanisms to implement autonomic actions. AM is the *Autonomic Manager*, the active component responsible for behavioural skeleton autonomic management (see [5] for a fuller description of both ABC and AM in behavioural skeletons). The inner components are the ones managed by the behavioural skeleton, in this case according to a functional replication/data parallel pattern.

- We assume that behavioural skeletons may be arbitrarily nested and therefore that a grid application can be abstracted as a skeleton tree. Each node in the tree is labelled with the pattern represented by the corresponding behavioural skeleton and each node has a number of descendant nodes representing the functional parameters of the behavioural skeleton.

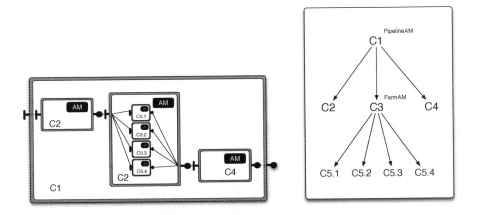

**Figure 2:** Sample application structure: component view (left) and skeleton view (right)

As an example, Fig. 2 depicts a grid application built as a three-stage pipeline. The first stage pre-processes the input and the last post-processes the results. The inner stage takes as input the output of the first stage and computes its result *in parallel* as the programmer recognizes that this is a highly demanding computation.

Autonomic managers in the behavioural skeleton components of the application enforce a performance contract that can either be provided by the user or agreed to by interacting AMs without any user intervention. For instance, in the sample application of Fig. 2 the contract of C1, the top level pipeline behavioural skeleton, is provided by the user, while the contracts of C2, C3 and C4 are derived from the contract of C1 and sent to the corresponding managers by the manager of C1.

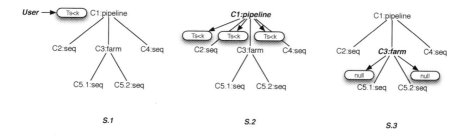

**Figure 3:** Contract propagation

We summarize the autonomic contract management activities in our nested behavioural skeleton context by the following abstract perspective, which was partially developed in [6].

## 2.1 Abstract perspective

The application is represented by means of a skeleton tree, such as the one of Fig. 2 right. The top level contract is provided by the application user, using the appropriate non-functional interfaces/ports. Contracts of managers in inner nodes come from parent nodes. The *propagation* of contracts from root to leaves happens either at compile time or at run time, depending on when the user provides the top level contract. In general, this is a non-trivial process. Sub-contracts for the inner component managers can be determined from the contract of the top level component manager only due to the fact that we are considering behavioural *skeletons*, that is, we are limiting the form of parallelism exploited within the top level component to a well known pattern. Figure 3 shows how a pipeline manager propagates contracts to the inner stage managers (steps S.1 and S.2). In this case, the same contract of the pipeline manager is passed to the stage managers, as pipeline service time is given by the maximum of the stage component service times ($T_{Spipeline} = max\{T_{Sstage_1}, \ldots, T_{Sstage_n}\}$). In the case of task farms, contract propagation is quite different. Farm service time is given by the aggregate service time of the inner worker components. In particular, in a farm with $n_w$ workers, the service time can be approximated as $T_{Sfarm} = (\sum_{i=1}^{n_w} T_{Sworker_i})/n_w{}^2$. Therefore a farm manager propagates to the worker components a null contract, basically stating worker components should do their best to exploit the available resources and then the farm manager will take care of ensuring the farm contract by varying the number of inner worker components (see Fig. 3, step S.3).

Once the application has been started, and the contracts have been propagated to the inner managers, the autonomic managers in the nodes determine whether the current contract is satisfied and, if it is not, they start an autonomic corrective action aimed at enforcing once again contract satisfaction. In this abstract perspective, verification of a contract basically requires three steps.

***Step 1*** The inner component autonomic managers are queried and the status of their contracts is obtained. Each inner manager provides both a boolean value (contract satisfied or not satisfied) together with a set of parameters concerning its monitoring status (e.g. the measures used to evaluate the contract, as provided by the component ABC). In this phase, the top level manager behaves as a master with respect to the slave inner components in the context of a *monitor* activity.

***Step 2*** The contract of the behavioural skeleton is evaluated making use of the values given by the inner managers (*monitor*). These values are periodically used to instantiate variables in the terms of a formula that represent the QoS contract (currently a first order logic formula). If the formula evaluates to `false` the contract is considered broken; otherwise it is considered satisfied.

***Step 3*** If the local contract is no longer satisfied, either a local action is taken aimed at reestablishing the existing contract or a failure is reported to the manager of the parent behavioural skeleton in the skeleton tree. The execution of a local action may involve distribution of new contracts to the inner components, as well as changing the current configuration of the behavioural skeleton component. The choice between performing local actions and reporting failure is driven by the *rules* embedded in the manager. These rules represent the AM knowledge base. Each rule is composed of a *precondition* (if satisfied the rule can be used), an *action* (if the rule is used the action states what steps have to be performed), a *cost* (the overhead incurred if the rule is applied) and finally an *expected benefit* (the benefit, in terms of the contract, that the AM can expect following rule application) [6].

The rules considered in the Step 3 above are related to the performance contract formulas. If the contract is violated, the formula representing the contract itself can be *analysed* to derive (one or more) assignments of the variables that may satisfy the formula and therefore the contract. Only variables that are likely to be altered due to a reconfiguration *plan* are considered in this process, and the plans suitably altering these variable values are considered for execution. The execution of a reconfiguration plan by a manager may consist in changing the assembly of inner components (e.g. adding a replica of a component) and/or enforcing a new contract on some inner component (via its manager). This corresponds to the inclusion in the AM knowledge base of a rule that has as a precondition the formula modelling plan feasibility and as an action the plan itself.

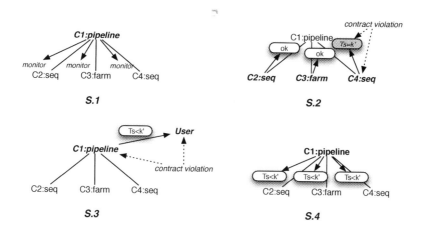

**Figure 4:** Sample inter-manager interactions: scenario 1

In the event that no plan is likely to induce the satisfaction of the formula at some point in the future, a broken contact event has to be propagated to the parent manager (to the user, if the top level AM is considered). This corresponds to the inclusion in the AM knowledge base of a (lowest priority) rule that has no precondition and has as action the report of the contract violation to the upper level manager.

Notice that in the general case the co-ordination of management plans is a difficult activity for several reasons. On the one hand, the satisfaction of a contract cannot be always guaranteed by the satisfaction of all the contracts of the inner components (for example, the interaction among components is usually not captured by any of the inner contracts in isolation, and the expected effect of reconfiguration plans is a forecast and its precision may be very coarse). On the other hand, starting from a contract it is not always easy to split it into sub-contracts (to be propagated to the inner components) in such a way that satisfaction of sub-contracts is likely to satisfy the contract (in this regard we are currently investigating an alternative logic that may easily support the projection of contract formulas into sub-contract formulas [7]). The proposed approach aims to ameliorate both problems via the behavioural skeleton concept since in these parametric components the general structure of contracts (formulas and plans) is pre-defined (up to parameterization).

## 2.2    Managers at work: sample scenarios

To illustrate how the whole process above works, consider again the application of Fig. 2 and let us assume that the user has provided a service time contract stating that service time should be less that $k$ msecs ($T_{S_{application}} =$

$T_{Spipeline} < k$) and that contract propagation has already been performed as shown in Fig. 3. Figures 4 and 5 illustrate some typical contract management scenarios within related autonomic managers.

In the first scenario (Fig. 4) the pipeline manager requests from the inner components the status of their contracts (this is the Step 1 in the abstract view above, *S.1* in the figure) and receives back two "contract satisfied" and one "contract violation" responses (*S.2*). The contract violation ($T_S = k'$ with $k' > k$) is raised by a sequential component manager (the manager of C4) that has no way to improve the performance (service time) of the controlled component. The pipeline manager has no means to ensure the user supplied contract and therefore reports a contract violation to the user console (*S.3*). If some "best effort" behaviour is requested by default, the pipeline manager may propagate a new, less strict contract ($T_S < k'$) to the inner stages, which possibly results in the release of resources previously required by the inner stages running with $T_S < k$.

In the second scenario (Fig. 5) the farm manager has a $T_S < k$ contract and requests contract values (service times) from the inner worker components (*S.1*). It receives two values that together make its contract false ($T_S = (T_S' + T_S'')/4 > k$ (*S.2*)). A rule with precondition $T_{Smonitored} > T_{Scontract}$ and action "add a fresh worker component instance" is applied (*S.3*). After the time needed to implement the rule (as estimated by the farm manager), the contracts of the inner components are monitored again (*S.4, S.5*) and this time the contract turns out to be satisfied (*S.6*).

## 3.    Prototype rule based autonomic management

A reference implementation of GCM is being developed on top of ProActive middleware [17] in the framework of the GridCOMP project [16]. Here, behavioural skeletons and autonomic managers within behavioural skeletons are implemented as described above. To date, however, the reference implementation of GCM does not explicitly use rules as described in Sec. 2. Rather, plain Java code is used within the manager to implement the rule concept. This was mainly due to implementation issues and the incremental nature of the design and implementation of the behavioural skeleton concept.

Recently, we implemented a single behavioural skeleton (one modelling the embarrassingly parallel computation pattern) on top of the Tuscany [3] SCA framework [1]. We wished to implement the behavioural skeleton concept as conceived in GCM without the restrictions and constraints of the ProActive-based reference implementation. At the same time, we wished to export GCM concepts to the service world and investigate the feasibility of implementing them on top of services. Tuscany looked like a viable proposition, being an open source component platform using state of the art, service based mechanisms.

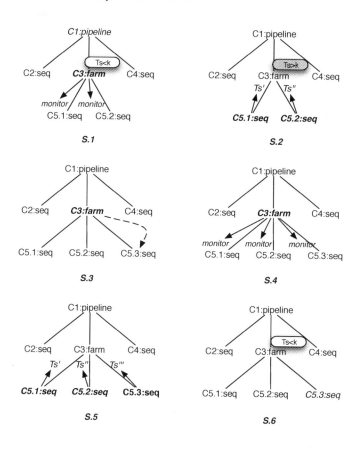

**Figure 5:** Sample inter-manager interactions: scenario 2

The general design of the SCA implementation of the GCM task farm behavioural skeleton was introduced in [20, 14]; in the current work we address in more detail the implementation of the rule-based autonomic manager. SCA allows programmers to make use of the component concept in the service framework. SCA components are perceived as plain services from the user viewpoint. We therefore developed an SCA service (the *WorkPoolService*) implementing a task farm behavioural skeleton according to the GCM specification as introduced in Sec. 2. The Workpool Service is outlined in Fig. 8. Two basic sets of services are provided: to submit tasks to be computed (this is the service functional interface, WorkpoolService in the figure) and to interact with the *WorkpoolService* manager (this is the non-functional one, WorkpoolManagerService in the figure).

The autonomic manager (*WorkpoolManager Component*) uses JBoss Rules, a "framework that provides an open source and standards-based business rules

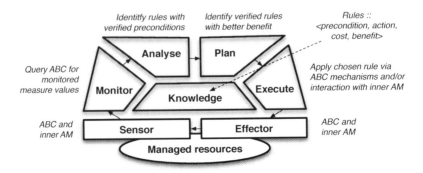

**Figure 6:** Autonomic cycle revisited

engine and business rules management system (BRMS) for easy business policy access, change, and management" [2]. The JBoss engine supports dynamic addition and removal of rules. The Drools Rule Language (DRL) implemented in JBoss uses Java to express field constraints, functions, and consequences in rules. In particular, Java beans are used to implement the getter methods needed to access variable values and the methods implementing functions (actions) used in the rules. A JBoss rule can be defined as a rule having a name, a condition enabling its application and an action to be taken if that condition holds. An example of a JBoss rule is the following:

```
rule "AdaptUsageFactor"
    when    $workerBean:WorkpoolBean(serviceTime > 0.25)
    then    $workerBean.addWorkerToLeastUsedNode();
end
```

The rule named "AdaptUsageFactor" can be used when the condition stating that the managed component `serviceTime` is more than 0.25 holds and, in this case, an `addWorkerToLeastUsedNode` is performed.

JBoss rules rely on the existence of a Java Bean (the one referenced by `$workerBean` in the example) to access the required values (e.g. the `service Time` instance variable of the bean) and `then` to implement the rule action (e.g. to invoke the `addWorkerToLeastUsedNode()` method on the same bean). To retain the possibility of using fully-fledged JBoss rules, we implemented the `WorkpoolManager` component in such a way that it uses an internal bean to support JBoss rules. The bean instance fields are set up periodically through the bean setter methods by the `WorkpoolManager`. In turn, the `WorkpoolManager` retrieves the relevant data through the methods exposed via the `WorkpoolService` interface. With respect to the GCM model (as outlined in Fig. 1), these methods (services) correspond to the non-functional, passive interface implemented by the ABC controller.

Our *WorkpoolManager Component* runs the JBoss rule engine. The rules (such as the one given above) constitute the manager knowledge base (see Fig. 6) and can be dynamically configured (added, deleted) through the `Workpool ManagerService` non-functional interface. For example, rules in component C3 of Fig 2 will be initially configured to include the sample rule shown above if the user contract requires from C1 a service time of at most 0.25 secs. If the C1 manager, while testing for contract integrity, discovers that the service time provided by the task farm is higher than both $T_{s_1}$ and $T_{s_3}$ (the service times of C1 and C3, respectively) it should interact with the C2 manager and send it a new `AdaptUsageFactor` differing only in the when clause

`when $workerBean:WorkpoolBean(serviceTime > max(TS1,TS2))`

that will eventually substitute the old `AdaptUsageFactor` rule.

To date we have experimented only with the SCA behavioural skeleton implementation alone (i.e. not in a behavioural skeleton nesting). However, the mechanism discussed above enables manager interaction via the submission of new contracts, in the form of rules. Submission of new rules can take place either during `Workpool` startup, to implement the initial propagation of the user-supplied top level contract, or at run time, during autonomic management actions reconfiguring the inner components of the behavioural skeleton. The mechanism has been proven effective by running a set of experiments that separately measured the scalability of the Tuscany/SCA task farm behavioural skeleton, and the overhead introduced by a typical, single reconfiguration enacted by its autonomic manager. We measured scalability of synthetic applications with variable computational grain. The computational grain $g = T_{seq}/T_{comm\_in\_out}$ is the ratio of the time spent to compute a task on the remote resource ($T_{seq}$), to the time spent to deliver the input data to the remote node plus the time spent to retrieve the results from the remote node ($T_{comm\_in\_out}$). The definition of scalability, $S(n)$, is the classical one: $S(n) = T(1)/T(n)$, where $T(n)$ represents the completion time of the application run with parallelism degree equal to $n$. Typical results are shown in Fig. 7 (left). Considering the high overhead in serializing (deserializing) service parameters with SOAP XML (we used no optimization), this represents a fairly good result.

Concerning the overhead related to reconfiguration of the behavioural skeleton, we measured the time spent in computing a set of 1K tasks, including a forced reconfiguration that doubled the number of farm workers ($4 \rightarrow 8$) when a given number of tasks had already been computed. The results are shown in Fig. 7 (right). The Exp1 (Exp2) line refers to an experiment where the workers were doubled after half (quarter) of the tasks were computed. In both cases the overhead involved is negligible, considering it includes both the time spent to activate (upon a timer) the JBoss rule engine and the time spent to perform the "add worker" rule four times.

| | 4 PE | 8 PE | 16 PE |
|---|---|---|---|
| *g = 10* | 0.96 | 0.89 | 0.6 |
| *g = 24* | 0.98 | 0.97 | 0.77 |
| *g = 40* | 0.99 | 0.97 | 0.87 |

| | Measured | Estimated | ε |
|---|---|---|---|
| *Exp 1* | 255.07 s | 252.07 s | 0.99 |
| *Exp 2* | 217.33 s | 209.76 s | 0.97 |

**Figure 7:** Scalability (left) and reconfiguration (right) efficiency results.

## 4.    Behavioural skeletons in SCA and interoperability

As stated at the beginning of Sec. 3, our implementation of GCM behavioural skeletons on top of SCA was also aimed at demonstrating the suitability of SCA to support GCM concepts and the interoperability we were able to achieve with the wider (i.e. beyond the GCM and grid community) service world.

SCA offers most of the mechanisms needed to implement a GCM behavioural skeleton. One facility missing is the means to change composite component assemblies at run time via XML composite component descriptors. For instance, when a new worker component has to be added to the `WorkpoolService`, we cannot simply produce a new composite descriptor to tell the framework the composite assembly has changed. Consequently, we implemented a component to deal with this kind of assembly change. The component provides means to instantiate a new (worker) component and to create the appropriate `connections` as defined by the schema of Fig. 8. The component uses the Tuscany API which, in turn, provides the mechanisms required to support new component integration with (as well as old component removal from) a component assembly. The SCA implementation of the task farm behavioural skeleton directly mirrors the GCM/ProActive implementation. The GCM/ProActive ABC is implemented via operations exported by the `Workpool` Service and the AM is implemented by the SCA component `WorkpoolManager` Service. All the components in Fig. 8 (the `WorkpoolService`, the `WorkpoolManager`, the `WorkerManagerNode` and the `WorkerService`) are exposed as services. They can be accessed through the automatically generated WSDL as plain services and, more importantly, they can be re-used to implement different behavioural skeletons in exactly the same way that the ABC and AM components may be re-used within the GCM/ProActive framework to implement other behavioural skeletons.

The overall design of the Workpool service (and of the associated support mechanisms) has been judged interesting by the Tuscany developers and our code has been included in the SCA `svn` as a Tuscany sample application.

Concerning interoperability, we verified that accessing a behavioural skeleton is as easy as accessing any other type of service on the network, as expected.

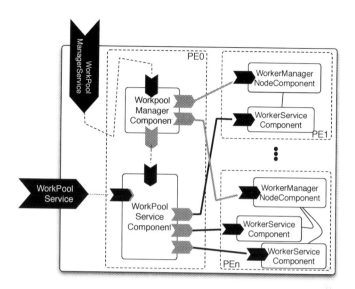

**Figure 8:** Workpool Service structure

Fig. 9 sketches the code needed to submit tasks to the WorkpoolService behavioural skeleton. The first part of the code (on the left) is that needed to set up a reference to the service (args[0] is the url of the service WSDL file). Here a service that will be invoked to post-process the results produced is passed to the WorkpoolService. The second part of the code (on the right) is that needed to submit the single task (in a Job) to the WorkpoolService. This code is of the same form as that required to access any other type of service from a Java program. Normal service application programmers require no additional effort to benefit from the advanced management supported in the WorkpoolService. Thus our implementation satisfies the requirement to *propagate the concept with minimal disruption* as stated by Murray Cole in his skeleton "manifesto" [11]. Service users may have the benefit of a fully-fledged autonomic implementation of embarrassingly parallel computations within a single service incorporating the best of the relevant GCM methodology and concepts.

## 5. Conclusions

We introduced rule-based autonomic management techniques for structured grid applications implemented using GCM Behavioural Skeletons. The general mechanism of rule exploitation for performance contract monitoring together with a significant sample case have been discussed. We then described a prototype implementation in SCA/Tuscany. We presented preliminary experimental results demonstrating the feasibility of the approach as well as the portability

```
...
// creates the workpool service stub
WorkpoolServiceStub wstub =
    new WorkpoolServiceStub(workpoolServiceWSDLuri);
// sets up services processing the results computed
WorkpoolServiceStub.AddTrigger sink = new
    WorkpoolServiceStub.AddTrigger();
WorkpoolServiceStub.CallableReferenceImpl callableReference =
    new WorkpoolServiceStub.CallableReferenceImpl();
WorkpoolServiceStub.EndpointReference endpoint =
    new WorkpoolServiceStub.EndpointReference();
endpoint.setURI(resultPostProcessServiceURI);
callableReference.setEndpointReference(endpoint);
sink.setParam0(callableReference);
wstub.addTrigger(sink);
// create a Job
MyJob j = new MyJob();
// set up serialization stuff
Serializer s = new Serializer();
OMElement element = s.serialize(j);
// create a submit request
WorkpoolServiceStub.Submit submit= new
    WorkpoolServiceStub.Submit();
// create the task
WorkpoolServiceStub.Job task= new
    WorkpoolServiceStub.Job();
// set up task and submit
task.setData(element);
submit.setParam0(task);
wstub.submit(submit)
...
```

**Figure 9:** Sample client code for the WorkpoolService

of GCM autonomic management aspects into the Service framework. The prototype implementation makes available a GCM task farm behavioural skeleton to service application programmers and thus helps broaden the applicability of CoreGRID results. As the intended target audience of the prototype is the service community, this also makes a bridge between the component and service worlds. The design of the prototype, fully exploiting component technology, allows reuse of its different parts to implement different behavioural skeletons. We are currently integrating the rule based implementation of behavioural skeletons into the GCM reference implementation being developed on top of ProActive in the GridCOMP project.

## References

[1] Service component architecture, 2007. http://www.ibm.com/developerworks/library/specification/ws-sca/.

[2] Jboss rules home page, 2008. http://www.jboss.com/products/rules.

[3] Tuscany home page, 2008. http://incubator.apache.org/tuscany/.

[4] M. Aldinucci, S. Campa, M. Danelutto, P. Dazzi, P. Kilpatrick, D. Laforenza, and N. Tonellotto. Behavioural skeletons for component autonomic management on grids. In *CoreGRID Workshop on Grid Programming Model, Grid and P2P Systems Architecture, Grid Systems, Tools and Environments*, Heraklion, Crete, Greece, June 2007.

[5] M. Aldinucci, S. Campa, M. Danelutto, M. Vanneschi, P. Dazzi, D. Laforenza, N. Tonellotto, and P. Kilpatrick. Behavioural skeletons in GCM: autonomic management of grid components. In *Proc. of Intl. Euromicro PDP 2008: Parallel Distributed and network-based Processing*, Toulouse, France, pages 54-63, Feb. 2008. IEEE.

[6] M. Aldinucci, M. Danelutto, and P. Kilpatrick. Towards hierarchical management of autonomic components: a case study. Technical Report TR-0127, CoreGRID, 2008. Available at http://www.coregrid.net/mambo/images/stories/TechnicalReports/tr-0127.pdf.

[7] S. Bistarelli, U. Montanari, F. Rossi, Semiring-Based Constraint Logic Programming: Syntax and Semantics, ACM TOPLAS, Vol. 23, 2001

[8] M. Beisiegel, H. Blohm, D. Booz *et al.* Service Component Architecture Building Systems using a Service Oriented Architecture, A Joint Whitepaper by BEA, IBM, Interface21, IONA, Oracle, SAP, Siebel, Sybase. 2000, available at http://www.iona.com/devcenter/sca/SCA_White_Paper1_09.pdf

[9] P. Boinot, R. Marlet, J. Noyé, G. Muller, and C. Cosell. A declarative approach for designing and developing adaptive components. In *Proc. of the 15th Intl. Conference on Automated Software Engineering*, pages 111–119. IEEE, 2000.

[10] J. Buisson, F. André, and J.-L. Pazat. Afpac: Enforcing consistency during the adaptation of a parallel component. *Scalable Computing: Practice and Experience*, 7(3):83–95, 2006

[11] M. Cole. Bringing skeletons out of the closet: A pragmatic manifesto for skeletal parallel programming. *Parallel Computing*, 30(3):389–406, 2004.

[12] CoreGRID NoE deliverable series, Prog. Model Institute. *D.PM.04 – Basic Features of the Grid Component Model (assessed)*, Feb. 2007. http://www.coregrid.net/mambo/images/stories/Deliverables/d.pm.04.pdf.

[13] CoreGRID NoE deliverable series, Prog. Model Institute. *D.PM.11 – GCM experience: inside the single component and beyond components*, Feb. 2008. http://www.coregrid.net/mambo/content/view/428/292/.

[14] M. Danelutto and G. Zoppi. Behavioural skeletons meeting Services. In *Proceedings of PAPP'08*. Springer Verlag, LNCS No. 5101, pages 146–153, June 2008. Krakow, Poland.

[15] H. González-Vélez. Self-adaptive skeletal task farm for computational grids. *Parallel Comput.*, 32(7):479–490, 2006.

[16] GridCOMP. GridCOMP web page, 2007. http://gridcomp.ercim.org.

[17] ProActive home page, 2006. http://www-sop.inria.fr/oasis/proactive/.

[18] S. S. Vadhiyar and J. J. Dongarra. Self adaptivity in grid computing: Research articles. *Concurr. Comput. : Pract. Exper.*, 17(2-4):235–257, 2005.

[19] G. Wrzesinska, J. Maassen, and H. E. Bal. Self-adaptive applications on the grid. In *PPoPP '07: Proceedings of the 12th ACM SIGPLAN symposium on Principles and practice of parallel programming*, pages 121–129, New York, NY, USA, 2007. ACM.

[20] G. Zoppi. Componenti Avanzati GCM/SCA, 2008. Dept. Computer Science, Univ. of Pisa. 2nd level graduation thesis, in Italian. http://etd.adm.unipi.it/theses/available/etd-01302008-103715/

# BEHAVIOURAL MODEL OF COMPONENT-BASED GRID ENVIRONMENTS

Alessandro Basso, Alexander Bolotov, Vladimir Getov
*Harrow School of Computer Science*
*University of Westminster*
*Watford Road, Northwick Park*
*Harrow HA1 3TP, London, U.K.*

[bassoa.bolotoa,v.s.getov]@wmin.ac.uk

**Abstract**    In component-based Grid environments, we analyse the problem of formal specification of their behaviour by introducing an automata-based model. We show how to construct this new framework from the analysis of states of components and how to apply it to a reconfiguration scenario in a dynamic distributed system environment. We aim at building a framework for future integration of these developments in a software tool for runtime automated specification and verification, ensuring a reliable dynamically reconfigurable component model.

**Keywords:**    GCM, Grid IDE, Reconfiguration, Temporal Deontic Specification, Dynamic Verification.

# 1.    Introduction

Component models enable modular design of software applications that can be easily reused and combined, ensuring greater reliability. This is important in distributed systems where asynchronous components must be taken into consideration, especially when there is need for reliable dynamic reconfiguration. In these models, components interact together by being bound through interfaces, however, there is a further need for a method which ensures correct composition and behaviour of components and their interaction with the environment.

Fractal [9] is a modular and extensible component model. The Fractal specification defines the Life Cycle controller interface as [8]: "A component interface to control the lifecycle of the component to which it belongs. The lifecycle of a component is supposed to be an automaton, whose states represent execution states of the component. This interface corresponds to an automaton with two states called **STARTED** and **STOPPED**, where all the four possible transitions are allowed. It is however possible to define completely different lifecycle controller Java interfaces to use completely different automatons, or to define sub interfaces of this interface to define automatons based on this one, but with more states and more transitions. A great number of component models in fact consider by default a number of substates to the most generic STARTED state, allowing for a deeper introspection on the behaviour of states of components (initialized, suspended, failed...).

The Grid Component model (GCM) [13] is an extension of Fractal built to accommodate requirements in distributed systems, in particular, those developed within and following the CoreGRID [12] project. The GCM specification defines a set of notions characterising this model, an API (Application Program Interface), and an ADL (Architecture Description Language) [4]. In Fractal, when changing the bindings of a component, this component must be stopped (in other words, to avoid disruption to the system, when unplugging a component, such component must be stopped before severing its connections to other components); at the same time, invocation on controller interfaces must be enabled when a component is stopped (in order to send the stop signal to the component), making de facto impossible to reconfigure the component controller. In GCM section 8.1 of [13], the life-cycle controller is extended allowing to separate partially the life-cycle states of the controller and of the content. When a component is functionally stopped (which corresponds to the stopped state of the Fractal specification), invocation on controller interfaces are enabled and the content of the component can be reconfigured. When a component is stopped, only the controllers necessary for configuration are still active (mainly binding, content, and lifecycle controllers), and the other components in the membrane can be reconfigured. We can make use of this extended capabilities and monitor the changes in states of components.

The recent development of a Grid Integrated Development Environment (GIDE) based on the GCM specification [3] opens new possibilities for the dynamic reconfiguration scenario in large distributed systems. We are able to take advantage of pre-built components in the GIDE (namely the component's hierarchical composition, their API, and the monitoring of both components and resources) to form a basis for a reconfiguration framework which exploits the underlying properties of the specification language and deductive reasoning verification methods used in our research. We consider the monitoring specification of [10] and the state information that can be retrieved through calls to the LifeCycleController interface (getFcState operation) for components, as well as other monitoring techniques for the environment.

The rest of this paper is organised as follows. In §2 we give some basic information on behaviour of stateful components/resources (§2.1), analyze the limitations of ADLs (§2.2) and the environment monitoring techniques which we utilize (§2.3). Further, in §3 we introduce the automaton model used for formal specification, detailing the component level automata in (§3.1) and the environment level one in (§3.2). In (§4.1) we outline the Specification process and its usage for reconfiguration purposes is introduced in (§4.2). Finally, we give some concluding remarks and identify future work in §5.

## 2. Background

## 2.1 Behaviour of stateful components/resources

The basic lifecycle of components, and thus the resources being managed, can be retrieved at runtime by the use of the Component Monitoring and Resources Monitoring systems, built in the GIDE, through: components state calls (implemented by all component objects), specialised parameters monitoring for some specific components, resources availability monitors and others. This state system is often restricted, in that it supports the deployment processes used by the framework and models only the deployment state of the system, not its operational characteristics. Each deployment component independently represents the state of the deployed resource which it is managing. The system as a whole must also represent a reasonable depiction of the overall state of many components. The core lifecycle is defined by the states, allowed transitions and operations shown in Figure 1.

As a component is such that it conforms to a set of defined states, and to the GCM, we can therefore consider composite components as components that inherit the same properties and conform to state composition. The analysis of the components' instances becomes now crucial. When a component is in the **instance** state, this component (and all its requirements) will be deployed to the appropriate system, and any operations will be performed that are part of the components instantiation process. This state also presumes that whatever

**Figure 1:** Component's Lifecycle States

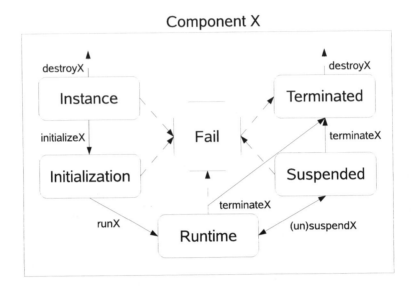

activation is required in order for the resource handler of the component to be valid has been performed (we will leave the detailed requirements for the resource monitoring system after more research into the effect of distributed properties at resource level). As shown in the diagram, the *initialize* and *destroy* state change commands are supported in this state. The component will then move to **initialization**, where it will wait until a call is made to run; passing on to the **runtime** state, which indicates that the services provided by the resources that are being deployed are available for use. This state does not indicate any information regarding the operational capabilities of the service, only that it has completed initialization and not failed. At any time, state actions may not complete correctly or the service itself may fail. In response to these failures, the component will transition to the **fail** state. The component may remain active in the system, but its managed resource is presumed to no longer be operational. Once the component is running or has failed it should either eventually or immediately terminated to stop its services. The **terminated** state represents a state where a component is no longer running and cannot be returned to the running state without redeployment. This state, however, does not eliminate the resource from the system. Upon invocation of the *destroy* command, the component's corresponding resource will be freed. In a system with multiple components, the lifecycle of the whole system is defined by the relationships between the individual component lifecycles. The state of each component is bound to the state of the components it relies on. The hierarchy of the system defines relationships where related components lifecycles are linked. The component model and the ADL specification help define explicit semantics for guiding lifecycle transitions.

**2.1.1    Suspended state.**    Further analysis should be considered into the **runtime** state above. We consider a special state in which the components my be transitioning to and from the running state. In this particular state, called the **suspended** state, special attention has to be made to the states of the resources relative to the component in question (ie. the resources may be released while a component is a suspended state). These properties help refine the way components and relative resources are handled in respect to their stateful behaviour.

**2.1.2    Wait state.**    The case of the **wait** state is a very particular one. This particular case is often referred to when a component is ready to receive the input required for continuing its process (although some other special cases could arise depending on the specific component). This state is often fallen back into the more generic **runtime** state, since resources are not released by the component although they may not even be "used" (ex. the component may be deployed on a node but not utilizing the processing power). We are currently forced to consider this state as a particular case of **runtime** state as there are no implemented ways to monitor this situation through the lifecycle controller.

## 2.2    The ADL limitations

It is well known that Architecture Description Languages (ADLs) generally cannot provide sufficient insight into the post-deployment / runtime reconfiguration [14]; although they can be used to describe components, connectors and configurations as well as the hierarchical structure of the system. We have to therefore rely on specific characteristics about the states of instantiated components (also known as "live components") using standard runtime monitoring tools. We can retrieve the specific state information (described in the previous section) as messages passed to the system thus describing the runtime behaviour of states of the component. Similarly, the overall view of behaviour of states of the components' system and resources, describes the runtime behaviour of the environment. We use "finite state on finite strings automata" for the former and "infinite state automata" for the latter, for our runtime behaviour specification.

## 2.3    Environment Monitoring

When considering the state of components and resources in a GCM model, and the runtime monitoring of the environment, we analyse the following introspections.

- For components, by accessing the `LifeCycleController` interface we are able to know the state of the requested component (namely **Started** and **Stopped**).

- For resources, we can monitor their availability status as long as these resources are specified during composition by some deployment descriptor, or at runtime some metadata provider. As the former is mandatory when using some specific components [1], it is not mandatory for all. We will assume that if the developer is interested in using this formal specification for safe reconfiguration of components, he will provide some accessibility to metadata information on runtime availability (as well as list of required resources for the corresponding components), which can be monitored at runtime.

## 3.    Automata Based Model

In building our specification protocol, we follow well known automata constructions. We take a simple finite state automaton on finite strings, for the components specification, and a more complex infinite state on finite strings automata to define the environment. The automata at component level are used for the creation of labels defining the various states in which the considered component is, and are then fed upon request on to the various states of the automata at environment level (Figure 2).

**Figure 2:** Automata Based Model

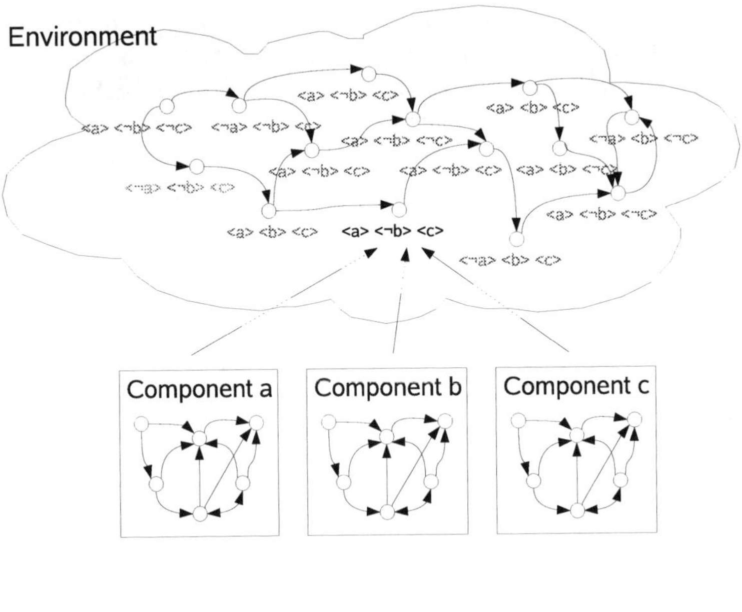

## 3.1    Component level automata

For a component level automaton we suggest to use a finite automaton on finite words. Let $\Sigma$ be a finite alphabet. A finite word over $\Sigma$ is an element of $\Sigma^{\star}$.

DEFINITION 1 (FINITE WORD AUTOMATON) *A finite word automaton, A, is a tuple $A = (\Sigma, Q, Q_i, Q_f, \Delta)$ where $\Sigma$ is a finite alphabet, $Q$ is a set of states, $Q_i \subseteq Q$ is a set of initial states, $Q_f \subseteq Q$ is a set of accepting states, and $\Delta : Q \times \Sigma \longrightarrow 2^S$ is a transition function.*

A run, $R$, of $A$ over a word $w = a_1, a_2, \ldots, a_n - 1$, $w \in \Sigma^{\star}$ is abbreviated as $R_w$ and it is a sequence of states $s_1, s_2, \ldots, s_n$ such that for any i, $(0 \leq i < n)$, $s_{i+1} \in \Delta(s_i, a_i)$. A run, $R = s_1, s_2, \ldots, s_n$, is successful if $s_1 \in Q_i$ and $s_n \in Q_f$. We say that an automaton $A$ accepts a word $w$ if it has a successful run $R_w$. In this case we also say that an automaton $A$ is not empty.

When we construct such an automaton at the component level, we would call it $A_c$ and we assume the following:

- Initial states, $Q_i$, are either 'running / waiting' or none of the previous;

- The set of states, $Q$, corresponds to the states of the component as defined in the previous section;

- The acceptance condition is defined as reaching of one of the following states: terminated, suspended state or fail. These states are in the set $Q_f$ and the acceptance condition is to reach one of these states in $Q_f$

- The transition conditions are determined by the state change calls of the component.

When the assumed automaton $A_c$ (non-)emptiness procedure establishes that the automaton is not empty, it returns a successful run of $A_c$. Thus, for any component cycle, when the corresponding automaton has an accepting run, it means that a component is in the one of the accepting states. We would define a simple function $Lab(A_c)$ which returns the following parameters:

- $< a_t >$ - when a component has met the acceptance condition "terminate"

- $< a_s >$ - when a component $a$ has met the acceptance condition "suspended"

- $< a_f >$ - when a component has met the acceptance condition "terminate after going through fail state"

- $< \neg a >$ - when component $a$ has not met any acceptance condition

These parameters generated by the function $Lab(A_c)$ will be subsequently passed to the environmental level automata which is described in the next section.

## 3.2    Environment level automata

For the environment level we consider automata on infinite trees. Namely, we consider Buchi tree automata [16]which is an extension of the standard tree automaton accepting infinite trees.

DEFINITION 2 (INFINITE TREE AUTOMATON) *A Buchi Tree automaton* $A_T = < \Sigma, D, S, M, s_0, Q_f >$, *where* $\Sigma$ *is an alphabet,* $D \subset N$ *is a finite set of branching degrees,* $M : S \times \Sigma \times D \longrightarrow 2^{S^*}$ *is a transition function satisfying* $M(s, \sigma, d) \in S^d$, *for every* $s \in S, \sigma \in \Sigma$, *and* $d \in D$, $s_0$ *is an initial state, and* $Q_f \subseteq S$ *is an acceptance condition.*

A run, $R$, of $A_T$ over a tree $\tau$ abbreviated as $R_\tau$ is an infinite tree. A run, $R_\tau$, is successful if there is a state $s_f \in Q_f$ such that $R_\tau$ hits $s_f$ infinitely often. We say that an automaton $A_T$ accepts a tree $\tau$ if it has a successful run $R_\tau$. In this case we also say that an automaton $A_T$ is not empty.

In the construction of this tree automaton, every state is labelled according to state of components (passed over from the component level automaton) and resources. In this case the transition function is not only related to the state transition of components, but is also tightly bound to the deontic logic accessibility relation. Here we expect that we would be able to specify the automaton in the normal form for CTL, SNF$_{CTL}$, developed in our previous papers [5]. Although we do not have a rigorous proof of this, we can anticipate that the situation here would be similar to the one in the linear-time case. Namely, in [6], it was shown that a Buchi word automaton can be represented in terms of SNF$_{PLTL}$, a normal form for PLTL. Similarly, we *expect that we will be able* to represent a Buchi tree automaton in terms of SNF$_{CTL}$. Subsequently, we enrich this representation of the automaton by deontic constraints [2] and apply a resolution based verification technique as a verification procedure.

## 4.    Runtime Reconfiguration

## 4.1    Systems States

Each deployment component **must** expose a state resource property which implements the Component's Monitoring capability. To satisfy this requirement, a deployment component must contain **States** and **State Transition** elements. Additionally, a deployment component may include additional information as an opaque quantity that an external consumer may be able to process. The **Component Status** property will be exposed by every component object of a system.

We can define these properties in the XML based system architecture as:

```
<ComponentStatus>
<State>InstanceState|InitializationState|RuntimeState|
SuspendedState|FailedState|TerminatedState</State>
<LifecycleTransition>StateTransition</LifecycleTransition>
</ComponentStatus>
```

where:

| Element | Description |
|---|---|
| InstanceState | State representing the presence of a component instance. |
| InitializationState | State in which a component has been properly initialized. |
| RuntimeState | Operational state. |
| SuspendedState | Operational state (in suspension). |
| FailedState | State in which the component has failed either a lifecycle operation or its operation has failed. |
| TerminatedState | State in which a component instance has been terminated. |

As the failed state may have been arrived at due to failures during many parts of the lifecycle, it is **recommended** that the component take action to ensure the services of the resources are not available while in this state, particularly if the transition occurred from the running state.

Similarly, we can map the state of resources and monitor changes through state change notifications fired by resource monitoring software implemented in the GIDE.

## 4.2  Formal Specification

We refer to reconfiguration as to the process through which a system halts operation under its current source specification and begins operation under a different target specification [15], and more precisely, after the deployment has taken place (dynamic reconfiguration). Some examples include the replacement of a software component by the user, or an automated healing process activated by the system itself. In either of these cases we consider the dynamic reconfiguration process as an unforeseen action at development time (known as ad-hoc reconfiguration [7]). When the system is deployed, the verification process should run continuously and the system will report back the current states for model mapping; if a reconfiguration procedure is requested or inconsistency detected, the healing process is triggered. The dynamic reconfiguration process works in a recursive way, constantly checking for update requests to the model and taking actions accordingly, enabling us to achieve an automated runtime reconfiguration through cycling deductive verification. The approach here is to specify general invariants for the infrastructure and to accept any change to the system, as long as these invariants hold. We assume that the infrastructure has some pre-defined set of norms which define the constraints for the system, in order to ensure system safety, mission success, or other crucial system properties which are critical to the system.

**Application scenario.** We could use this type of specification to construct a normative framework for reconfiguration where a model is requested to be updated. Once an automaton at the bottom level is constructed, it feeds the upper layer automaton with the labels for the states. Then this upper layer automaton can be checked by given its presentation in the normal form with the subsequent application of the resolution procedure to the derived specification. Once this process has been carried out, we could use it for reconfiguration; when a request for reconfiguration is received, we can consider it as an update to the model, which is carried out by verifying the new specification against the system one, stopping the components in question (in essence modifying their state) and updating the model. The reconfiguration process is then left in the hands of the resource handler and the components can be started again to carry on their task with the updated model.

## 5.   Conclusions

The need for a safe and reliable way to dynamically reconfigure systems at runtime, especially distributed, resource-depending and long-running, has led to the need for a formal way to describe and verify them before risking to take some action. In this paper we have given a novel approach to the formal specification of behaviour in GCM environments. Furthermore, by defining our automata-based approach, we have laid the grounds for a solid prototyping of such a specification system. The method introduced will be used to prevent inconsistency and suggest corrections to the system in a static and/or dynamic environment during reconfiguration procedures. Indeed, if the verification technique discovers inconsistencies in the configuration then the "healing" process is triggered: the process of "reconfiguring" of the computation tree model that conforms the protocol. As a next step, we are planning to embed all these features in a prototype plug-in for the GridComp GIDE and test it on case studies proposed by industry partners. While we have applied this framework to a GCM system, such procedure could be applied to other systems, giving the deductive reasoning a chance to assist other verification methods such as model checking by filling the gaps in those areas where these other well established methods cannot be used.

### Acknowledgement

This research work was carried out under the FP6 network of excellence CoreGRID (Contract IST-2002-004265) and the FP6 research and development project GridCOMP (Contract IST-2005-034442) funded partially by the European Commission.

# References

[1] M. Aldinucci, S. Campa, M. Danelutto, M. Vanneschi, P. Kilpatrick, P. Dazzi, D. Laforenza, N. Tonellotto. Behavioural Skeletons in GCM: Autonomic Management of Grid Components PDP '08: Proc. 16th Euromicro Conference on Parallel, Distributed and Network-Based Processing, pp. 54-63, 2008.

[2] A. Basso and A. Bolotov. Towards GCM reconfiguration - extending specification by norms. To appear in: CoreGRID Springer Volume of the CoreGRID Workshop at Heraklion, June 2007.

[3] A. Basukoski, V. Getov, J. Thiyagalingam, S. Isaiadis. Component-Based Development Environment for Grid Systems: Design and Implementation Making Grids Work, Springer, 2008 (to appear).

[4] T. Barros, L. Henrio, A. Cansado, E. Madelaine, M. Morel, V. Mencl and F. Plasil Extension of the Fractal ADL for the Specification of Behaviours of Distributed Components Accepted for poster presentation at the 5th Fractal Workshop (part of ECOOP'06), July 3rd, 2006, Nantes, France, Jul 2006.

[5] A. Bolotov and M. Fisher. A Clausal Resolution Method for CTL Branching Time Temporal Logic Journal of Experimental and Theoretical Artificial Intelligence, volume 11, 1999, pages 77-93, Taylor & Francis.

[6] A. Bolotov, C.Dixon and M. Fisher. On the Relationship between Normal Form and $w$-automata (with M.Fisher and C.Dixon). Journal of Logic and Computation, Volume 12, Issue 4, August 2002, pp. 561-581, Oxford University Press.

[7] T. Batista, A. Joolia, and G. Coulson. Managing Dynamic Reconfiguration in Component-based Systems Proceedings of the European Workshop on Software Architectures, June, 2005, Springer-Velag LNCS series, Vol 3527, pp 1-18.

[8] E. Bruneton. Fractal - Tutorial. Electronic resource: http://fractal.objectweb.org/tutorials/fractal/index.html. September 2003.

[9] E. Bruneton, T. Coupaye, and J.B. Stefani. Recursive and dynamic software composition with sharing. In Seventh Int. Workshop on Component-Oriented Programming (WCOP02), at ECOOP 2002, Malaga, Spain, 2002.

[10] E. Bruneton, T. Coupaye, and J.B. Stefani. The Fractal component Model. Electronic resource: http://fractal.objectweb.org/specification/fractal-specification.pdf. February 2004.

[11] H. Comon, M. Dauchet, R. Gilleron, C. Loding, F. Jacquemard, D. Lugiez, S. Tison, M. Tommasi. Tree Automata Techniques and Applications. Available on: http://www.grappa.univ-lille3.fr/tata, release October, 12th 2007.

[12] CoreGRID - The European Research Network on Foundations, Software Infrastructures and Applications for large scale distributed, GRID and Peer-to-Peer Technologies. http://www.coregrid.net/

[13] Basic Features of the Grid Component Model Deliverable D.PM.04, CoreGRID, March 2007.

[14] J. Matevska-Meyer, W. Hasselbring, R.H. Reussner. Software architecture description supporting component deployment and system runtime reconfiguration. Proceedings of the Ninth International Workshop on Component-Oriented Programming, Oslo, Norway, 2004.

[15]  E.A. Strunk and J.C. Knight. Assured Reconfiguration of Embedded Real-Time Software. DSN '04: Proceedings of the 2004 International Conference on Dependable Systems and Networks (DSN'04), 2004, p. 367, IEEE Computer Society.

[16]  M.Y. Vardi. Automata-Theoretic Techniques for Temporal Reasoning From: Handbook of Modal Logic, Studies in Logic and practical Reasoning, volume 3, chapter 17, Blackbourn, Van Benthem, Wolter editors, 2006.

# TOWARDS A FORMAL SEMANTICS FOR AUTONOMIC COMPONENTS

Marco Aldinucci
*Department of Computer Science, University of Pisa, Italy*
aldinuc@di.unipi.it


Emilio Tuosto
*Department of Computer Science, University of Leicester, UK*
et52@mcs.le.ac.uk

**Abstract**      Autonomic management can improve the QoS provided by parallel/distributed applications. Within the CoreGRID Component Model, the autonomic management is tailored to the automatic – monitoring-driven – alteration of the component assembly and, therefore, is defined as the effect of (distributed) management code.

     This work yields a semantics based on *hypergraph* rewriting suitable to model the dynamic evolution and non-functional aspects of Service Oriented Architectures and component-based autonomic applications. In this regard, our main goal is to provide a formal description of adaptation operations that are typically only informally specified. We advocate that our approach makes easier to raise the level of abstraction of management code in autonomic and adaptive applications.

**Keywords:**    Components, adaptive applications, autonomic computing, grid, semantics, graph rewriting.

## 1. Introduction

Developers of grid applications cannot rely neither on fixed target platforms nor on stability of their status [14]. This makes dynamic adaptivity of applications an essential feature in order to achieve user-defined levels of Quality of Service (QoS). In this regard, component technology has gained increased impetus in the grid community for its ability to provide a clear separation of concerns between application logic and QoS-driven adaptation, which can also be achieved *autonomically*. As an example, GCM (the Grid Component Model defined within the CoreGRID NoE) is a hierarchical component model explicitly designed to support component-based autonomic applications in highly dynamic and heterogeneous distributed platforms [7].

An assembly of components may be naturally modelled as a graph and, if components are autonomic, the graph can vary along with the program execution and may change according to input data and/or grid hardware status. These changes can be encoded as reaction rules within the component *Autonomic Manager* (hereafter denoted as $AM$). A proper encoding of these rules effectively realises the management policy, which can be specific of a given assembly or pre-defined for parametric assemblies (such as *behavioural skeletons*) [2, 1]. In any case, the management plan relies on the reconfiguration operation exposed by the component model run-time support.

A major weakness of current component models (including GCM) is that the semantics of these operations are informally specified, thus making hard to reason about QoS-related management of components. In this work

- We introduce few operations useful for component adaptation; the chosen operations are able to capture typical adaptation patterns in parallel/distributed application on top of the grid. These are presented as *non-functional interfaces* of components that trigger component assembly adaptation (Sec. 2).

- We detail a semantics for these operations based on *hypergraph* rewriting suitable for the description of component concurrent semantics and the run-time evolution of assemblies of autonomic components along adaptations (Sec. 3, 4, and 5).

- We discuss the appropriateness of the level of abstraction chosen to describe adaptation operations to support the design of component-based applications and their autonomic management (Sec. 6).

The key idea of our semantical model consists in modelling component-based applications by means of *hypergraphs* which generalise usual graphs be allowing *hyperedges*, namely arcs that can connect more than two nodes. Intuitively, hyperedges represent components able to interact through *ports* represented by nodes of hypergraphs. The *Synchronised Hyperedge Replacement* (SHR) model specifies how hypergraphs are rewritten according to a set of *productions*. Basically, rewritings represent adaptation of applications possibly triggered by the underlying grid middleware events (or by the applications themselves).

SHR has been shown suitable for modelling non-functional aspects of service oriented computing [10–11] and is one of the modelling and theoretical tools of the SENSORIA project [20]. For simplicity, we consider a simplified version of SHR where node fusion is limited and restriction is not considered. Even if, for the sake of simpleness, the SHR framework used in this work is not the most general available, it is sufficient to give semantics to the management primitives (aka adaptation operations) addressed here. The autonomic manager – by way of these adaptation operations – can structurally reconfigure an application to pursue the (statically or dynamically specified) user intentions in terms of QoS.

## 2.     Autonomic Components and GCM

Autonomic systems enable dynamically defined adaptation by allowing adaptations, in the form of code, scripts or rules, to be added, removed or modified at run-time. These systems typically rely on a clear separation of concerns between adaptation and application logic [15]. An autonomic component will typically consist of one or more managed components coupled with a single autonomic manager that controls them. To pursue its goal, the manager may trigger an adaptation of the managed components to react to a run-time change of application QoS requirements or to the platform status. In this regard, an assembly of self-managed components implements, via their managers, a distributed algorithm that manages the entire application.

The idea of autonomic management of parallel/distributed/grid applications is present in several programming frameworks, although in different flavours: ASSIST [22, 3], AutoMate [18], SAFRAN [9], and GCM [7] all include autonomic management features. The latter two are derived from a common ancestor, i.e. the Fractal hierarchical component model [17]. All the named frameworks, except SAFRAN, are targeted to distributed applications on grids.

GCM builds on the Fractal component model [17] and exhibits three prominent features: hierarchical composition, collective interactions and autonomic management. GCM components have two kinds of interfaces: functional and non-functional ones. The functional interfaces host all those ports concerned with implementation of the functional features of the component. The non-functional interfaces host all those ports needed to support the component management activity in the implementation of the non-functional features, i.e. all those features contributing to the efficiency of the component in obtaining the expected (functional) results but not directly involved in result computation. Each GCM component therefore contains an $AM$, interacting with other managers in other components via the component non-functional interfaces. The *AM* implements the autonomic cycle via a simple program based on reactive rules. These rules are typically specified as a collection of when-*event*-if-*cond*-then-*adapt_op* clauses, where *event* is raised by the monitoring of component internal or external activity (e.g. the component server interface received a request, and the platform running a component exceeded a threshold load, respectively); *cond* is an expression over component internal attributes (e.g. component life-cycle status); *adapt_op* represents an adaptation operation (e.g. create, destroy a component, wire, unwire components, notify events to another component's manager) [9].

We informally describe some common adaptation operations that may be assigned to configuration interfaces:

**Migration** A component is required to change its running location (e.g. platform, site). The request must include the new location and can be performed while keeping its attached external state (**go**) or restating from a fresh default state (**start**).

**Replication** A component (either composite or primitive) is replicated. Replication operation is particularly targeted to composite components exhibiting the parametric replication of inner components (such as behaviour skeletons), and can be used to change their parallelism degree (and thus their performance and fault-tolerance properties). Replication events are further characterized with respect to their relation with replicated component state, if any. A component replica may be created with a fresh external state, carry a copy of the external state (**copy**), or share the external state with the source component (**share**).

**Kill** A component is killed. Due to this kind of action disconnected components (and in particular storage managers) can subject to garbage collection.

Described primitives make possible the implementation of several adaptation paradigms. In particular, migration may be used to adapt the application to changes of grid topology as well as to performance drop of resources. Replication and kill may be used to adapt both data and task parallel computation. In particular, replication with share makes it possible the redistribution of sub-task in data parallel computations; replication with copy enables hot-redundancy. Both stateful and stateless farm computation (parameter-sweeping, embarrassingly parallel) may be reshaped both in parallelism degree and location run by using replication and kill.

EXAMPLE 1 *Let* P, C, SF, S, $AM$, $W_1$, $W_2$, $W_3$ *components (Producer, Consumer, Stateful Farm[1], Storage, Autonomic Manager, and Workers);* $L_1 \cdots L_8$ *locations (e.g. sites, platforms). Thee kinds of bindings are used in the assembly (see also Sec. 4).*

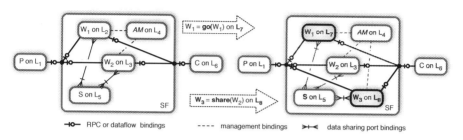

The described assembly of components (left) is paradigmatic of many producer-filter-consumer applications, where the producer (P) generates a stream of data and the filter is parallel component (SF) exhibiting a shared state among its inner components (e.g. a database). The original assembly (left) can be dynamically adapted (right) by way of two adaptation operations to react to runtime events, such as a request of increasing the throughput. The **go** operation moves $W_1$ from $L_2$ to $L_7$ (as an example to move a component onto a more powerful machine); the **share** operation that replicates $W_2$ and place it in the new location $L_8$ (to increase the parallelism degree). Both operations preserve the external state of the migrated/replicated component, which is realised by way of a storage component) attached via a data sharing interface [4].

Example 1 illustrates how the management can be described from a *global viewpoint.* Indeed, the system is described by in a rather detailed way, e.g., components are explicitly enumerated along with their connections. Even if this global viewpoint is useful (and sometime unavoidable) when designing distributed systems, it falls short in describing what single components are supposed to do when a reconfiguration is required. In other terms, it is hard to tell what the *local* behaviour of each component should be in order to obtain the reconfiguration described by the *global* view.

Also, it is worth remarking that, though the diagram clearly describes the changes triggered by $AM$ in this scenario, the lack of a formal semantics leaves some ambiguities. For example, it is not clear if the reconfiguration should take place if, and only if, the system is configured as on the lhs or this is rather a "template" configuration (e.g., should the system reconfigure itself also when $W_2$ is connected to $W_1$? What if $W_2$ was not present?). Of course, such ambiguous situations can be avoided when a formal semantics is adopted.

---

[1]This component is a composite component, and in particular it is an instance of a behavioural skeleton [2].

## 3.     A Walk through SHR

*Synchronised Hyperedge Replacement* (SHR) can be thought of as a rule-based framework for modelling (various aspects of) of distributed computing [11] modelled as *hypergraphs*, a generalisation of graphs roughly representing (sets of) relations among nodes. While graphs represent (sets of) binary relations (labelled arcs connect exactly two nodes), labelled *hyperedges* (hereafter, edges) can connect any number of nodes. We give an informal albeit precise description of *hypergraphs* and SHR through a suitable graphical notation. The interested reader is referred to [11, 16] and references therein for the technical details.

EXAMPLE 2 *In our graphical notation, a hypergraph is depicted as*

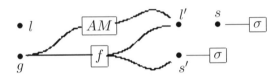

*Edges (labelled by $f$, $AM$ and $\sigma$) are connected to nodes ($g$, $l$, $l'$, $s$ and $s'$). Specifically, $AM$ connects $g$ and $l'$, $f$ connects $g$, $l'$ and $s'$ while two $\sigma$-labelled edges are attached to $s$ and $s'$. Notice that nodes can be isolated (e.g., $l$).*

Hyperedges represent (distributed) components that interact through *ports* represented by nodes. Connections between edges and nodes, called *tentacles*, allow components sharing ports to interact (e.g., in Example 2, $f$ and $AM$ can interact on $g$ and on $l'$).

EXAMPLE 3 *The hypergraph in Example 2 represents (part of) a system where a manager $AM$ and a component $f$ are located at $l'$ and can interact on port $g$. The component $f$ has access to the store at $s'$ (e.g. by way of a data port [4]). In the system are also present another location $l$ and store $s$.*

As in string grammars, SHR rewriting is driven by *productions*. In fact, strings can be rewritten according to a set of *productions*, i.e. rules of the form $\alpha \rightarrow \beta$, where $\alpha$ and $\beta$ are strings (over fixed alphabets of terminal and non-terminal symbols). Similarly, in SHR hypergraph rewritings are specified by productions of the form $L \rightarrow R$, where the lhs $L$ is a hyperedge, the rhs $R$ is a hypergraphs and states that occurrences of $L$ can be replaced with $R$. Intuitively, edges correspond to non-terminals and can be replaced with a hypergraph according to their productions. In SHR, hypergraphs are rewritten by *synchronising* productions, namely edge replacement is *synchronised*: to apply the productions of edges sharing nodes, some conditions must be fulfilled.

More precisely, an SHR production can be represented as follows:

where on the lhs is a decorated edge and on the rhs a hypergraph. The production above should be read as a rewriting rule specifying that edge $f$ on the lhs can be replaced with the hypergraph on the rhs provided that the conditions on the tentacles are fulfilled. More precisely, **copy** and $\overline{\text{rep}}$ must be satisfied on node $g$ and $s$, respectively while $f$ is *idle* on node $l$, namely it does not pose any condition on $l$. According to our interpretation, this amounts to say that when component $f$ is said to replicate with copy by its $AM$ (condition **copy** on node $g$), it tells its store to duplicate itself (condition **rep** on node $s$). When such conditions are fulfilled, edge $f$ is replaced with the hypergraph on the rhs which yield two instances of $f$ one of which connected to the communicated nodes as prescribed by the rhs of the production. Indeed, $f$ exposes three nodes on condition **copy** and one on **rep**; these represent nodes that are communicated, i.e. $g$ and $l$ are node communication accounts for mobility as edges can dynamically detach their tentacles from nodes and connect them elsewhere.

SHR has a declarative flavour because programmers specify synchronisation conditions of components independently from each other. Once the system is built (by opportunely connecting its components) it will evolve according to the possible synchronisations of the edges. Global transitions are obtained by parallel application of productions with "compatible" conditions where compatibility depends on the chosen synchronisation policy[2]. Conditions on $L \rightarrow R$ make it possible to introduce the concept of "*context-freeness*": the productions with a left-hand-side (lhs) which is either a node or an edge confer a context-free flavour to graph grammars. Indeed, such productions do not consider the "surroundings" of their lhs. This makes it possible to design graph rewritings that can be *locally* applied, whereas other graph rewriting mechanisms (such as double-pushout) requires to be applied in a context, which may the be in the worst case the entire graph [11, 16]. As we shall discuss in Sec. 6, the context-freeness of the approach is one of key features making SHR well-suited to describe autonomic component in a grid framework.

---

[2]SHR is parametric with respect to the synchronisation mechanism adopted and can even encompass several synchronisation mechanisms.

## 4.    Productions for Non-functional Interfaces

SHR can adequately formalise the non-functional interface mechanisms informally described in Sec. 2. Three conceptually distinct interfaces can be
considered: $i$) interfaces between components and $AM$ (for management non-
functional bindings); $ii$) interfaces toward the external state (for data sharing
functional bindings); $iii$) interfaces for communicating with other components
(for RPC/dataflow functional bindings).

Since interfaces $iii$ are application dependent, we focus on the coordination-
related interfaces $i$ and $ii$.

A main advantage of our approach is that all aspects of non-functional interfaces are captured in a uniform framework based on SHR. Indeed,

- components are abstracted as edges connected to form a hypergraph;

- the coordination interface of each component is separately declared and
  is not mingled with its computational activity;

- being SHR a *local* rewriting mechanism, it is possible to specify confined
  re-configuration of systems triggered by *local* conditions;

**Migration.**    The migration of a component $f$ is triggered when its $AM$ raises
a signal **go** with the new location on node $g$. The synchronisation of $f$ on the
**go** signal is given by following production:

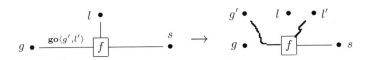

specifying that $f$ running at $l$ accepts to migrate to $l'$ (lhs); the "location" tentacle of $f$ is disconnected from $l$ and attached to $l'$ (rhs). Notice that $f$ maintains
the connection to the previous state $s$ and $l$ is still present. The tentacle connected to $g$ on the lhs is connected to $g'$ on the rhs; however, it might well be that
$g' = g$ ($f$ is still connected to the original $AM$) or $g \neq g'$ ($f$ changes manager).
Similarly, **start** moves the component to a new location $l'$. However, a new
external state $\sigma$ is created together with its attaching node:

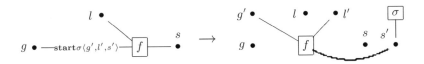

**Replication.** Unlike migration, replication of $f$ preserves the location of the original edge (i.e. a component):

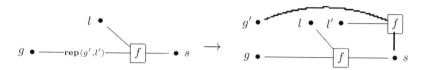

the effect of the above production is to add a new instance of $f$ at $l'$ with $AM$ connected to $g'$; of course, $l = l'$ and $g = g'$ are possible. The newly generated instance shares external state with the original one.

Replication can also activate the new instance with a different state:

The production above creates a fresh replica of $f$ at $l'$ and assigns to it the manager at $g'$; notice that the two instances of $f$ share the state $s$.

Replication can also trigger a new instance of $f$ that acts on a copy of the state original state as described in the production of page 37 where $f$ must notify to its state to duplicate itself and connect the new copy on $s'$. Hence, the state connected to $s$ duplicate itself on the node $s'$ when the action complementary to $\overline{\text{rep}}$ is received, as stated below.

**Component killing.** Components are killed using the following production:

stating that $f$ disappears when its corresponding $AM$ sends a **kill** signal.

## 5.    Synchronising productions

The operational semantics of SHR is illustrated through an example that highlights the following steps:

1 individuate the adjacent tentacles labelled by compatible conditions;

2 determine the synchronising productions and replace the (instances of) edges on their lhs with the hypergraphs on their rhs;

3 fuse the nodes that are equated by the synchronisations.

Let us apply the previous steps to show how migration works in a situation represented by the following hypergraph

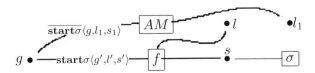

where component $f$ is running at $l$ and shares $g$ with a manager $AM$ located at $l_1$. For brevity, tentacles are decorated with the conditions triggering the rewriting (step 1). Indeed, the tentacles of $AM$ and of $f$ incident on node $g$ yield compatible output and input conditions respectively so that $AM$ orders $f$ to migrate to $l_1$ and to use the store at $s_1$ while staying connected to $g$.

Productions synchronisation consists in replacing the occurrences of the edges on the lhs with the hypergraphs specified in the rhs of the productions and applying the node fusions obtained by the node communicated. For instance, in the previous example the synchronising productions are the $\mathbf{start}\sigma$ production of $f$ given in Sec. 4 and the production of $AM$ whose lhs and rhs consist of $AM$ connected to $g$ and $l_1$ (step 2). Hence, after the synchronisation, the node fusions $g' = g, l' = l_1$ and $s' = s_1$ are applied (step 3), so that the hypergraph is rewritten as

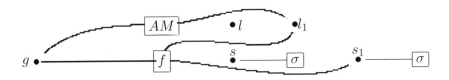

Let us remark that $l$, $\sigma$ and $s$ remain in the final hypergraph. In fact they should not be removed because other edges can be allocated on $l$ or access $\sigma$.

The intuitive description of SHR given in this section suggests the following design style and execution style:

- assign an edge to each component and specify their productions;

- represent the system as a hypergraph;

- decorate the tentacles with the synchronisation conditions;

- synchronise the productions until possible.

It is worth remarking that, unlike other semantical frameworks (e.g., process calculi), in SHR synchronisation conditions may require more than two (productions of) components to be synchronised. This actually depends on the synchronisation policy at hand. For instance, in the migration rewriting described in this section, it is possible to use broadcast interactions on the node $g$ so that *all* the components connected on $g$ will move at $l'$ when the productions are synchronised.

## 6.    SHR provides a suitable abstraction for GCM Managers

We envision the GCM applications as composed of assemblies autonomic components. These components are *locally* managed by their own $AM$, whereas the *global* managing of the application is distributely realised via the cooperation of all $AM$s. This cooperation may happen in different fashions, although an arrangement in a hierarchical fashion appears quite natural for GCM applications due to the hierarchic nature of the model [7].

Irrespectively of any given schema chosen for managing orchestration, each manager can be described in terms of the adaptations that it can locally induce, and the coordination actions it can handle towards other managers. Observe, however, that the ultimate nature of those coordination actions consist in give rise to a broader adaptation involving (also) not directly managed components[3]. As discussed in Sec.3, SHR enables the system designer to uniformly formalise and encode *adapt_op* as local rules in the $AM$. These rules may

- drive the adaptation of directly managed components, via the synchronisation with nodes included in the managed (composite) component, such as **go**, **start**, **rep**, **copy**, and **kill**;

- drive broader adaptations via the synchronisation with other $AM$s. The formalisation of these rules is currently under investigation and it not fully discussed in this work. Preliminary results suggest the feasibility of a design based on just two rules for interaction among managers: a

---

[3]Indeed, both classes of operations have been denoted as *adapt_op* (see Sec. 2).

rule to (dynamically) send a new set of rules to other $AM$s, and a rule to raise exception/violation toward other $AM$s.

An implementation of GCM exploiting described principles is currently on-going. The feasibility of the approach has been prototyped with SCA/Tuscany [19, 21] leveraging on a JBoss-based [13] encoding of when-*event*-if-*cond* -then-*adapt_op* rules. [8]. This kind of encoding makes easy the serialisation of rules to support their portability across different $AM$s.

A distinguished feature of our approach is the high level of abstraction that can be achieved through SHR formalisation of adaptation operations. This results in:

- The possibility to model very different attributes related to QoS management. As an example, in the previous sections we uniformly used nodes of the graphs to model locations, storage ports, functional ports, and non-functional ports. The concept can be easily and uniformly extended to cover other attributes that may be of interest of a particular instance of the model, inter alia attributes concerning security, robustness, and platform configuration.

- The possibility to describe autonomic behaviour irrespectively of any particular implementation. This is mostly due to the neutrality of the description with respect to lower level detail of the component model behaviour, inter alia component life-cycle, interactions between functional and non-functional ports. As an example, the proposed description of adaptation operation is suitable for GCM/P [2], ASSIST [3], and SCA/-Tuscany [8] implementation of autonomic components.

In regard to the latter point, observe that our approach substantially differs from other formalisation efforts aiming to model and check a particular implementation of an adaptive component framework (such as [6]). In particular, the SHR description cannot be directly checked before being mapped onto a concrete model. We believe, however, this is a strength of the approach rather than a limitation. On the one hand, because the concrete model can be automatically generated through compilation once implementation-specific details has been fixed, whereas in other approaches the model is entirely manually designed. On the other hand, because it can support different concrete models matching different implementations.

EXAMPLE 4 *The reference implementation of GCM (GCM/P [12], developed on top of the Proactive middleware [5]) and ASSIST [3] exploit slightly different autonomic component models and substantially different implementations. $i$) ASSIST is implemented in C++ whereas GCM/P in Java. $ii$) ASSIST does not require a component subject of a* **copy** *to be in stopped state, whereas GCM/P* *does. iii*) *ASSIST implements* **kill** *as component destruction, whereas GCM/P as logical marking. iv*) *ASSIST provides a native Distributed Shared Memory for external storage in* **share***, whereas GCM/P does not. v*) *ASSIST does not implements* **go** *for all components, whereas GCM/P does. However, they both implement the same set of adaptation operations, which is the one described in the previous sections. As expected, the same operation exhibits different limitations and overheads in the two implementations*[4].

Finally, observe that proposed approach to formalisation of autonomic components slightly extends classic (run-time) autonomic approach. We believe that the GCM equipped with those adaptation operations make it possible the definition of a malleable component model in which adaptations may be either applied autonomically at run-time (under the control of the $AM$s) or statically exploited to achieve static or launch-time optimisation targeted to generate/configure a particular component assembly for a well-known running environment (e.g. a cluster), thus potentially achieving a significant reduction of overhead in the running code while keeping the full ubiquity potential of the GCM applications.

## 7.    Conclusions

In this work we introduced a SHR formalisation of adaptation operations suitable to support the definition and the evolution autonomic components, and in particular GCM-based autonomic components, which has been defined within the CoreGRID NoE.

A reference implementation of GCM (GCM/P) autonomic components is currently ongoing within the GridCOMP STREP project [12]. In this implementation, the autonomic manager of a component is currently defined as a chunk of plain Java code (wrapped into a proper placeholder) invoking monitor and adaptation operations. This approach, despite already fully functional [2], is excessively low-level and implementation-dependent, thus is unlikely to properly support the design of management for large/complex component assemblies, to sustain the design of reusable management policies, and to survive to the porting of these policies to other implementations of the same (or similar) component models.

The proposed formalisation aims to raise the level of abstraction of adaptation operations and their effects (i.e. their semantics), thus providing

- the application designer with a theoretical tool to design management policies, and reason about their effects (effectiveness, correctness, etc.);

---

[4]On the whole, GCM/P focuses on generality whereas ASSIST on performance [3, 2].

- the component model developers with a formal specification of adaptation operations as reference for their implementation and manipulation (parsing, serialisation, dynamic installation, etc.)

SHR has been previously exploited in [10] for managing application level *service level agreement* (SLA) in a distributed environment, and in [11] to tackle several programming and modelling facets arising in service oriented computing. Here, we shown that SHR is a suitable tool to describe adaptation operations at the "proper" level of abstraction, thus making possible to achieve

- the uniform description of the attributes involved in component assembly adaptation (such as location, storage ports, etc.);

- describe adaptations at the level of the component model (as opposed to its implementation);

- the design of effective and reusable autonomic management policies.

The presented adaptation operations are currently implemented (as Java code) in GCM/P; their effectiveness and overhead in managing the QoS of grid applications is discussed in [1–2].

## Acknowledgments

This research has been supported by the FP6 Network of Excellence Core-GRID, the FP6 GridCOMP project funded by the European Commission (IST-2002-004265 and FP6-034442), and the SENSORIA project funded by the European Commission (FET-GC II IST-2005-16004).

## References

[1] M. Aldinucci, S. Campa, M. Danelutto, P. Dazzi, P. Kilpatrick, D. Laforenza, and N. Tonellotto. Behavioural skeletons for component autonomic management on grids. In M. Danelutto, P. Frangopoulou, and V. Getov, editors, *Making Grids Work*, CoreGRID. Springer, May 2008.

[2] M. Aldinucci, S. Campa, M. Danelutto, M. Vanneschi, P. Dazzi, D. Laforenza, N. Tonellotto, and P. Kilpatrick. Behavioural skeletons in GCM: autonomic management of grid components. In D. E. Baz, J. Bourgeois, and F. Spies, editors, *Proc. of Intl. Euromicro PDP 2008: Parallel Distributed and network-based Processing*, pages 54–63, Toulouse, France, Feb. 2008. IEEE.

[3] M. Aldinucci and M. Danelutto. Algorithmic skeletons meeting grids. *Parallel Computing*, 32(7):449–462, 2006.

[4] G. Antoniu, H. Bouziane, L. Breuil, M. Jan, and C. Pérez. Enabling transparent data sharing in component models. In *6th IEEE Intl. Symposium on Cluster Computing and the Grid (CCGRID)*, pages 430–433, Singapore, May 2006.

[5] L. Baduel, F. Baude, D. Caromel, A. Contes, F. Huet, M. Morel, and R. Quilici. *Grid Computing: Software Environments and Tools*, chapter Programming, Deploying, Composing, for the Grid. Springer, Jan. 2006.

[6]  T. Barros, L. Henrio, and E. Madelaine. Behavioural models for hierarchical components. In P. Godefroid, editor, *Model Checking Software, Proc. of the 12th Intl. SPIN Workshop*, volume 3639 of *LNCS*, pages 154–168, San Francisco, CA, USA, Aug. 2005. Springer.

[7]  CoreGRID NoE deliverable series, Institute on Programming Model. *Deliverable D.PM.04 – Basic Features of the Grid Component Model (assessed)*, Feb. 2007. http://www.coregrid.net/mambo/images/stories/Deliverables/d.pm.04.pdf.

[8]  M. Danelutto and G. Zoppi. Behavioural skeletons meeting services. In *Proc. of ICCS: Intl. Conference on Computational Science, Workshop on Practical Aspects of High-level Parallel Programming*, volume 5101 of *LNCS*, pages 146–153, Krakow, Poland, June 2008. Springer.

[9]  P.-C. David and T. Ledoux. An aspect-oriented approach for developing self-adaptive fractal components. In W. Löwe and M. Südholt, editors, *Proc. of the 5th Intl Symposium Software on Composition (SC 2006)*, volume 4089 of *LNCS*, pages 82–97, Vienna, Austria, Mar. 2006. Springer.

[10]  R. De Nicola, G. Ferrari, U. Montanari, R. Pugliese, and E. Tuosto. A formal basis for reasoning on programmable Qos. In *Intl. Symposium on Verification – Theory and Practice – Honoring Z. Manna's 64th Birthday*, volume 2772 of *LNCS*. Springer, June 2003.

[11]  G. Ferrari, D. Hirsch, I. Lanese, U. Montanari, and E. Tuosto. Synchronised hyperedge replacement as a model for service oriented computing. In F. de Boer, M. Bonsangue, S. Graf, and W. de Roever, editors, *Formal Methods for Components and Objects: 4th Intl. Symposium, FMCO*, volume 4111 of *LNCS*, Amsterdam, The Netherlands, Nov. 2006. Springer. Revised Lectures.

[12]  GridCOMP Project. Grid Programming with Components, An Advanced Component Platform for an Effective Invisible Grid, 2008. http://gridcomp.ercim.org.

[13]  JBoss rules home page. http://www.jboss.com/products/rules, 2008.

[14]  K. Kennedy, M. Mazina, J. Mellor-Crummey, K. Cooper, L. Torczon, F. Berman, A. Chien, H. Dail, O. Sievert, D. Angulo, I. Foster, D. Gannon, L. Johnsson, C. Kesselman, R. Aydt, D. Reed, J. Dongarra, S. Vadhiyar, and R. Wolski. Toward a framework for preparing and executing adaptive Grid programs. In *Proc. of NSF Next Generation Systems Program Workshop (IPDPS 2002)*, 2002.

[15]  J. O. Kephart and D. M. Chess. The vision of autonomic computing. *IEEE Computer*, 36(1):41–50, 2003.

[16]  I. Lanese and E. Tuosto. Synchronized Hyperedge Replacement for Heterogeneous Systems. In J. Jacquet and G. Picco, editors, *International Conference on Coordination Models and Languages*, volume 3454 of *LNCS*, pages 220 – 235. Springer, April 2005.

[17]  ObjectWeb Consortium. *The Fractal Component Model, Technical Specification*, 2003.

[18]  M. Parashar, H. Liu, Z. Li, V. Matossian, C. Schmidt, G. Zhang, and S. Hariri. AutoMate: Enabling autonomic applications on the Grid. *Cluster Computing*, 9(2):161–174, 2006.

[19]  Service component architecture. http://www.ibm.com/developerworks/library/specification/ws-sca/, 2008.

[20]  Sensoria Project. Software Engineering for Service-Oriented Overlay Computers, 2008. http://sensoria.fast.de/.

[21]  Tuscany home page. http://incubator.apache.org/tuscany/, 2008.

[22]  M. Vanneschi. The programming model of ASSIST, an environment for parallel and distributed portable applications. *Parallel Computing*, 28(12):1709–1732, Dec. 2002.

# INTEGRATING APPLICATION AND SYSTEM COMPONENTS WITH THE GRID COMPONENT MODEL

Michal Ejdys, Ula Herman-Izycka, Namita Lal, Thilo Kielmann*
*Vrije Universiteit*
*Dept. of Computer Science*
*De Boelelaan 1083*
*1081HV Amsterdam, The Netherlands*
kielmann@cs.vu.nl


Enric Tejedor, Rosa M. Badia
*Univ. Politècnica de Catalunya*
*C/ Jordi Girona, 1–3*
*E-08034 Barcelona, Spain*

**Abstract**     The Grid Component Model (GCM) is becoming a promising development platform for flexible and adaptable grid applications. Recently, a set of mediator components has been proposed for providing a uniform and integrated platform to access grid middleware, services, and resources from an application. In this paper, we present our experiences with building such mediator components using GCM, focusing on two functionality areas. First, we show how application adaption support can be realized via mediator components, based on a set of component controllers through which the application components can be adapted and steered. Second, we show how a service and resource abstraction layer can be controlled at runtime from the mediator components.

**Keywords:**     Grid Component Model (GCM), Mediator Components, Grid Application Toolkit (GAT)

---

*Contact author.

## 1.    Introduction

Developing grid applications has proven to be a hard problem. What distinguishes grids from other environments is their heterogeneity, dynamic variability of resource quality, and their non-negligible failure rates, in their totality requiring approaches to application development that take these non-functional properties into account [14].

Many grid programming models have been proposed. Component models like CCA [4]or Fractal [6]provide the flexibility that is needed to address the challenges of grid programming. The Grid Component Model (GCM) [8]is becoming a promising development platform for flexible and adaptable grid applications. Recently, an integrated toolkit for grid applications has been proposed [9], using both a set of mediator components and a service and resource abstraction layer to integrate GCM-based applications with grid middleware environments.

In this paper, we present our experiences with building such mediator components using GCM, focusing on two functionality areas. First, we show how application adaption support can be realized via mediator components, based on a set of component controllers through which the application components can be adapted and steered. Second, we show how a service and resource abstraction layer can be controlled at runtime from the mediator components. We show how both GCM-aware and GCM-unaware applications can be used with our mediator component toolkit.

The remainder of this paper is organized as follows. Section 2 and Section 3 briefly present the GCM component model, and survey the integrated toolkit, respectively. Section 4 describes a more detailed design for the integration of the mediator components with application components. In Section 5, we describe how GCM components can be used to dynamically adapt the service and resource abstraction layer, too, shown on the example of the JavaGAT [16]implementation. Section 6 discusses related work. Section 7 concludes.

## 2.    The Grid Component Model (GCM)

GCM allows applications to be written in a way that they can cope with the specific requirements of grid environments, most prominently resource heterogeneity, performance variability, and fluctuating availability. GCM is addressing these issues by the following properties.

First, GCM is a *hierarchical* component model. This means that users of GCM (programmers) have the possibility of building new GCM components as compositions of existing GCM components. The new, composite components programmed in this way are first class components, in that they can be used in every context where non-composite, elementary components can be used.

Programmers need not necessarily perceive these components as composite, unless they explicitly want to consider this feature.

GCM allows component interactions to take place with several distinct mechanisms. In addition to classical use/provide (or client/server) ports, GCM allows *data*, *stream* and *event ports* to be used in component interaction. Using data ports, components can express data sharing between components while preserving the ability to properly perform ad hoc optimization of the interaction among components sharing data. While stream ports can be easily emulated by classical use/provide ports, their explicit inclusion allows much more effective optimizations to be performed in the component run-time support (framework). Event ports may be used to provide asynchronous interaction capabilities to the component framework. Events can be subscribed and generated. Furthermore, events can be used just to synchronize components as well as to synchronize *and* to exchange data while the synchronization takes place.

Regarding collective interaction patterns, GCM supports several kinds of collective ports, including those supporting implementation of structured interaction between a single use port and multiple provide ports (multicast collective) and between multiple use ports and a single provide port (gathercast collective). The two parametric (and therefore customizable) interaction mechanisms allow the implementation of most (hopefully all) of the interesting collective interaction patterns deriving from the usage of composite (parallel) components.

GCM is intended to be used in grid contexts, that is in highly dynamic, heterogeneous and networked target architectures. GCM therefore provides several levels of *autonomic managers* in components, that take care of the *non-functional* features of the component programs. GCM components have thus two kind of interfaces: a functional one and a non-functional one. The functional interface includes all those ports contributing to the implementation of the functional features of the component, i.e. those features directly contributing to the computation of the result expected of the component. The non-functional interface comprises all those ports needed to support the component manager activity in the implementation of the non-functional features, i.e. all those features contributing to the efficiency of the component in the achievement of the expected (functional) results but not directly involved in actual result computation. Each GCM component therefore contains one or more managers, interacting with other managers in other components via the component's non-functional interfaces and with the managers of the internal components of the same component using the mechanism provided by the GCM component implementation. Each component has a manager whose job it is to ensure efficient execution of the component on the target grid architecture.

## 3.    The Mediator Component Toolkit

The goal of the mediator component toolkit is to integrate system-component capabilities into application code, achieving both steering of the application and performance adaptation by the application to achieve the most efficient execution on the available resources offered by the Grid.

By introducing such a set of components, resources and services in the Grid get integrated into one overall system with homogeneous component interfaces. The advantage of such a component system is that it abstracts from the many software architectures and technologies used underneath.

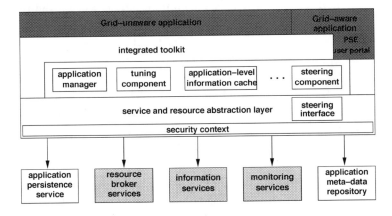

**Figure 1:** The generic component platform with mediator components, from [9].

The strength of such a component-based approach is that it provides a homogeneous set of well-defined (component-level) interfaces to and between all software systems in a Grid platform, ranging from portals and applications, via mediator components to the underlying system software. The set of envisioned mediator components, with their embedding in the generic component platform, can be seen in Figure 1; a detailed description can be found in [9]. We briefly summarize the mediator components in the following.

### Application-level information cache

This component is supposed to provide a unified interface to deliver all kinds of meta-data (e.g., from a GIS, a monitoring system, from application-level meta data) to the application. Its purpose is twofold. First, it is supposed to provide a unifying component interface to all data (independent of its actual storage), including mechanisms for service and information discovery. Second, this application-level cache is supposed to deliver the information really fast, cutting down access times of current implementations like Globus GIS (up to multiple seconds) to the order of a method invocation. For the latter purpose, this component may have to prefetch (poll) information from the various sources to provide them to the application in time. An implementation of such a component, albeit without a "real," e.g. GCM, component interface, has been described in [2].

### Application steering and tuning components

Controlling and steering of applications by the user, e.g. via application managers, user portals, and problem solving environments (PSE's), requires a component-level interface to give external components access to the application. Besides the steering interface, also dedicated steering components are necessary, both for mediating between application and system components, but also for implementing pro-active steering systems, carrying their own threads of activity. The steering components thus provide a framework for performance tuning, which can be used to improve the execution time of applications automatically as well as for improving services and tools which are involved in the environment.

### Application manager component

The envisioned application manager component establishes a pro-active user interface, in charge of tracking an application from submission to successful completion. Such an application manager is in charge of guaranteeing such successful completion in spite of temporary error conditions or performance limitations. (In other settings, such an active component might be referred to as an agent.) For performing its task, the application manager will need to interoperate with most of the other mediator components, like the application itself (via the steering interface), the application meta data repository and cache, as well as an application persistence service, like the one published in [15].

The components as described so far denote the core of the mediator set. In the course of ongoing work, this set is being refined and enriched as new experience will be gained.

## 4.  Application Adaptation Support

The generic component platform, along with the mediator components, provides a platform for grid applications to adapt themselves to changing conditions and resources at runtime. In this section, we propose how to interface application components to this platform. We assume a parallel application that can adapt itself via its data distribution or by migration to other compute nodes. An example for such an application could be *Successive Over Relaxation* (SOR) which is based on nearest-neighbour communication. Applications with other communication patterns (like master/worker) would also be applicable. We also assume that the application shall be steered by its user.

For both adaptation by tuning and management components, as well as by the user via the steering component, the application components have to be called by the mediator components. For this purpose, we propose the interface shown in Figure 2, with specialized controllers that are added to the application components' membrane.

Based on experience gathered when investigating the GCM component framework, we propose the following extensions. First, in order to effectively modify the structure of a running application, we propose to implement an *explorer component*. Thus, the user could switch between different implementations of his/her algorithms without the need to stop and re-run their application.

Second, the mediator toolkit can greatly benefit from implementing different control aspects of the application separately, namely by using controllers. We propose to introduce into the architecture the following controllers, as depicted in Figure 2:

- steering – for modifying application parameters, which would allow for computational steering during runtime

- persistence – for handling checkpoints: initiating checkpoints, as well as starting (from checkpoint or from scratch) and stopping the application

- distribution – for optimal utilization of allocated resources, and for adapting to changes in environment (releasing and acquiring resources, changes in quality of network connections)

- component – for investigating the application's structure (in terms of components) and modifying it (e.g. switching to alternative implementation, replacing subcomponents)

Note that the component controller is already implemented in GCM. However, the other controllers have to be added according to the necessary functionality. Another important observation is that communication with the application is via its controllers only.

## 4.1    Persistence Controller and Life Cycle Controller

The *Persistence Controller* is the manager of an application instance. Not only is it responsible for checkpointing, but also for starting (from scratch or from a checkpoint) and stopping an application. For this to be accomplished, we propose bounding the Persistence Controller with GCM's *LifeCycleController*. The latter is a simple state automaton (with two states: *started* and *stopped*). We propose extending the state-cycle to service checkpointing. See Figure 3.

We propose to extend the *started* state of the component by adding substates representing different stages of the running application (*created*, *initialized*, *running*, and *finished*), and *checkpointing*.

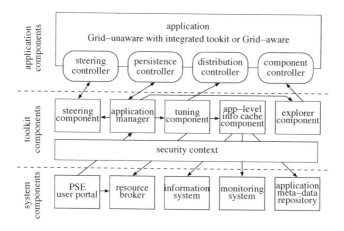

**Figure 2:** Generic component platform with application controllers.

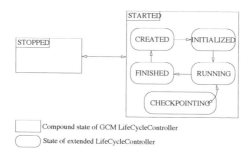

**Figure 3:** Extended states of LifeCycleController.

The GCM LifeCycleController is responsible for starting and stopping the component. There are certain conditions under which a component can be stopped. For example, all method invocations on this component should have finished (a special interceptor keeps a counter of active method invocations). Similarly, only a component with all mandatory interfaces bound can be started.

Our system also benefits from this approach. Transitions between *stopped* and *started* states are limited to only a few *started* substates. The component must not be allowed to stop while checkpointing is in progress. Additionally, stopping an application in the *running* state could mean interrupting the application (transition to *finished*) first.

## 4.2    Application controllers

The proposed application controllers (steering – *sc*, persistence – *pc*, distribution – *dc*, and component – *cc*) are implemented as GCM-controllers, part of the membrane, shown in Figure 4 (left). Alternatively, the controllers can also be implemented as components inside a compound component, together with the application component itself, shown in Figure 4 (right). This design can be used for GCM-unaware applications as discussed below.

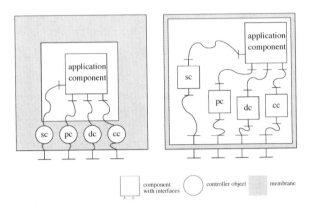

**Figure 4:** Controllers inside the component membrane (left) or as subcomponents (right).

## 4.3    Dealing with GCM-aware and unaware applications

The GCM Mediator Toolkit is ready to run not only with applications that have been developed with GCM in mind, but also with application *objects* (rather than components), from "legacy" applications, as shown in Figure 5.

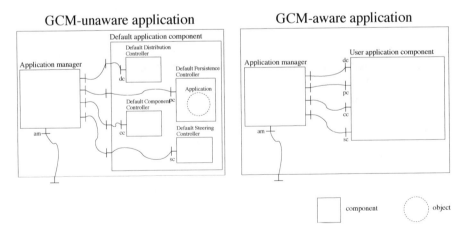

**Figure 5:** Integrating applications with mediator controllers.

**GCM-unaware applications.**    The framework is able to cooperate with applications that do not use the GCM framework, shown in Figure 5, left. In that case, a set of default controllers is created. A user application is encapsulated by the default persistence controller as this component is responsible for starting and stopping the application, and it has direct access to the application object. This controller, together with the default distribution, component, and steering controllers, are integrated to a default application component, which is bound to the rest of the framework via the application manager.

The default implementations of controllers are very simple. Only the persistence controller is able to perform some actions – starting and terminating the application. All other methods in this and the remaining controllers throw a *not implemented* exception, as they cannot be provided without specific knowledge about the application.

**GCM-aware applications.**    These are very easy to connect to the framework. The only requirement towards the application developer is to deliver a GCM component (*user application component*, see Figure 5, right) with exported interfaces for each of the controllers (dc, pc, cc, and sc). Internally, they are expected to be bound to the user's implementation of the controllers.

## 5.    Service and Resource Abstraction

The mediator component toolkit is using a *service and resource abstraction layer* for the boundary between system and application components on one side, and (remote) services and resources, on the other side. The Java Grid Application Toolkit (JavaGAT) [16] is an implementation of such a layer. It provides an object-oriented, high-level, and middleware-independent interface to the grid.

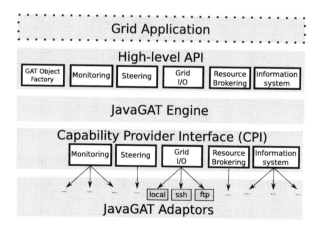

**Figure 6:** Structure of the JavaGAT implementation, from [16].

JavaGAT uses nested exceptions and intelligent dispatching of method invocations to automatically select the most suitable grid middleware that implements the requested operations [16]. For instance, file transfers are typically faster with GridFTP than with SSH, as GridFTP can use parallel data streams. Another reason for a particular preference could be security: the most secure transfer protocol could be tried first (much like SSH does). Figure 6 illustrates the structure of the JavaGAT implementation. The JavaGAT engine is using adaptor selection policies to express preferences for different adaptors and the middleware they interface to. We propose to modify the engine such that the configuration of these policies is more dynamic than its current implementation.

In JavaGAT, the selection process of the appropriate middleware (adaptors) is done at runtime using a default ordering policy that defines the order in which the adaptors are tried. This default ordering can be overridden by a user-defined policy allowing the user to define the order in which the adaptors are tried to service a particular request call. This can be done by defining an *AdaptorOrderingPolicy* class and specifying the name of the new ordering class using a command line option that sets a Java system property.

However, since the user-defined ordering policy is specified as a system property when the application is started, it is a one-time configuration that cannot be changed while the application is running. In order to make this configuration more flexible, we investigate how we can utilize GCM's component architecture in order to make the policy more dynamic.

In order to make this possible we define a GCM component that exposes an interface that can allow the user of the application to provide a new adaptor ordering policy for a particular GATobject. Internally to the engine, each GATobject provides a method that can be invoked internally by the component to change the ordering of the adaptors in the adaptor list. Access to this list has to be synchronized since the list can be concurrently modified through the GCM component while it is being used by the adaptor selection process. This setup is illustrated in Figure 7.

## 6.    Related Work

The work presented in this paper is presenting our experiences with integrating application and system components into a homogeneous system of components. It is directly based on work within CoreGRID, namely the Grid Component Model (GCM) [8], and the set of mediator components [9]. We are using the ProActive/GCM implementation from the GridCOMP project [10].

What distinguishes grids from other environments is their heterogeneity, dynamic variability of resource quality, and their non-negligible failure rates, in their totality requiring approaches to application development that take these non-functional properties into account [14]. In consequence, approaches to

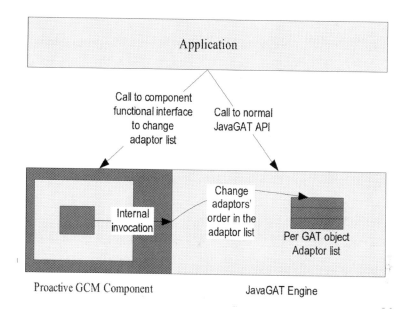

**Figure 7:** Dynamic adaptor ordering using GCM components.

dynamically adapt applications to changing grid environments are legion. Here, we can only mention a few.

First of all, the GCM model provides the core mechanisms for our work. Important, in this respect, is the work on skeleton-based, autonomic management of grid components within GCM [1]. Behavioural skeletons are closely related to higher-order components (HOC's) that are likewise proposed for performance adaptation of grid applications [3]. Both skeletons and HOC's are providing structural frameworks in which application components can be inserted and being leveraged from directly dealing with adaptation issues. In contrast, mediator components do not require applications to fit into certain structures but let them provide application-specific code to be interfaced with the provided controllers.

Of course, there also exist many approaches to adapting grid applications that are not based on components. Examples providing some form of application frameworks or infrastructures are [5, 11, 12, 18, 19]. The most puristic approach is to modify the application code itself, or to develop new, grid-aware applications [7, 17]. In contrast to these approaches, we propose to build both applications and their supportive environments from the same grid component model (GCM), and to tightly integrate them for flexible composition of efficient and adaptive grid applications.

Whereas application performance is the predominant goal of running applications in grids, it is not the only purpose for which dynamic adaptation is required. Via service and resource abstraction, applications become independent of and portable across different grid middleware and infrastructure. This purpose is addressed by the Grid Application Toolkit (the JavaGAT) [16], or by the implementation of the recently standardized SAGA API [13]. Both SAGA and the JavaGAT need some form of configuration information from the user in order to identify and select proper middleware adaptors. Our mediator component-based framework provides an integrated mechanism to provide all necessary information to a resource and service abstraction layer, like SAGA or JavaGAT.

## 7.    Conclusions

With the Grid Component Model (GCM), applications can be written in ways to cope with specific requirements of grid environments, namely resource heterogeneity, performance variability, and fluctuating availability. The integrated toolkit for grid applications is providing both a set of mediator components and a service and resource abstraction layer, allowing to integrate application components with grid middleware systems.

In this paper, we have presented our design for integrating the mediator components with the application itself. We have also shown, on the example of the JavaGAT, how the service and resource abstraction layer can be made adaptive, too. As of the time of writing, the mediator component toolkit has been implemented partially. With the advent of a complete GCM platform implementation, a fully integrated component platform will become available.

## Acknowledgments

This research work is carried out under the FP6 Network of Excellence *CoreGRID* funded by the European Commission (Contract IST-2002-004265).

## References

[1]  M. Aldinucci, S. Campa, M. Danelutto, M. Vanneschi, P. Dazzi, D. Laforenza, N. Tonellotto, and P. Kilpatrick. Behavioural skeletons in GCM: autonomic management of grid components. In *Intl. Euromicro PDP 2008: Parallel Distributed and network-based Processing*, pp. 54–63, Toulouse, France, Feb. 2008. IEEE.

[2]  G. Aloisio, Z. Balaton, P. Boon, M. Cafaro, I. Epicoco, G. Gombas, P. Kacsuk, T. Kielmann, and D. Lezzi. *Integrating Resource and Service Discovery in the CoreGrid Information Cache Mediator Component*. CoreGRID Integration Workshop 2005, Pisa, Italy, 2005.

[3]  M. Alt, C. Dumitrescu, S. Gorlatch, A. Kertesz, G. Sipos, and D. Epema. Towards user-transparent performance prediction for workflows of higher-order components. In *Proceedings of the CoreGRID Integration Workshop*, pp. 345–356. CYFRONET Poland, 2006. ISBN 83-915141-6-1.

[4] R. Armstrong, G. Kumfert, L.C. McInnes, S. Parker, B. Allen, M. Sottile, T. Epperly, and T. Dahlgren. The CCA component model for high-performance scientific computing. *Concurrency and Computation: Practice and Experience*, 18(2):215–229, 2006.

[5] F. Berman, R. Wolski, H. Casanova, W. Cirne, H. Dail, M. Faerman, S. Figueira, J. Hayes, G. Obertelli, J. Schopf, G. Shao, S. Smallen, N. Spring, A. Su, and D. Zagorodnov. Adaptive Computing on the Grid using AppLeS. *IEEE Trans. on Parallel and Distributed Systems*, 14(4):369–382, 2003.

[6] E. Bruneton, T. Coupaye, M. Leclercq, V. Quéma, and J.-B. Stefani. The Fractal Component Model and Its Support in Java. *Software Practice and Experience*, special issue on Experiences with Auto-adaptive and Reconfigurable Systems, 36(11-12), 2006.

[7] W. Chrabakh and R. Wolski. GridSAT: A Chaff-based Distributed SAT Solver for the Grid. In *ACM/IEEE Conference on Supercomputing*, page 37, 2003.

[8] CoreGRID Institute on Programming Models. *Basic Features of the Grid Component Model (assessed)*, Deliverable D.PM.04, CoreGRID Network of Excellence, 2007. http://www.coregrid.net/mambo/images/stories/Deliverables/d.pm04.pdf.

[9] CoreGRID Institute on Grid Systems, Tools, and Environments. *Design of the Integrated Toolkit with Supporting Mediator Components*. Deliverable D.STE.05, CoreGRID Network of Excellence, 2007. http://www.coregrid.net/mambo/images/stories/Deliverables/d.ste05.pdf.

[10] The GridCOMP project, http://gridcomp.ercim.org/, 2008.

[11] E. Heymann, M.A. Senar, E. Luque, and M. Livny. Adaptive scheduling for master-worker applications on the computational grid. In *1st IEEE/ACM International Workshop on Grid Computing*, pp. 214–227, LNCS 1971, Springer Verlag, 2000.

[12] E. Huedo, R.S. Montero, and I.M. Llorente. A framework for adaptive execution in grids. *Software – Practice and Experience*, 34(7):631–650, May 2005.

[13] S. Jha, H. Kaiser, A. Merzky, and O. Weidner. Grid Interoperability at the Application Level Using SAGA. *International Grid Interoperabilty and Interoperation Workshop 2007(IGIIW 2007)*.

[14] T. Kielmann. Programming Models for Grid Applications and Systems: Requirements and Approaches. *IEEE John Vincent Atanasoff International Symposium on Modern Computing (JVA 2006)*, Sofia, Bulgaria, October 2006, pp. 27-32.

[15] E. Krepska, T. Kielmann, R. Sirvent, R.M. Badia. A Service for Reliable Execution of Grid Applications. In *Achievements in European Research on Grid Systems*, Springer Verlag, 2007.

[16] R.V. van Nieuwpoort, T. Kielmann, and H.E. Bal. User-friendly and reliable grid computing based on imperfect middleware. *ACM/IEEE Conference on Supercomputing (SC'07)*, 2007.

[17] A. Plaat, H.E. Bal, and R.F.H. Hofman. Sensitivity of parallel applications to large differences in bandwidth and latency in two-layer interconnects. In *5th International Symposium on High Performance Computer Architecture*, pp. 244–253, 1999.

[18] S.S. Vadhiyar and J.J. Dongarra. Self adaptivity in Grid computing. *Concurrency and Computation: Practice and Experience*, 17(2–4):235–257, 2005.

[19] G. Wrzesinska, J. Maassen, and H.E. Bal. Self-adaptive applications on the Grid. In *ACM SIGPLAN Symposium on Principles and Practices of Parallel Programming (PPoPP'07)*, San Jose, CA, USA, March 2007.

II

# RESOURCE MANAGEMENT AND SCHEDULING

# AN EVALUATION OF AVAILABILITY COMPARISON AND PREDICTION FOR OPTIMIZED RESOURCE SELECTION IN THE GRID*

Farrukh Nadeem, Radu Prodan, Thomas Fahringer
*Institute of Computer Science, University of Innsbruck, Austria*
farrukh@dps.uibk.ac.at

Vincent Keller
*Ecole Polytechnique Federale de Lausanne, LIN-STI, Switzerland*
Vincent.Keller@epfl.ch

**Abstract**     Resources in the Grid exhibit different availability properties and patterns over time, mainly due to their administrators' policies for the Grid, and the different domains to which they belong, e.g. non-dedicated desktop Grids, on-demand systems, P2P systems etc. This diversification in availability properties makes availability-aware resource selection, for applications with different fault tolerance capabilities, a challenging problem. To address this problem, we introduce new availability metrics for resource availability comparison. We further predict resource availability considering their availability policies. We introduce a new resource availability predictor based on pattern matching through availability *pattern recognition and classification* for resource *instance* and *duration* availability, and compare it with other methods. Notably we are able to achieve an average accuracy of more than 80% in our predictions.

**Keywords:**     Resource Availability Comparison, Resource Stability and Dependability, Availability Prediction, Pattern Recognition and Classification

---
*This work is partially supported by the European Union through IST-2002-004265 CoreGRID and IST-034601 edutain@grid projects. Part of this work is also supported by Higher Education Commission (HEC) of Pakistan.

## 1.    Introduction

With the growing maturity of the Grid technology, the composition, functionality, utilization and scale of computational Grids continue to evolve. The
large scale computational Grid environments and testbeds under centralized administrative controls, such as, Cern LCG, Tera Grid, Grid'5000, Austrian Grid
etc. amass hundreds/thousands of resources, which vary considerably in terms
of their computation power and their availability patterns. A large number of
these resources may be unavailable at any time, mainly due to wide range of
policies for *when* and *how* to make their resources available to the Grid. These
policies are usually based on resources' usage patterns and owners' other preferences, like shutting down the resources during night. Resources may also
be made available to the Grid on demand [1] and may even be temporarily
removed partially or completely from the Grid to accommodate other tasks or
projects.

The Grid schedulers and resource brokers need information about resource
availability properties and predictions about their future availability, besides
application execution time predictions on them, to compare and select the most
suitable resources. Knowing the resource availability properties, *how* often and
*when* the resources become unavailable, they can be more cogent, especially if
this knowledge is coupled with information about application characteristics.
For example, the applications that do not implement checkpointing mechanism
and have long run times require resources with more steady and reliable availability, whereas, the applications which require heavy checkpointing may be
scheduled to the resources with a longer availability durations and applications
with light checkpointing and easily replicable processes might even be scheduled on less powerful and more intermittently available resources. Similarly,
considering resource availability patterns, heavy weight checkpointing could be
created on demand rather than periodically, thereby circumventing unnecessary
overheads.

Predicting the resources' availability and comparing them on this basis is a
hard problem due to its dependency on multiple factors like resource's components stability, Grid middleware maturity, varying resource maintenance and
manageability. Particularly, the wide range of policies for resource availability
in the Grid makes the problem even more challenging. To address this problem,
we present in this paper resource availability comparison framework and a new
prediction method *Pattern Matching* from *pattern recognition and classifications*, for resource *instance* and *lifetime* availability predictions. We compare
resource availability using different metrics, in particular with *resource stability*, which better compares resources for their availability as a function of time.
Availability trace from Austrian Grid is undertaken for our present study. Please
note that in this paper we use the terms *machine* and *resource* interchangeably.

We compare the effectiveness of our prediction technique by designing and building different predictors that take advantage of different availability properties. Results from the prototype implementation of our system in ASKALON [14] show that more specific information is critical for better predictions. On average, we are able to get more than 95% accuracy in our *instance* availability predictions and more than 75% accuracy in *duration* predictions.

## 2. Austrian Grid Availability Trace

Here we describe the availability trace of resources in a large-scale Grid: Austrian Grid. Austrian Grid is a nation-wide, multi-institutional, -administrative and -VO Grid platform, consisting of 28 Grid-sites geographically distributed in Austria, and collectively there are over 1.5 thousand processors. To better expose resource availability properties, we include (external) knowledge of high level resource availability policies for the Grid. Based on these policies, we identify three main classes of resources in Austrian Grid: the *dedicated resources*, which are meant to be always available to the Grid users; the *temporal resources*, the resource from the university labs, are available in the Grid as long as they are turned on; and the *on-demand resources*, which are made available to the Grid only on demand from the Grid users for large scale jobs or experiments. The names of the resource classes reflect their respective availability policies.

The complete resource availability trace, in which each event (for every individual Grid-sites) separated by 5 minutes time represents resource state (available or unavailable), was analyzed for a duration of approx. one year from mid-June 2006 to mid-April 2007. Altogether this trace is comprised of more than 23 million events that occurred on the whole Austrian Grid. In the presented work, a resource is considered available if it is turned on and accessible remotely (e.g. through GRAM), otherwise it is considered unavailable.

## 3. Resource Availability Comparison

The main purpose of resource comparison based on the availability properties is to provide the resource broker and meta-scheduler a ranking of Grid resources to assist the optimized resource selection process for advance reservations and execution planning respectively. We compare the Grid resources for their availability in two dimensions: the static availability comparison through MTBF (mean time before failure) and MTR (mean time to reboot); the dynamic availability comparison through resource stability (for different job durations), and the resource dependability (as a function of time). We argue that the later two metrics are more suitable for resource comparisons as they include better probabilities approximations about resources' availability. These are described in the following sections.

## 3.1    Resource Stability

Stability of a Grid resource for a time duration reflects its suitability for executing jobs of that duration. We define stability (of availability) of a Grid resource for a duration $t_k$, having a set of $n$ durations $t = \{t_1, t_2, t_3, ..., t_n\}$, as:

$$\zeta(t_k) = \sum_{\forall t_i \geq t_k} \left\lfloor \frac{t_i}{t_k} \right\rfloor \times P(t_i)$$

where $P(t_i)$ denotes the probability of duration $t_i$ for the resource.

We present the resource stability comparison at resource class level in Figure 1. The on-demand resources have the lowest stability while the dedicated resources have the highest. For job duration of 60 minutes the dedicated resources have a stability of 44 (more than 8 times that of on-demand resources), and temporal resources exhibit that of 11 (more than 2 times that of on-demand resources). The space limit does not allow us to present individual resource comparisons here.

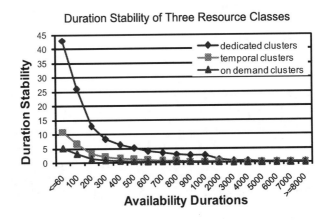

**Figure 1:** Resource stabilities for jobs of different durations at resource class level

## 3.2    Resource Consistent Availability over Time

In contrast to existing works [8, 17] which use only simple availability properties like daily and hourly availability to compare resources, we consider mean duration of availability as MTBF and mean duration of unavailability as MTR for the Grid resources too. Duration of availability of Grid resources is of critical importance for execution of long jobs. Likewise, duration of unavailability is also an important measure for ahead of time planning for job executions as in advance reservations. We define the duration of availability as the time elapsed between the occurrence of resource turned *on* or recovered after the failure and

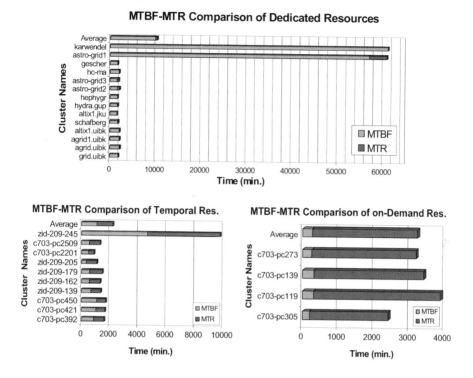

**Figure 2:** MTBF and MTR comparison of resources in three resource classes

again turn *off/failed*. Likewise, we formulate our definition for duration of un-availability. It is noteworthy that our definitions coincide with that of time to repair by [13, 12] and of recovery time used in [5]. Figure 2 shows average availability duration(MTBF), and average unavailability durations(MTR), for each of the individual resource classes. The MTBF(MTR) of resources at Grid level, is observed about 4 days(1008 min). At resource classes level, these estimates clearly give a better view of resource duration availability. Intuitively, the class of dedicated resources show the highest (of three classes) MTBF of 7 days on average, with max.(min.) of 42 days (1609 min). These also exhibited the lowest (of three classes) MTR of 45 min., with max.(min.) of 89 (26) min. Temporal resources, at class level showed almost equal MTBF and MTR and highest MTR of the three classes. They showed an average MTBF and MTR of 18 hrs. Max.(min.) of MTBF were 77(6) hrs., whereas those of MTR are 5149(381) min. On demand resources on average showed the lowest (of three classes) MTBF of 269 min. and an MTR of 2944 min. We found on-demand resources with higher MTR than temporal resources. The SD was quite low for both MTBF and MTR in case of dedicated resources, whereas these were quite high for temporal and on-demand resource classes. It is also important to note that the failure durations may include the night hours during which the system administrators of the Grid sites are not available, and the durations for which the machines are automatically turned off. Furthermore, it may also include the durations for Grid-sites' maintenance/repair etc.

## 3.3    Resource Dependability

The resource dependability describes the extent to which a resource can be depended for being available. We define resource dependability as a function of time duration, as its probability of availability for a given time duration or higher. For a resource exhibiting a set of different consistent life times $l = l_1, l_2, l_3...l_m$

$$\eta(t) = \sum_i^m P(l_i) \mid l_i > t$$

A comparison of resource dependability at the level of resource classes is shown in Figure 3 as a sum of probabilities of the different lifetimes($t$) and their greater lifetimes $P(x \geq t)$. On average, classes of dedicated, temporal and on-demand resources have a maximum dependability of approx. $65$ days, $4$ days and $1000$ min. respectively. It is interesting to note that dedicated resources on average have $35\%$ dependability for a job lasting a little more than a day. The temporal resources are $50\%$ dependable for the jobs of $6$ hours or more, and on-demand resources have $50\%$ dependability for the jobs lasting more than $90$ min.

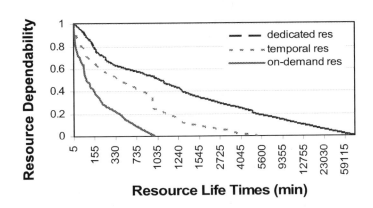

**Figure 3:** Dependability comparison of three resource classes

# 4.   Resource Availability Prediction

In this section we present our resource availability prediction methods. We employ three methods from *pattern recognition and classification* for resource availability predictions, to serve resource *instance* or *point* availability and *duration* availability predictions: the *Bayes' Rule*, *Nearest Neighbor Rule* and *Pattern Matching*. The motivation behind employing these methods is the shape of the auto-correlation function of availability of the three resource classes (figure not shown), which indicates that there are strong patterns in the availability of the resources.Instance or point availability describes resource availability at a certain point of time; in our presented work it refers to the next monitoring instance. Whereas, the duration availability describes resource availability for a certain time duration, in our presented work it refers to the immediate next duration of a certain time span. These methods exploit different patterns of resource availability to serve its future availability predictions. Below we describe some patterns in resource availability at resource class level.

## 4.1   Patterns in Resource Availability

We observed different resource availability patterns over time– in a day and over different days of week. Figure 4 depicts diurnal resource availability patterns in a day; availability peaks during 8a.m. to 8p.m. and recesses during the remaining hours. The maximum availability was found at 4p.m., 2p.m., 3p.m. and the minimum at 4a.m., 8a.m., 4a.m. respectively for the three classes. We observed interesting patterns at resource class level as well at Grid level. The availability remains comparatively in a small range during the night hours with the minimum value between 4a.m. and 8a.m. This is the time when most of the resources are turned off or given a restart. After the minimum value it starts increasing towards the peak value (except one decrease in dedicated resources), and from the maximum it decreases towards a certain level to be maintained till the minimum occurs.

The availability patterns on 28 machines (machine names are irrelevant) over different week days are shown in Figure 5. Two classes of patterns can be visualized from this figure; first, with lower availability at week ends, and higher during the working week days. This class has an increasing availability till Tuesday or Wednesday and then decreasing till weekend. Second, with higher availability on weekends and lower during the working weekdays. This class has a decreasing availability till Wednesday and then again increasing availability till Saturday.

The average SD over different hours of the day was 4.16 as compared with that of 1.37 on a specific hour of the day. Moreover, at Grid level, an average SD over different week days was 12.3 and that of 6.6 was observed in availabilities on specific week days. This remarkable lower SD in availabilities on a specific

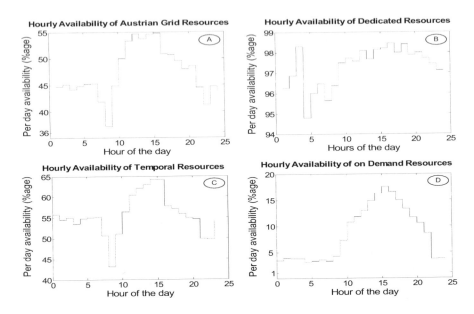

**Figure 4:** Resource hour-of-the-day availability at resource class and Grid level

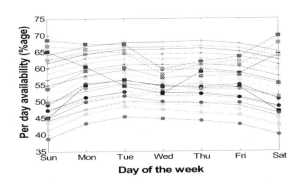

**Figure 5:** Resource availability patterns over different days of week

day of the week than that on all week days, indicates strong availability pattern on specific week days. In sequel, lower SD in availabilities on specific hour of the day than that on all hours, shows similar availability patterns over specific hours of the day. In the following sections we present different prediction methods we employed.

## 4.2    Prediction Methods

In this paper we present a new prediction method from *pattern recognition and classification*: *pattern matching* and compare the results with our previous work in [7]. The pattern matching is a well recognized technique from pattern recognition and classification [4]. It considers resource's recent patterns of availability of certain duration and searches for the same from the past trace. It predicts the resource behavior as its most likely behavior subsequently after the same patterns in the past. For *instance* availability prediction the first subsequent resource status is considered, whereas for *duration* prediction the subsequent duration of interest is taken into account. We employ *Boyer-Moore String Matching* algorithm with *bad-character heuristic* and *good-suffix heuristic* [4] for pattern matching. The main advantage of this algorithm is that it has a complexity just of $O(n)$, and is much faster than similar others.

## 5. Performance Evaluation

This section describes the evaluation results for the prediction methods presented in the last section. We evaluated these methods for their prediction accuracy, calculated as *Accuracy =(no. of true predictions)/(total number of prediction queries)* represented as percentage. In case of instance availability prediction, a prediction is treated true if the resource immediate next status is the same as predicted, otherwise it is considered false. In case of duration availability prediction, prediction is treated as true if a resource is predicted to be available for a certain immediate duration and resource is available for that duration or longer, otherwise it is considered false. In case when resource is available for a duration lesser than the predicted, the accuracy of prediction is calculated as the ratio of actual available duration to the predicted. Furthermore, the accuracy is recorded for different predictors which use different features from the feature vector described in [7].

## 5.1 Instance Availability Prediction

We made a greedy evaluation of accuracy of predictions made through Bayes' rule [7]. The accuracy was evaluated for all the resources in every resource class and accuracy at class level is presented by taking their average. For one resource, the prediction was evaluated on all the days of monitoring period (more than 300) and the accuracy was recorded on daily basis, where prediction query time in a day was selected at random. Thus, every resource was evaluated for more than 300 times, while the class-level daily accuracy was averaged from all the resources in the resource class. The daily accuracy of predictions for three resource classes using predictor hourOfDay_cur [7] is presented in Figure 6(A). For dedicated resources, the average accuracy was 97%. Accuracy for temporal resources averaged to 90% and on-demand resources exhibited that of 94%. We found for the all three classes that prediction accuracy decreases as more historical data distant from the prediction query time is included in calculating the priories.

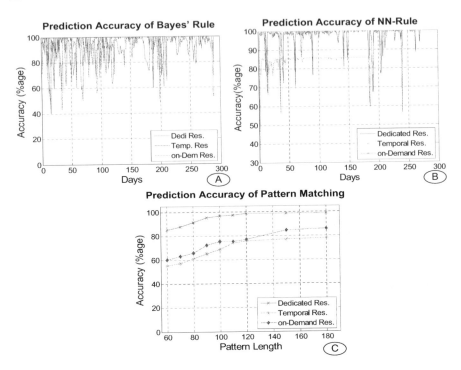

**Figure 6:** Resource instance availability prediction through Bayes' rule, NN-rule and pattern matching: Prediction accuracy comparisons of the three resource classes

A similar greedy setup was made for evaluation of instance availability predictions through NN-rule [7], as the same for Bayes' rule. Prediction accuracy results for the three resource classes using NN-rule are depicted in Figure 6(B). The average accuracies were recorded as $99.98\%$, $82.4\%$ and $98.4\%$ respectively for dedicated, temporal and on-demand resources at class level. The very high prediction accuracy for dedicated and on-demand resources is due to their high MTBF and high MTR, respectively. NN-rule gives higher accuracies for instance availability predictions for all three resource classes as compared with those through Bayes' rule.

Accuracy of instance availability predictions through pattern matching was also evaluated through a similar test phase. The accuracy results for the three resource classes are shown in Figure 6(C). Pattern matching showed $94.41\%$ accuracy for dedicated resources, while the same for temporal and on-demand resources was $68.13\%$ and $73.34\%$ respectively. The lower accuracy of temporal resources is due to a higher variation in their patterns of (un)availability over time. The pattern matching yielded the least accuracy of $78.63\%$ at Grid level, as compared with the three methods.

## 5.2    Duration Availability Prediction

Prediction accuracy results of the the three methods, for duration availability, are evaluated extensively through a series of experiments. For every resource, predictions were evaluated for the time durations starting from 10 min. to 24 hrs. with the increments of 5 min. Prediction for every duration was repeated 100 times, where date and time were randomly selected from the resource monitoring duration. These 100 repetitions were later averaged to record accuracy for that duration for the selected resource. Average accuracy for each time duration on all resources in a resource class, was recorded as accuracy of the class for that duration. The prediction accuracy of Bayes' rule with the predictor dayOfWeek using different amount of trace data, for the three resource classes is shown in Figure 7(a). We have noted that the prediction accuracy decreases as amount of historical data more distant from the prediction query time is included

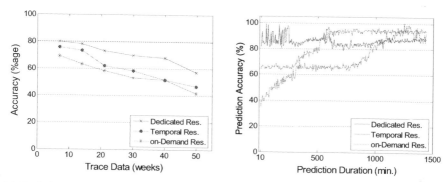

(a) Prediction accuracy through Bayes' rule using different amount of trace data

(b) Prediction accuracy through NN-rule for different durations

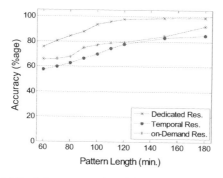

(c) Prediction accuracy through Pattern Matching for different pattern lengths

**Figure 7:** Accuracies comparison of duration availability predictions of the three resource classes through different methods.

while calculating priories. This was also conformed by ACF (auto-correlation function) of availability durations(not shown here). The highest accuracy of duration availability predictions was observed in class of dedicated resources, which is due to their better stability for jobs of different durations, as shown in Figure 1. Bayes' rule exhibited a better accuracy of duration availability predictions for temporal resources than on-demand resources, which shows that on-demand resources were made available for quite different time durations.

We present the accuracy of predictions for duration availability through NN-rule for the time durations of 10min-24hrs. The Figure 7(b) presents the prediction accuracy results at resource class level. Dedicated resources, as in all other evaluations showed the highest accuracy, within the range of $79\% - 99\%$. NN-rule prediction accuracy increases from a minimum of $64\%$ to a maximum of $93\%$ for temporal resources, whereas, in case of on-demand resources, it increases from a minimum of $36\%$ to a maximum of $100\%$. The increase in prediction accuracy by NN-rule, for temporal and on-demand resources is as expected– because resources in these two classes were available for relatively shorter time durations and NN-rule made availability predictions with higher accuracy for longer durations than for smaller durations.

The average accuracy of predictions for different durations, through pattern matching, using patterns of different lengths, are shown in the Figure 7(c). We observed accuracies of $93.18\%$, $69.39\%$ and $75.56\%$ for dedicated, temporal and on-demand resources respectively. We observed an increase in the accuracy when the pattern length was increased. This shows that resources exhibit more consistent behavior over longer time durations than shorter durations. Pattern matching resulted in better accuracy than NN-rule for duration predictions.

## 6.    Related Work

Several other studies characterize or model availability in different environments like cluster of computers [3], multi-computers [13], meta-computers (also called desktop Grids) [9], Grid [11], [2], super-computers [13], and peer-to-peer systems [8]. Most of these studies are about early systems considering only short term availability data, and ignoring machine availability policies. The two most closely related studies to ours are [2] and [11]. These works consider the availability characteristics at Grid level only, whereas we identify different classes of resources based on their policies of availability in the Grid, and analyze their properties on the class level, and achieve better representative aggregates. Another closely related study to ours is [16] that analyzes resource availability through CPU failures, and finds its implications on large-scale clusters. We further compare resources based on their daily availability, hourly availability, MTBF, MTR, their dependability for different jobs and are the first to compare resources based on their stability for jobs of different durations.

Predictions from availability models give probability of resource in available state and are most of the times insufficient to decide whether the resource will be available or not [7]. Works in [10], [15] and [11] have made predictions based on previous weekday or weekend only, and have got moderate accuracy in their predictions. In contrast we employ methods from pattern recognition and classification, which exploit knowledge from our resource availability characterization phase, and takes into account patterns from resource past behavior as well as its current behavior, and yield very promising results.

## 7.    Conclusion

Besides that the Grid technology is getting more matured day by day, different policies for resource availability in the Grid, and resources' working *stability* raise serious issues about their suitability for different jobs. In this work we compare resources based traditional and new metrics- their MTBF, MTR in general and their *stability* and *dependability* for jobs of different durations in particular. Different comparison criteria suit to different needs. We argue the later two metrics better compare the resources considering the job durations. Dedicated resources revealed the highest *stability* for all jobs of different durations and showed the highest MTBF and the lowest MTR, the converse it true for on-demand resources. Stability of temporal resources falls in the mid range of other two resource classes, and they showed an almost equal MTBF and MTR. Next, we find patterns in resource availability and make resource instance and duration availability predictions by using three methods from *pattern recognition and classification*; Bayes' Rule, Nearest Neighbor Rule and Pattern Matching. We extensively evaluated the accuracy for these methods using different predictors and different amount of historical data. On average, more than $90\%$ and $70\%$ accuracy is found for instance and duration predictions respectively, when minimum of historical data was used.

As future work, we will try to integrate resource computational metrics (MFlops and others) with availability metrics to come up with a unified metric to compare the resources in a generic way as well. We would also like to validate our resource availability prediction methods using availability traces from other Grids. We also plan to evaluate improvements in job execution performance through availability aware resource selection, and availability aware data storage.

## References

[1]  The Austrian Grid Consortium. http://www.austriangrid.at.

[2]  Alexandru Iosup et al. On the dynamic resources availability in grids. In *CCGrid*, Rio de Janeiro, Brazil, May 14-17, 2007.

[3]  Anurag Acharya et al. The utility of exploiting idle workstations for parallel computation. In *international conference on measurement and modeling of computer systems*, Seattle, Washington, USA, 1997.

[4]  Duda, Richard O. et al. *Pattern Classification (2nd Edition)*. Wiley-Interscience, November 2000.

[5]  C. Ebeling. *An Introduction to Reliability and Maintainability Engineering*. McGraw-Hill, Boston, MA, 1997.

[6]  Farrukh Nadeem et al. Soft benchmarks-based application performance prediction using a minimum training set. In *e-Science 2006*, Amsterdam, Netherlands.

[7]  F. Nadeem, R. Prodan, and T. Fahringer. Characterizing, Modeling and Predicting Dynamic Resource Availability in a Large Scale Multi-Purpose Grid. In *Proc. of CCGrid 2008*, Lyon, France, May 2008.

[8]  R. Bhagwan et al. Understanding availability. In *Proceedings of the 2nd International Workshop on Peer-to-Peer Systems*, Feb 2003.

[9]  R. Wolski et al. Automatic methods for predicting machine availability in desktop grid and peer-to-peer systems. In *CCGrid2004*, Chicago, Illinois, USA.

[10] X. Ren and R. Eigenmann. Empirical studies on the behavior of resource availability in fine-grained cycle sharing systems. In *International Conference on Parallel Processing*, Washington, DC, USA, 2006.

[11] B. Rood and M. J. Lewis. Multi-state grid resource availability characterization. In *International Conference on Grid Computing*, Austin, TX, September 17-19, 2007.

[12] B. Schroeder and G. A. Gibson. A large-scale study of failures in high-performance computing systems. In *International Conference on Dependable Systems and Networks*, Washington, DC, USA, 2006.

[13] D. Tang and R. K. Iyer. Dependability measurement and modeling of a multicomputer system. *IEEE Trans. Comput.*, 42(1), 1993.

[14] Thomas Fahringer et al. Askalon: a grid application development and computing environment. In *GRID05*.

[15] Xiaojuan Ren et al. Resource availability prediction in fine-grained cycle sharing systems. In *International Performance and Distributed Computation*, 2006.

[16] Yanyong Zhang et al. Performance implications of failures in large-scale cluster scheduling. 2004.

[17] D. Kondo et al. Characterizing and evaluating desktop grids: An empirical study, 2004.

# ONLINE HIERARCHICAL JOB SCHEDULING ON GRIDS

Andrei Tchernykh
*Computer Science Department, CICESE Research Center, Ensenada, BC, México*
chernykh@cicese.mx


Uwe Schwiegelshohn
*Robotics Research Institute, Technische Universität Dortmund, Dortmund, Germany*
uwe.schwiegelshohn@udo.edu


Ramin Yahyapour
*IT and Media Center, Technische Universität Dortmund, Dortmund, Germany*
ramin.yahyapour@udo.edu


Nikolai Kuzjurin
*Institute of System Programming RAS, Moscow, Russia*
nnkuz@ispras.ru

**Abstract**      In this paper, we address non preemptive online scheduling of parallel jobs on a Grid. The Grid consists of a large number of identical processors that are divided into several machines. We consider a Grid scheduling model with two stages. At the first stage, jobs are allocated to a suitable machine while at the second stage, local scheduling is applied to each machine independently. We discuss strategies based on various combinations of allocation strategies and local scheduling algorithms. Finally, we propose and analyze a relatively simple scheme named adaptive admissible allocation. This includes competitive analysis for different parameters and constraints. We show that the algorithm is beneficial under certain conditions and allows an efficient implementation in real systems. Furthermore, a dynamic and adaptive approach is presented which can cope with different workloads and Grid properties.

**Keywords:**    Grid Computing, Online Scheduling, Resource Management, Algorithmic Analysis, Job Allocation

## 1.    Introduction

Due to the size and dynamic nature of Grids, allocating computational jobs
to available Grid resources requires an automatic and efficient process. Various scheduling systems have been proposed and implemented in different types
of Grids. However, there are still many open issues in this field, including
the consideration of multiple layers of scheduling, dynamicity, and scalability.
Grids are typically composed of heterogeneous resources which are decentralized and geographically dispersed. Academic studies often propose a completely distributed resource management system, see, for instance, Uppuluri et
al. [13] while real installations favor a combination of decentralized and centralized structures, see, for instance, GridWay [4]. A hierarchical multilayer
resource management can represent such a system well. Therefore, we use
this model to find a suitable tradeoff between a fully centralized and a fully
decentralized model. The highest layer is often a Grid-level scheduler that
may have a more general view of the resources while the lowest layer is the
local resource management system that manages a specific resource or set of
resources, see Schwiegelshohn and Yahyapour [10]. Other layers may exist in
between. At every layer, additional constraints and specifications must be considered, for instance, related to the dynamics of the resource situation. Thus,
suitable scheduling algorithms are needed to support such multilayer structures
of resource management.

Grids are typically based on existing scheduling methods for multiprocessors
and use an additional Grid scheduling layer [10]. The scheduling of jobs on
multiprocessors is generally well understood and has been studied for decades.
Many research results exist for different variations of this single system scheduling problem; some of them provide theoretical insights while others give hints
for the implementation of real systems. However, the scheduling in Grids is
almost exclusively addressed by practitioners looking for suitable implementations. There are only very few theoretical results on Grid scheduling and
most of them address divisible load scheduling like, for instance, Robertazzi
and Yu [7].

In this paper, we propose new Grid scheduling approaches and use a theoretical analysis to evaluate them. As computational Grids are often considered as
successors and extensions of multiprocessors or clusters we start with a simple
model of parallel computing and extend it to Grids. One of the most basic
models due to Garey and Graham [2] assumes a multiprocessor with identical
processors as well as independent, rigid, parallel jobs with unknown processing
times, where a suitable set of concurrently available processors exclusively executes this job. Although this model neither matches every real installation nor
all real applications the assumptions are nonetheless reasonable. The model
is still a valid basic abstraction of a parallel computer and many applications.

Our Grid model extends this approach by assuming that the processors are arranged into several machines and that parallel jobs cannot run across multiple machines. The latter assumption is typically true for jobs with extensive communication among the various processors unless special care has been devoted to optimize the code for a multisite configuration.

While a real Grid often consists of heterogeneous parallel machines, one can argue that an identical processor model is still reasonable as most modern processors in capacity computing mainly differ in the number of cores rather than in processor speed. Our model considers two main properties of a Grid: separate parallel machines and different machine sizes. Therefore, the focus of this paper is on these properties of Grids.

From a system point of view, it is typically the goal of a Grid scheduler to achieve some kind of load balancing in the Grid. In scheduling theory, this is commonly represented by the objective of makespan minimization. Although the makespan objective is mainly an offline criterion and has some shortcomings particularly in online scenarios with independent jobs, it is easy to handle and therefore frequently used even in these scenarios, see, for instance, Albers [1]. Hence, we also apply this objective in this paper. For such a model, Schwiegelshohn et al. [9] showed that the performance of Garey and Graham's list scheduling algorithm is significantly worse in Grids than in multiprocessors. They present an online non-clairvoyant algorithm that guarantees a competitive factor of 5 for the Grid scenario where all available jobs can be used for local scheduling. The offline non-clairvoyant version of this algorithm has an approximation factor of 3. This "one-layer" algorithm can be implemented in centralized fashion or use a distributed "job stealing" approach. Although jobs are allocated to a machine at their submission times they can migrate if another machine becomes idle.

In this paper, we use a two layer hierarchical online Grid scheduling model. Once a job is allocated to a machine it must be scheduled and executed on this machine, that is, migration between machines is not allowed. Tchernykh et al. [11] considered a similar model for the offline case and addressed the performance of various 2-stage algorithms with respect to the makespan objective. They present algorithms with an approximation factor of 10.

In Section 2, we present our Grid scheduling model in more details. The algorithms are classified and analyzed in Section 3. We propose a novel adaptive two-level admissible scheduling strategy and analyze it in Section 4. Finally, we conclude with a summary and an outlook in Section 5.

## 2. Model

As already discussed, we address an online scheduling problem with the objective of minimizing the makespan: $n$ parallel jobs $J_1, J_2, \ldots$ must be scheduled on $m$ parallel machines $N_1, N_2, \ldots, N_m$. $m_i$ denotes the number of identical processors of machine $N_i$. W.l.o.g. we index the parallel machines in ascending order of their sizes $m_1 \le m_2 \le \ldots \le m_m$, and introduce $m_0 = 0$.

Each job $J_j$ is described by a triple $(r_j, size_j, p_j)$: its release date $r_j \ge 0$, its size $1 \le size_j \le m_m$ that is referred to as its *degree of parallelism*, and its execution time $p_j$. The release date is not available before a job is submitted, and its processing time is unknown until the job has completed its execution (non-clairvoyant scheduling).

We assume that job $J_j$ can only run on machine $N_i$ if $size_j \le m_i$ holds, that is, we do not allow multi-site execution and co-allocation of processors from different machines. Finally, $g(J_j) = N_i$ denotes that job $J_j$ is allocated to machine $N_i$. Let $n_i$ be the number of jobs allocated to the machine $N_i$.

We assume a space sharing scheduling mode as this is typically applied on many parallel computers. Therefore, a parallel job $J_j$ is executed on exactly $size_j$ disjoint processors without preemptions.

Let $p_{max}$ be $\max_{1 \le j \le n}\{p_j\}$. Further, $W_j = p_j \cdot size_j$ is the work of job $J_j$, also called its area or its resource consumption. Similarly, the total work of a job set $I$ is $W_I = \sum_{J_j \in I} W_j$. $c_j(S)$ denotes the completion time of job $J_j$ in schedule $S$. We omit schedule $S$ if we can do so without causing ambiguity.

All strategies are analyzed according to their competitive factor for makespan optimization. Let $C^*_{max}$ and $C_{max}(A)$ denote the makespan of an optimal schedule and of a schedule determined by strategy $A$, respectively. The competitive factor of strategy $A$ is defined as $\rho_A = \sup \frac{C_{max}(A)}{C^*_{max}}$ for all problem instances.

The notation $GP_m$ describes our Grid machine model. In the short three field notation *machine model-constraints-objective* proposed by Graham et al. [3], this problem is characterized as $GP_m|r_j, size_j|C_{max}$. We use the notation $MPS$ to refer to this problem while the notation $PS$ describes the parallel job scheduling on a single parallel machine ($P_m|r_j, size_j|C_{max}$).

## 3.  Classification of Algorithms

In this section, we first split the scheduling algorithm into an allocation part and a local scheduling part. Then we introduce different strategies to allocate jobs to machines. We classify these strategies depending on the type and amount of information they require. Finally, we analyze the performance of these algorithms.

### 3.1  Two Layer MPS Lower Bound

Before going into details we add some general remarks about the approximation bounds of $MPS$. We regard $MPS$ as two stage scheduling strategy: $MPS = MPS\_Alloc + PS$. At the first stage, we allocate a suitable machine for each job using a given selection criterion. At the second stage, algorithm $PS$

is applied to each machine independently for jobs allocated during the previous stage.

It is easy to see that the competitive factor of the $MPS$ algorithm is lower bounded by the competitive factor of the best $PS$ algorithm. Just consider a degenerated Grid that only contains a single machine. In this case, the competitive factors of the $MPS$ algorithm and the best $PS$ algorithm are identical as there is no need for any allocation stage.

But clearly, an unsuitable allocation strategy may produce bad competitive factors. Just assume that all jobs are allocated to a single machine in a Grid with $k$ identical machines. Obviously, the competitive factor is lower bounded by $k$.

The best possible $PS$ online non-clairvoyant algorithm has a tight competitive factor $2 - 1/m$ with $m$ denoting the number of processors in the parallel system; see Naroska and Schwiegelshohn [6]. Hence, the lower bound of a competitive factor for any general two-layer online $MPS$ is at least $2 - 1/m$.

Schwiegelshohn et al. [9] showed that there is no polynomial time algorithm that guarantees schedules with a competitive bound $< 2$ for $GP_m|size_j|C_{\max}$ and all problem instances unless $P = NP$. Therefore, the multiprocessor list scheduling bound of $2 - 1/m$, see Garey and Graham [2] for concurrent submission as well as Naroska and Schwiegelshohn [6] for online submission, does not apply to Grids. Even more, list scheduling cannot guarantee a constant competitive bound for all problem instances in the concurrent submission case [9, 11].

## 3.2 Job Allocation

Now, we focus on job allocation with the number of parallel machines and the information about the size of each machine being known. Further, we distinguish four different levels of additionally available information for job allocation.

Level 1: The job load of each machine, that is the number $n_i$ of jobs waiting to run on machine $N_i$, is available. We use the job allocation strategies $Min\_L$ and $Min\_LP$. $Min\_L$ allocates a job to the machine with the smallest job load. This strategy is similar to static load balancing. $Min\_LP$ takes into account the number of processors and selects the resource with the lowest job load per processor ($\arg\{\min_{1\leq i\leq m}\{\frac{n_i}{m_i}\}\}$). Note that neither strategy considers the degree of parallelism or the processing time of a job.

Level 2: Additionally to the information of Level 1, the degree of parallelism $size_j$ of each job is known. The $Min\_PL$ strategy selects a machine with the smallest parallel load per processor ($\arg\{\min_{1\leq i\leq m}\{\sum_{g(J_j)=N_i}\frac{size_j}{m_i}\}\}$).

Level 3: In addition to the information of Level 2, we consider clairvoy-
ant scheduling, that is, the execution time of each job is available. The
$Min\_LB$ strategy allocates a job to the machine $N_i$ with the least remaining total workload of all jobs already allocated to this machine, that
is

$$\arg\{\min_{1 \leq i \leq m}\{\sum_{g(J_j)=N_i}\frac{size_j \cdot p_j}{m_i}\}\}.$$

If the actual processing time $p_j$ of job $J_j$ is not available, we may use
an estimate of the processing time instead. Such an estimate may be
generated automatically based on history files or provided by the user
when the job is submitted.

Level 4: We have access to all information of Level 3 and to all local schedules
as well. The $Min\_CT$ job strategy allocates job $J_j$ to the machine with
the earliest completion time of this job using the existing schedules and
the job queues [8, 14].

Levels 1 and 2 describe non-clairvoyant problems. Strategies of Levels 1 to
3 are based only on the parameters of jobs, and do not need any information
about local schedules.

## 3.3    Two Layer MPS Strategies

In this section, we analyze a two layer online $MPS$ for different $PS$ algorithms and the $MPS$-allocation strategies $Min\_L$, $Min\_LP$, $Min\_PL$,
$Min\_LB$, and $Min\_CT$.

Tchernykh et al. [11] discussed the combination of allocation strategies with
the simple online scheduling algorithm $FCFS$, that schedules jobs in the order of their arrival times. Clearly, this strategy cannot guarantee a constant
approximation factor as $FCFS$ is already not able to do this. Even if all jobs
are available at time 0 and they are sorted in descending order of the degree of
parallelism, we cannot achieve a constant competitive factor [11, 9].

Let us consider now the case of an arbitrary online local $PS$ algorithm.
Based on the simple example considered by Tchernykh et al. [11] for offline
strategies and Schwiegelshohn et al. [9] for online strategies, it can be shown
that $Min\_L$, $Min\_LP$, and $Min\_PL$ allocation strategies combined with $PS$
cannot guarantee a constant approximation factor of $MPS$ in the worst case.

Let us now consider the two allocation strategies $Min\_LB$ and $Min\_CT$
that take into account job execution times. Fig. 1 shows an example of sets
of machines and a set of jobs for which constant approximation factors are
not guaranteed for $Min\_LB + PS$ and $Min\_CT + PS$. In this figure, the
vertical axis represents time while the bars and their widths denote machines
and their numbers of processors, respectively. The example has an optimal

makespan of 2, see Fig. 1. If the jobs are released in ascending order of their degrees of parallelism, algorithms $Min\_LB + PS$ and $Min\_CT + PS$ allocate them to machines as shown in Fig. 2. If the processing time is identical for all jobs the makespans of algorithms $Min\_LB + PS$ and $Min\_CT + PS$ equal the number of job groups with different degrees of parallelism. Additional information about the schedule in each machine (application of $Min\_CT$) does not help to improve the worst case behavior of $MPS$. Results are the similar for the offline [11] and the online [9] cases.

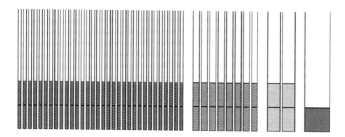

**Figure 1:** Optimal schedule of a bad instance.

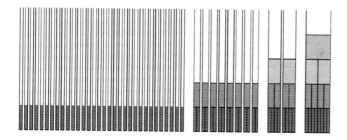

**Figure 2:** $Min\_LB + PS$ schedule for the instance of Fig.1.

## 4. Adaptive Admissible Allocation Strategy

Based on the example shown in Figure 2, it can be seen that one reason of the inefficient online job allocation is the occupation of large machines by sequential jobs causing highly parallel jobs to wait for their execution.

Tchernykh et al. [11] proposed a relatively simple scheme named *admissible selection* that can be efficiently implemented in real systems. This scheme excludes certain machines with many processors from the set of machines available to execute jobs with little parallelism.

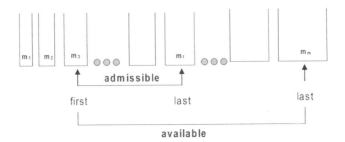

**Figure 3:** Concept of the admissible model

Let the machines be indexed in non-descending order of their sizes ($m_1 \leq m_2 \leq \ldots \leq m_m$). We define $f(j) = \text{first}(j)$ to be the smallest index $i$ such that $m_i \geq size_j$ holds for job $J_j$. Note that due to our restriction $size_j \leq m_m \forall J_j$, we have $l \leq m$. The set of available machines $M_{available}(j)$ that are available for allocation of job $J_j$ corresponds to the set of machine indexes $s(f(j), m) = \{f(j), f(j) + 1, \ldots, m\}$, see Fig. 3. Obviously, the total set of machines $M - total$ is represented by the integer set $s(1, m) = 1, \ldots, m$. $m(f, l) = \sum_{i=f}^{l} m_i$ is the total number of processors that are in machines $m_f$ to $m_l$.

Tchernykh et al. [11] defined the set $M_{admissible}(j)$ of admissible machines for a job $J_j$ to be the machines with their indexes being in the set $s(f(j), r(j))$, see Fig. 3. $r(j)$ is the smallest number with $m(f(j), r(j)) \geq \frac{1}{2}m(f(j), m)$. In this paper, the definition is generalized by introducing a new parameter $0 \leq a \leq 1$ that parameterizes the admissibility ratio used for the job allocation. Hence, we call $s(f(j), r(j))$ the index set of admissible machines if $r(j)$ is the minimum index such that $m(f)j), r(j)) \geq a \cdot m(f(j), m)$ holds. The choice $a = 0.5$ produces the original definition of Tchernykh et al. [11].

A worst case analysis of adaptive admissible selection strategies is presented in Section 4.2.

## 4.1    Workload

Before going into details of admissible job allocation strategies, we define different types of possible workloads. First, we combine all machines of the same size into group. Let $i$ be a machine index such that $m_{i-1} < m_i$. Then group $G_i$ contains all machines $M_j$ with $m_j = m_i$. The size of $G_i$ is the total number of processors of all machines in $G_i$. Further, we can partition the set of all jobs into sets $Y_i$ such that $J_j \in Y_i$ if and only if $m_{i-1} < size_j \leq m_i$ holds, that is, all jobs of $Y_i$ can be executed by machines of $G_i$ but do not fit on any machine of a group $G_h$ with $h < i$. Note that some sets $Y_i$ may be empty.

The workload is *balanced* for a set of machines $G = \bigcup_{i=1}^{k} G_i$ with some $k > 0$ if the ratio of the total work of set $Y_i$ and the size of group $G_i$ is the same for all groups of $G$.

The workload is *perfect* for $G$ if it is balanced and each set $Y_i$ can be scheduled in a nondelay fashion on $G_i$ such that makespans of all machines in $G$ are identical. Fig. 1 shows an example of a balanced workload for each set of machines that do not include the last machine.

## 4.2    Analysis

In this section, we consider the allocation strategies of Section 3.3 for admissible machines. Formally, we denote this extension by appending the letter $a$ to the strategy name, for instance, $Min\_L - a$. Tchernykh et al. [11] showed that strategies $(Min\_L - a, Min\_PL - a) + FCFS$ cannot guarantee constant approximations for $a = 0.5$. This result also holds for arbitrary $a$ and algorithm $Best\_PS$. We already showed in Section 3.3 that $Min\_LB$ cannot guarantee a constant approximation even in combination with the $Best\_PS$. We now consider the case when the selection of a suitable machine for executing job $J_j$ is limited by its admissible set of machines $M_{admissible}(j)$.

**4.2.1    Online Allocation and Online Local Scheduling.**    First, we determine the competitive factor of algorithm $Min\_LB - a + Best\_PS$.

THEOREM 1 *Assume a set of machines with identical processors, a set of rigid jobs, and admissible allocation range $0 \le a \le 1$. Then algorithm $Min\_LB - a + Best\_PS$ has the competitive factor*

$$\rho \le \begin{cases} 1 + \frac{1}{a^2} - \frac{1}{m(1,m)} & \text{for } a \le \frac{m(f,m)}{m(f_0,m)} \\ 1 + \frac{1}{a(1-a)} - \frac{1}{m(1,m)} & \text{for } a > \frac{m(f,m)}{m(f_0,m)} \end{cases}$$

*with $1 \le f_0 \le f \le m$ being parameters that depend on the workload, see Fig. 4.*

**Proof.** Let us assume that the makespan of machine $N_k$ is also the makespan $C_{\max}$ of the Grid. Then let job $J_d$ be the last job that was added to this machine. We use the notations $f = f(d)$ and $r = r(d)$. $I_f, \dots, I_r$ are the sets of jobs that had already been scheduled on machines $N_f, \dots, N_r$ before adding job $J_d$. Remember that machines $N_f, \dots, N_r$ constitute the set $M_{admissible}(d)$. Since $J_d$ was added to machine $N_k$, $Min\_LB - a$ guarantees $\frac{W_{I_k}}{m_k} \le \frac{W_{I_i}}{m_i}$ for all

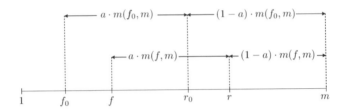

**Figure 4:** Admissible allocation with factor $a$

$i = f, \ldots, r$. Therefore, we have

$$
\begin{aligned}
W(f,r) &= \sum_{i=f}^{r} W_{I_i} = \sum_{i=f}^{r} \frac{W_{I_i}}{m_i} m_i \\
&\geq \sum_{i=f}^{r} \frac{W_{I_k}}{m_k} m_i = \frac{W_{I_k}}{m_k} \sum_{i=f}^{r} m_i = \frac{W_{I_k}}{m_k} m(f,r).
\end{aligned}
$$

Let $W_{idle}^{opt}$ be the idle workload space of the optimal solution on the machine $N_k$. We use the notation $W_i' = W_i + W_{idle}^{opt}$ and obtain

$$
\begin{aligned}
W'(f,r) &= \sum_{i=f}^{r} (W_i + W_{idle}^{opt}) = \sum_{i=f}^{r} W_i' = \sum_{i=f}^{r} \frac{W_i'}{m_i} m_i \\
&\geq \sum_{i=f}^{r} \frac{W_k'}{m_k} m_i == \frac{W_k'}{m_k} \sum_{i=f}^{r} m_i = \frac{W_k'}{m_k} m(f,r). \quad (1)
\end{aligned}
$$

It is known from the literature [5, 12] that in the schedule of machine $N_k$, there are two kinds of time slots which can be combined conceptually into two successive intervals $C_1$ and $C_2$, see Fig. 5.

Let $size_{\max}$ be the maximum size of any job assigned to machine $N_k$. Then the intervals correspond to the parts of the schedule when at most $size_{\max} - 1$ processors are idle and when strictly more than $size_{\max} - 1$ processors are idle, respectively.

Tchernykh et al. [12] showed that $C_2$ is limited by the maximum job execution time $p_{\max}$ and that for an arbitrary list schedule, $W_k \geq (m_k - size_{\max} + 1)C_1 + C_2$ yields the competitive bound $\frac{2m_k - size_{\max}}{m_k - size_{\max} + 1}$.

Algorithm $Best\_PS$ produces the makespan $C = \frac{W_k + W_{idle}^{opt} + W_{idle}}{m_k}$ with $W_{idle}$ being the additional idle space due to $Best\_PS$. To be $2 - \frac{1}{m}$ competitive, algorithm $Best\_PS$ must generate schedules that increase the idle space of the

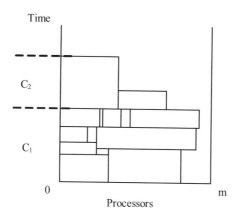

**Figure 5:** Scheduling Rigid Jobs in Space Sharing Mode [12]

optimal schedule by not more than
$$W_{idle} \leq p_{\max} \cdot (m_k - 1).$$

Hence, for $W_k' = W_k + W_{idle}^{opt}$ and $W_k' \geq m_k \cdot C_1 + C_2$, we obtain an upper bound of the total completion time:

$$C \leq \frac{W_k' + p_{\max} \cdot (m_k - 1)}{m_k} = \frac{W_k'}{m_k} + p_{\max} \cdot \left(1 + \frac{1}{m_k}\right) \qquad (2)$$

Due to $C_{\max}^* = \frac{W_k'}{m_k}$ and $C_{\max}^* \geq p_{\max}$, Equation 2 implies a competitive bound $2 - \frac{1}{m}$ for single machine scheduling.

Let $J_b$ be the job having the smallest size among all jobs executed at machines $N_f, \ldots, N_r$. We use the notation $f_0 = f_b$. Hence jobs packed at $N_f, \ldots, N_r$ cannot be allocated to a machine with a smaller index than $f_0$. As $J_b$ is executed on one of the machines $N_f, \ldots, N_r$ we have $r_b \geq f$, see Fig. 4 and $C_{\max}^* \geq \frac{W'(f,r)}{m(f_0,r)}$. Substituting Equation 1 in this formula, we have

$$C_{\max}^* \geq \frac{W_k' m(f,r)}{m_k m(f_0,m)}.$$

Finally, we consider two cases:

- $a \leq \frac{m(f,m)}{m(f_0,m)}$

  From our definition $m(f,r) \geq a \cdot m(f,m)$, we obtain $m(f_0,m) \leq m(f,r)/a^2$. This yields

  $$C_{\max}^* \geq \frac{W_k' \cdot m(f,r)}{m_k \cdot m(f_0,m)} \geq \frac{W_k' \cdot a^2}{m_k}$$

As we have $C^*_{\max} \geq p_{\max}$, Equation 2 implies

$$\rho \leq \frac{W'_k}{m_k C^*_{\max}} + p_{\max}\frac{1 - \frac{1}{m_k}}{C^*_{\max}} \leq 1 + \frac{1}{a^2} - \frac{1}{m(1,m)}$$

- $a > \frac{m(f,m)}{m(f_0,m)}$

  We have $m(f_0, m) \leq m(f, m) + a \cdot m(f_0, m)$, see Fig. 4. This yields

$$C^*_{\max} \geq \frac{W'_k \cdot m(f,r)}{m_k \cdot m(f_0,m)} \geq \frac{W'_k \cdot a \cdot m(f,m)}{m_k \cdot \frac{m(f,m)}{1-a}} = \frac{W'_k \cdot a \cdot (1-a)}{m_k}$$

and

$$\rho \leq \frac{W'_k}{m_k C^*_{\max}} + p_{\max}\frac{1 - \frac{1}{m_k}}{C^*_{\max}} \leq 1 + \frac{1}{a \cdot (1 - a)} - \frac{1}{m(1,m)}$$

*(End)*

Note that both bounds produce the same result $\rho = 5 - \frac{1}{m(1,m)}$ for $a = 0.5$.

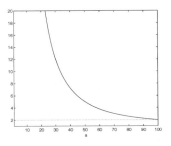 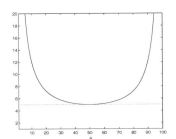

**Figure 6:** $\rho \leq 1 + \frac{1}{a^2} - \frac{1}{m(1,m)}$        **Figure 7:** $\rho \leq 1 + \frac{1}{a(1-a)} - \frac{1}{m(1,m)}$

Fig. 6 to 8 show the bounds of the competitive factor of strategy $Min\_LB - a + Best\_PS$ as a function of the admissible value $a$ in percent.

**4.2.2    Worst Case Performance Tune Up.**    Finally, we analyze the worst case performance for various workload types. We consider two intervals for the admissible factor $a$: $(0, \frac{m(f,m)}{m(f_0,m)}]$ and $(\frac{m(f,m)}{m(f_0,m)}, 1]$. We distinguish only few cases of workload characteristics to determine workload dependent worst case deviations.

- $f = m$ and $f_0 = 1$ produce $\frac{m_m}{\sum_{i=1}^m m_i} \leq a \leq 1$ and $\rho \leq 1 + \frac{1}{a(1-a)} - \frac{1}{m(1,m)}$. These characteristics are normal for a balanced workload. Clearly,

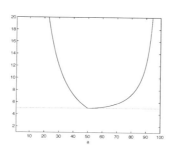

**Figure 8:** $\rho \leq 1 + \frac{1}{a^2} - \frac{1}{m(1,m)}$ for $a \leq 0.5$ and $\rho \leq 1 + \frac{1}{a(1-a)} - \frac{1}{m(1,m)}$ for $a > 0.5$

if $a = 1$ holds, as in traditional allocation strategies, a constant approximation cannot be guaranteed. The example in Fig. 2 shows such a schedule in which highly parallel jobs are starving due to jobs with little parallelism. However, a constant approximation $\rho = 5 - \frac{1}{m(1,m)}$ can be achieved with $a = 0.5$.

- If $f = f_0 = 1$ holds we say that the workload is *predominantly sequential*. In such a case, we have $\rho \leq 1 + \frac{1}{a^2} - \frac{1}{m(1,m)}$. For $a = 1$, we obtain $\rho = 2 - \frac{1}{m(1,m)}$. This bound is equal to the bound of list scheduling on a single machine with the same number of processors. Hence, for this type of workload, $Min\_LB$ is the best possible allocation algorithm.

- If $f = f_0 = m$ holds we say that the workload is *predominantly parallel*. In such a case, we have $\rho \leq 1 + \frac{1}{a^2} - \frac{1}{m(1,m)}$. Again $a = 1$ yields $\rho = 2 - \frac{1}{m(1,m)}$. Therefore, $Min\_LB$ is also the best possible allocation algorithm for this type of workload.

- In a real Grid scenario, the admissible factor can be dynamically adjusted in response to the changes in the configuration and/or the workload. To this end, the past workload within a given time interval can be analyzed to determine an optimal admissible factor $a$. The time interval for this adaptation should be set according to the dynamics in the workload characteristics and in the Grid configuration. One can iteratively approximate the optimal admissible factor.

## 5. Concluding Remarks

Scheduling in Grids is vital to achieve efficiently operating Grids. While scheduling in general is well understood and has been subject of research for many years, there are still only few theoretical results available. In this paper, we analyze the Grid scheduling problem and present a new algorithm that is based on an adaptive allocation policy. Our Grid scheduling model uses a two layer hierarchical structure and covers the main properties of Grids, for instance, different machine sizes and parallel jobs. The theoretical worst-case analysis yields decent bounds of the competitive ratio for certain workload configurations. Therefore, the proposed algorithm may serve as a starting point for future heuristic Grid scheduling algorithms that can be implemented in real computational Grids. In future work, we intend to evaluate the practical performance of the proposed strategies and their derivatives. To this end, we plan simulations using real workload traces and corresponding Grid configurations. Further, we will compare our approach with other existing Grid scheduling strategies which are typically based on heuristics.

# References

[1] S. Albers. Better bounds for online scheduling. SIAM Journal on Computing, 29(2):459-473, 1999.

[2] M. Garey and R. Graham. Bounds for multiprocessor scheduling with resource constraints. SIAM Journal on Computing, 4(2):187-200, 1975.

[3] R. Graham, E. Lawler, J. Lenstra, and A.R. Kan. Optimization and approximation in deterministic sequencing and scheduling: A survey. Annals of Discrete Mathematics, 15:287-326, 1979.

[4] E. Huedo, R.S. Montero and I.M. Llorente. A modular meta-scheduling architecture for interfacing with pre-WS and WS Grid resource management services. Future Generation Computing Systems 23(2):252-261, 2007.

[5] E. Lloyd. Concurrent task systems, Operational Research 29(1):189-201, 1981.

[6] E. Naroska and U. Schwiegelshohn. On an online scheduling problem for parallel jobs. Information Processing Letters, 81(6):297-304, 2002.

[7] T. Robertazzi and D. Yu. Multi-Source Grid Scheduling for Divisible Loads. Proceedings of the 40th Annual Conference on Information Sciences and Systems, pages 188-191, 2006.

[8] G. Sabin, R. Kettimuthu, A. Rajan, and P. Sadayappan. Scheduling of Parallel Jobs in a Heterogeneous Multi-Site Environment, Proceedings of the 8th International Workshop on Job Scheduling Strategies for Parallel Processing (JSSPP), pages 87-104, 2003.

[9] U. Schwiegelshohn, A. Tchernykh, and R. Yahyapour. Online Scheduling in Grids, Proceedings of the IEEE International Parallel and Distributed Processing Symposium (IPDPS'2008), CD-ROM, 2008.

[10] U. Schwiegelshohn and R. Yahyapour. Attributes for communication between grid scheduling instances. In J. Nabrzyski, J. Schopf, and J. Weglarz (Eds.), Grid Resource Management - State of the Art and Future Trends, Kluwer Academic, pages 41-52, 2003.

[11] A. Tchernykh, J. Ramírez, A. Avetisyan, N. Kuzjurin, D. Grushin, and S. Zhuk. Two Level Job-Scheduling Strategies for a Computational Grid. In Parallel Processing and Applied Mathematics, Wyrzykowski et al. (Eds.): Proceedings of the Second Grid Resource Management Workshop (GRMW'2005) in conjunction with the Sixth International Conference

on Parallel Processing and Applied Mathematics - PPAM 2005. LNCS 3911, Springer-Verlag, pages 774-781, 2006.

[12] A. Tchernykh, D. Trystram, C. Brizuela, and I. Scherson. Idle Regulation in Non-Clairvoyant Scheduling of Parallel Jobs to be published in Discrete Applied Mathematics, 2008.

[13] P. Uppuluri, N. Jabisetti, U. Joshi, and Y. Lee. P2P Grid: Service Oriented Framework for Distributed Resource Management. Proceedings of the 2005 IEEE International Conference on Services Computing (SCC'05), pages 347-350, 2005.

[14] S. Zhuk, A. Chernykh, N. Kuzjurin, A. Pospelov, A. Shokurov, A. Avetisyan, S. Gaissaryan, D. Grushin. Comparison of Scheduling Heuristics for Grid Resource Broker. Proceedings of the third International IEEE Conference on Parallel Computing Systems (PCS2004), pages 388-392, 2004.

# GLOBAL OPTIMIZATION FOR SCHEDULING MULTIPLE CO-RESERVATIONS IN THE GRID

Thomas Röblitz
*Zuse Institute Berlin*
*Takustr. 7, D-14195 Berlin, Germany*
roeblitz@zib.de

*CoreGRID Institute on Resource Management and Scheduling*

**Abstract**     Co-reservations are an efficient means to support guarantees on the allocation of resources in order to execute complex distributed application scenarios. Scheduling multiple moldable co-reservations involves several steps leading to guarantees of resource allocation. Previous work has provided either mechanisms for individual steps only or for selecting co-reservations, but with more limited application scenarios. In this work, we extend previous work by studying the problem as generic optimization problem, by developing a mixed integer linear programming model which allows more freedom in the specification of the goals of requests, resources and the broker, and by performing extensive experiments to analyze important parameters on the time to solve various problem instances.

**Keywords:**     Co-reservation, Grid Resource Management, Workflow Management, Optimization, Mixed Integer Linear Programming.

## 1. Introduction

In many disciplines of science and business, large scale simulations and workflows for analyzing petascale data sets necessitate the adoption of Grid technologies to meet their demanding resource requirements. The use of Grid resources, however, poses new challenges, because of their heterogeneity, geographic distribution and autonomous management. Specifically, we consider complex applications developed within the AstroGrid-D project [4] such as large simulations of black holes with Cactus or distributed observations of astronomic objects with robotic telescopes. These applications require the *co-allocation* of multiple Grid resources. Figure 1(a) and 1(b) exemplify two types of applications and the temporal relationships among the applications' parts.

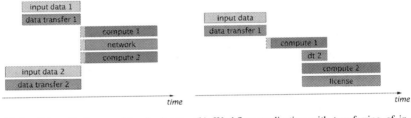

(a) Parallel application requiring the input data to be transferred from a remote archive.

(b) Workflow application with transferring of input data, streaming of intermediate results and co-allocation of licenses.

**Figure 1:** Parallel and workflow application scenarios.

Because Grid resources are autonomously managed, the allocation of them at the same time or in some sequence with hard time constraints cannot be guaranteed by standard Grid job management schemes. That is, a broker decides where to submit a job, but has no control on when the job is actually executed. This problem can be circumvented by acquiring reservations for the required resources. A reservation guarantees that a specific resource can be allocated to a request at the desired time.

This paper contributes a generic approach for modeling the co-reservation problem. In particular, it supports flexible constraints and objectives of all involved parties – users submitting requests, providers of resources and the broker of a virtual organization. We consider requests to be flexible in four dimensions – the resource to reserve, the start time, the service level and the duration. However, once a co-reservation has been acquired, its parameters may not be changed without confirmation. The relationships among the parts of an application are modeled by temporal and spatial relationships.

**Outline.** The remainder of the paper is structured as follow. Firstly, we briefly present a framework for processing requests for co-reservations in Section 2.

In Section 3, we incrementally develop a mixed integer linear programming model for the third processing phase. Thereafter, we present the results of an extensive experimental evaluation of solving various problem instances with CPLEX 10.1 in Section 4. We discuss related work in Section 5 and conclude in Section 6.

## 2. Framework for Processing Requests

Figure 2 shows a framework for processing co-reservation requests. The three main components are the *Grid Reservation Service* (GRS), the *Resource Catalog* (RC) and the *Local Reservation Service* (LRS). The Grid Reservation

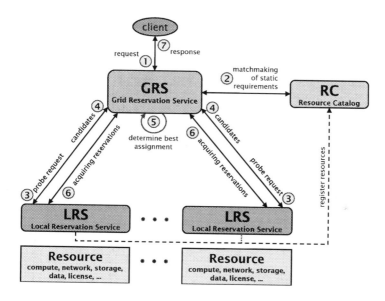

**Figure 2:** Components of the reservation framework and their interplay in the processing of a co-reservation request.

Service (GRS) receives co-reservation requests and coordinates their processing. A GRS may be deployed on all levels in the Grid resource management hierarchy – from small groups of researchers to large virtual organizations. Thus, it can incorporate domain specific knowledge about both the applications of the researchers and the resources they wish to use. After receiving a request (step (1)), the GRS performs a matchmaking on the static properties of requests and resources (step (2)). Next, it sends flexible probe requests to the LRS of each matched resource (step (3)). The LRS determines reservation candidates for given ranges of start times, service levels and durations. For each reservation candidate, the LRS calculates certain metrics – like availability, reservation fee, cancelation fee, etc. – and sends the information back to the GRS [10–

11](step (4)). When the GRS has received the reservation candidates, it selects the best combination (step (5)) and finally acquires the reservations (step (6)).

In this work, we study methods for selecting the best combination (step (5)).

## 3. Modeling the Application Scenarios

In this section, we explore the modeling of the application scenarios as a linear problem (LP) and a mixed integer linear problem (MILP). Independent of the chosen tool for solving problem instances, a solution must provide the same information – for each atomic request, it states the assigned resource, the allocated start time and duration as well as the agreed service level.

We consider three classes of problem instances: single-atomic-request (SAR, cf. Sec. 3.1), multiple-atomic-requests (MAR, cf. Sec. 3.2) and multiple-co-requests (MCR, cf. Sec. 3.3). The classes SAR and MAR are used to incrementally develop the full model MCR, which implements a mixed integer linear program of the co-reservation problem. With one exception, we assume that for each atomic request $r$ multiple resources $S_r$ are found through the matchmaking (step (2)). As we will see, linear programming can only be applied to the class of single atomic requests for which only a single resource was obtained from the matchmaking step. For each class and the availability of multiple resources, we study mixed integer linear programming (MILP).

## 3.1 Single Atomic Requests

First, we develop a linear programming model for the unusual scenario involving a single request and a single resource. Thereafter, we extend the model to fully support the class of single atomic requests by modeling multiple resources with a mixed integer linear programming model.

**Linear programming.** We restrict the number of requests as well as the number of resources to one. Let $T \subset \mathbb{R}_{\geq 0}$, $Q \subset \mathbb{R}_{\geq 0}$ and $D \subset \mathbb{R}_{\geq 0}$ denote the sets of the start times, the service levels and the durations, respectively. We assume that all properties, constraints and objectives are linear functions, i.e., $f(t, q, d) := c_1 t + c_2 q + c_3 d + c_4$ with $t \in T$, $q \in Q$, $d \in D$ and the coefficients $c_{1,2,3,4} \in \mathbb{R}$. The matrices $C^=$ and $C^{\geq}$ contain the coefficients of the linear equality and inequality constraints (one constraint per row), respectively. Similarly, the matrices $O_{vo}$, $O_r$ and $O_s$ contain the coefficients of the objectives of the broker, the request and the resources, respectively. The dimensions of these matrices are $4 \times n_{vo}$, $4 \times n_r$ and $4 \times n_s$, respectively, with the $n$s being the number of objectives. The $1 \times n_{vo/r/s}$ vectors $o_{vo}^{\omega}$, $o_r^{\omega}$ and $o_s^{\omega}$ contain the weights of these objectives, with $n_{vo/r/s}$ being the number of objectives of the corresponding party. Using the weighted sum as objective criteria, the co-reservation problem can be modeled as follows.

$$\min \quad O_r \begin{pmatrix} t \\ q \\ d \\ 1 \end{pmatrix} o_r + O_s \begin{pmatrix} t \\ q \\ d \\ 1 \end{pmatrix} o_s + O_{vo} \begin{pmatrix} t \\ q \\ d \\ 1 \end{pmatrix} o_{vo}$$

subject to $\qquad\qquad\qquad\qquad\qquad\qquad\qquad\qquad\qquad$ (1)

$$C^= \begin{pmatrix} t \\ q \\ d \\ 1 \end{pmatrix} = 0 \quad \wedge \quad C^{\geq} \begin{pmatrix} t \\ q \\ d \\ 1 \end{pmatrix} \geq 0$$

Note, the constant components in the objective – the "1" in the vectors – are not required. However, they were left in for illustrative purposes, i.e., to show the similarity between the objectives and the constraints. Furthermore, they will be replaced by other constructs in the following models. Due to the limitation to a single request no temporal and spatial relationships need to be modeled.

**Removing model restrictions.** The presented model has two limitations – the used functions are linear and only a single resource is modeled. We briefly introduce piecewise linear functions as a means to model non-linear functions. Thereafter, we describe two means for modeling multiple resources. In the remainder of the paper, we will implement the latter of these means.

While some properties such as the availability of a resource or the available budget depending on the finish time could be roughly approximated by a linear function, others may not so. For example, the costs for reserving network bandwidth may follow a periodic function (day/night or working day/weekend). Another example is given by the execution time of a parallel program, which may be modeled by a non-linear function derived from Amdahl's law.

This problem may be circumvented by approximating the actual functions with piecewise linear functions (PLF). PLFs over a single domain are often modeled by special ordered sets of type 2 (SOS2). In our scenarios, however, the properties are defined over three domains (start time, service level and duration). Hence, we would need special ordered sets of type 4. Alternatively, the problem can be partitioned such that all properties are linear over a single partition. However, the full exploitation of PLFs is beyond the scope of this paper.

For extending model 1 to the class SAR, we need to model multiple resources. The canonical means for supporting multiple resources are:

- constructing an instance of model 1 for each resource, solve all instances individually and select the resource with minimal objective as solution, *or*

- developing an integrated model which uses, for each resource, one binary variable, one time variable, one service level variable and one duration variable.

We will focus on the latter possibility, since the essential part of the former was already defined by model 1.

**Mixed integer linear programming.**    Let $K := |S|$ denote the number of resources. We model the class SAR by associating four variables $x_k \in \{0, 1\}$, $t_k \in T$, $q_k \in Q$ and $d_k \in D$ with each resource $s_k \in S$. The values of the solution variables $s$, $t$, $q$ and $d$ are derived as follows $s = \sum_{k=1}^{K} k\, x_k$, $t = \sum_{k=1}^{K} t_k\, x_k$, $q = \sum_{k=1}^{K} q_k\, x_k$. and $d = \sum_{k=1}^{K} d_k\, x_k$.

We rewrite the linear model 1 by modeling multiple resources and modifying the constraints and objectives such that only those of the selected resource are taken into account. The new constraints are as follows

$$\forall k \leq K : C_k^= \begin{pmatrix} t_k \\ q_k \\ d_k \\ x_k \end{pmatrix} = 0 \quad \wedge \quad \forall k \leq K : C_k^\geq \begin{pmatrix} t_k \\ q_k \\ d_k \\ x_k \end{pmatrix} \geq 0 , \quad (2)$$

where $C_k^=$ and $C_k^\geq$ contain all constraints on the assignment of the request to resource $s_k$. The variables of the start times, the service levels and durations are bounded by their domains $T$, $Q$ and $D$, respectively. We assume that corresponding constraints are already included in $C^=$ and $C^\geq$. Thus, the following constraint ensures that only a single tuple $\langle x_k, t_k, q_k, d_k \rangle$ is set to non-zero values.

$$\sum_{k=1}^{K} x_k \leq 1 \tag{3}$$

The objectives (cf. equation 1) are adapted in a similar fashion by adding indices to the variables, replacing the '1' in the vectors by $x_k$ and building the sum over all resources. Thus, the new objective looks as follows

$$\min \quad \sum_{k=1}^{K} \left( O_r^k \begin{pmatrix} t_k \\ q_k \\ d_k \\ x_k \end{pmatrix} o_r + O_s^k \begin{pmatrix} t_k \\ q_k \\ d_k \\ x_k \end{pmatrix} o_s + O_{vo}^k \begin{pmatrix} t_k \\ q_k \\ d_k \\ x_k \end{pmatrix} o_{vo} \right) . \tag{4}$$

## 3.2    Multiple Atomic Requests

We adapt the model of the class SAR to support multiple atomic requests. The main difference between the classes SAR and MAR is that MAR requires to model multiple requests. Thus, we need to parametrize the variables, the coefficient matrices, the constraints and the objectives with the resource and the request. That is, we model any possible assignment of a request $r_l$ to a resource $s_k$ by a tuple $\langle t_{l,k}, q_{l,k}, d_{l,k}, x_{l,k} \rangle$. A variable $x_{l,k}$ is set to one iff the request $r_l$ is assigned to the resource $s_k$. In that case, the variables $t_{l,k}, q_{l,k}$ and $d_{l,k}$ may be set to non-zero values. Let $L$ denote the number of requests. We replace the single constraint 3 by the following set of constraints

$$\forall l \leq L : \sum_{k=1}^{K} x_{l,k} \leq 1 \tag{5}$$

The set of constraints 5 ensures that each request is assigned to at most one resource. The constraints in 2 are changed to

$$\forall l \leq L : \forall k \leq K : C_{l,k}^{=} \begin{pmatrix} t_{l,k} \\ q_{l,k} \\ d_{l,k} \\ x_{l,k} \end{pmatrix} = 0$$

$$\wedge \quad \forall l \leq L : \forall k \leq K : C_{l,k}^{\geq} \begin{pmatrix} t_{l,k} \\ q_{l,k} \\ d_{l,k} \\ x_{l,k} \end{pmatrix} \geq 0 \,,$$

where $C_{l,k}^{=}$ and $C_{l,k}^{\geq}$ contain all constraints on the assignment of the request $r_l$ to resource $s_k$. The objective function in equation 4 is replaced by

$$\min \sum_{l=1}^{L} \sum_{k=1}^{K} \left( O_r^{l,k} \begin{pmatrix} t_{l,k} \\ q_{l,k} \\ d_{l,k} \\ x_{l,k} \end{pmatrix} o_r + \right.$$

$$\left. O_s^{l,k} \begin{pmatrix} t_{l,k} \\ q_{l,k} \\ d_{l,k} \\ x_{l,k} \end{pmatrix} o_s + O_{vo}^{l,k} \begin{pmatrix} t_{l,k} \\ q_{l,k} \\ d_{l,k} \\ x_{l,k} \end{pmatrix} o_{vo} \right).$$

## 3.3    Multiple Co-Reservation Requests

Compared to the class MAR, we need to model temporal and spatial relationships between any two requests – more precisely between two assignments of a request to a resource. Particularly, we will extend the model MAR by two new types of constraints. The existing model for the class MAR is not changed.

**Temporal relationships.** Temporal relationships can use the start time, the end time, any offset to them or the duration. For example, the requirement that the requests $r_1$ and $r_2$ shall start at the same time can be formulated as the constraint $t_1 - t_2 = 0$. Since, a time variable $t_i$ models the start time of a request, we need to add the request's duration to model its end time. For example, the requirement that request $r_1$ shall precede request $r_3$ can be formulated as the constraint $t_3 - (t_1 + d_1) \geq 0$. We implement temporal relationships by fully exploiting the multi-dimensional definition of constraints, i.e., $c^j : (R \times S \times T \times Q \times D)^L \longrightarrow \mathbb{R}$. Here, $R$ and $L$ denote the set of requests and their number, respectively.

The corresponding coefficient matrices $TC^{=,\geq}$ contain $4L$ columns, where the elements $tc_{z,4(l-1)+1}, \ldots, tc_{z,4l}$ contain the coefficients of request $l \in [1, L]$ of the temporal relationship $z$. For example, the 'precede' condition of the above problem with three requests would be written as the row vector

$$(-1, 0, -1, 0 \ , \ 0, 0, 0, 0 \ , \ 1, 0, 0, 0) \, .$$

Let $Y$ denote the vector

$$\left( \sum_{k=1}^{K} t_{1,k}, \sum_{k=1}^{K} q_{1,k}, \sum_{k=1}^{K} d_{1,k}, \sum_{k=1}^{K} x_{1,k}, \ldots, \sum_{k=1}^{K} t_{L,k}, \sum_{k=1}^{K} q_{L,k}, \sum_{k=1}^{K} d_{L,k}, \sum_{k=1}^{K} x_{L,k} \right),$$

which contains the aggregated values of the variables for each request. The temporal relationships can be formulated as

$$TC^= \cdot Y^T = 0 \qquad \wedge \qquad TC^{\geq} \cdot Y^T \geq 0 \, .$$

**Spatial relationships.** Spatial relationships are used to co-locate two requests at the same site – e.g., input data with the compute part – and to ensure connectivity for a network request and the participants on both ends. We introduce a generic model, which applies to both types of spatial relationships. We use two vectors left and right and the matrix coloc for supporting spatial relationships. The vectors contain information about the left and the right 'end' (or location) of a resource. These differ for network resources, but are the same for other resources. The matrix coloc contains one row for each spatial relationship.

The vectors LEFT $:= (\text{left}_1, \ldots, \text{left}_K)$ and RIGHT $:= (\text{right}_1, \ldots, \text{right}_K)$ define the left and right location of all resources $s_k$. Each row in coloc contains $2L$ elements. The elements $2l - 1$ and $2l$ represent the left and the right end of the request $l$. If the left/right side of request $v$ shall be co-located with the left-/right side of request $w$, the corresponding elements of request $v$ and request $w$ are set to 1 and -1, respectively. Let $Z$ define the vector of the locations of the resources assigned to all requests, i.e.,

$$\left( \sum_{k=1}^{K} x_{1,k}\text{left}_k \ , \ \sum_{k=1}^{K} x_{1,k}\text{right}_k \ , \quad \ldots \quad , \ \sum_{k=1}^{K} x_{L,k}\text{left}_k \ , \ \sum_{k=1}^{K} x_{L,k}\text{right}_k \right) \, .$$

**Table 1:** Parameters of the experiments for the classes MAR and MCR.

| parameter | values for the class | |
| --- | --- | --- |
| | MAR | MCR |
| application sce-nario | independent tasks | $S1, S2, S3, S4, S5, S6, S7, S8$ |
| no. of requests | $1, 2, 3, 4, 5, 10, 20, 30, 40, 50, 100$ | $1, 2, 3$ |
| no. of resources | $1, 2, 3, 4, 5, 10, 20, 30, 40, 50, 100$ | $1, 2, 3$ |
| no. of constraints | $6, 9, 12$ | $6, 9, 12$ |
| no. of objectives | $1, 2$ | $1, 2$ |
| no. of runs | $10$ | $3$ |

The spatial relationships can be formulated as the constraint

$$\mathsf{coloc} \cdot Z^T = \vec{0}^T \, ,$$

where $\vec{0}$ contains as many elements as spatial relationships are defined.

## 4.    Experimental Evaluation

Many optimization problems, in particular integer problems, suffer from a large search space. We performed 9,556 experiments using CPLEX 10.1 to study which instances are solvable in a reasonable time and which parameters influence the solving time most. In the experiments, we varied the number of requests, the number of resources, the number of the constraints per entity (requests and resources) and the structure of the requests. Because we generated random numbers for the coefficients, we repeated each experiment up to 10 times.

The experiment parameters for the classes MAR and MCR are shown in Table 1. Because, the experiments for the class MCR required much longer solving times we had to shrink the number of requests and resources significantly. The application scenarios S1-S8 are depicted in Fig. 3. Because of the limited space, we can only present results for a few datasets for each class. The experiments were carried out on a SUN Galaxy 4600 16 core system with 64 Gbytes of RAM. The solution times ranges from a few milliseconds to several hours.

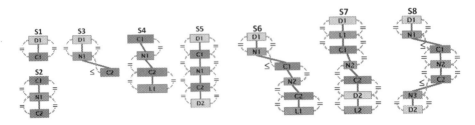

**Figure 3:** Application scenarios S1 to S8 used in the experimental evaluation of the class MCR. Solid red lines indicate spatial relationships. Temporal relationships are shown by dashed blue lines plus a comparison operator. The type of a requested resource is given by the first letter of the tag in a box – C for compute, D for data, N for network and L for license.

## 4.1    Results for Multiple Atomic Requests (Class MAR)

Figures 4a and 4b show the times needed for scheduling 1 to 100 requests to 10 and 100 resources, respectively. We use a logarithmic scale for the vertical axis (solution time) and partially logarithmic scale for the horizontal axis (number of requests) to optimize the presentation of the data. For each number of requests, we plotted three error bars (6, 9 and 12 constraints per party, i.e., request/resource). An error bar indicates the average ('center'), the minimum and the maximum measured solving time for 10 runs.

The graphs show several important information. First, the more requests are to be scheduled the more time the solver needs to find the optimal solution. However, the time increases nearly linearly with the number of requests. The solving time for the experiments with 100 resources is approximately one order of magnitude larger than for the experiments with 10 resources. This is not surprising, since the problem sizes (number of resources) also differ by one order of magnitude. More notable are the different increases of the solving time for the transitions from 6 to 9 and from 9 to 12 constraints. This behavior is caused by the different nature of the constraints. In each experiment, six constraints are used to bound the variables of the problem – two for each of the start time $t$, the service level $q$ and the duration $d$. The remaining constraints are derived randomly and resemble linear combinations of the three variables. In summary, we see that mixed integer linear programming is well applicable to smaller Grid environments (requiring not more than one second for up to 50 requests). It is still applicable in larger environments, but achieving fast response times for scheduling decisions may require to limit either the number of constraints or the number of requests.

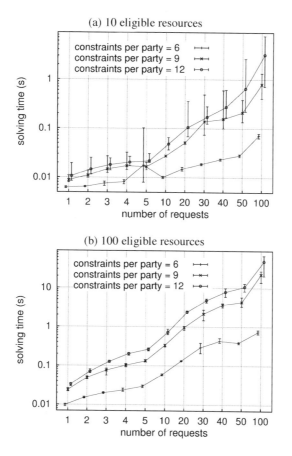

**Figure 4:** Solving time vs. the number of requests for different numbers of eligible resources per request. Each error bar shows the average, minimum and maximum times measured for 10 runs. The lines connect the average values of experiments differing in the number of requests only.

## 4.2 Results for Multiple Co-Reservation Requests (Class MCR)

Figures 5a and 5b show the times needed for scheduling requests of different application scenarios requiring two to six non-network resources and none to three network resources. The number of eligible non-network resources per request is one and three in Fig. 5a and Fig. 5b, respectively. We use a logarithmic scale for the vertical axis (solution time). The scenarios are ordered such that their complexity increases along the horizontal axis. For each scenario we plotted four error bars, each one corresponding to a combination of the number of requests and the number of constraints.

Although, the experiments involved only a few number of requests and resources, we observed large solving times. The solving time increases exponentially, except for co-reservation requests requiring only two resources, i.e., for scenario S1 (cf. Fig. 3). Studying the graphs in more detail, we find that the problem instances with a single eligible resource per atomic request (all instances in Fig. 5a) are solvable in reasonable time. The problem instances with three eligible resources per atomic request, generally, require more time for finding an optimal solution. Most of the smaller instances (S1 to S4) and instances with a single request are solved in reasonable time, i.e., in less than 30 seconds. However, the slightly more complex scenarios require significantly more time. We also considered even more complex scenarios involving multiple steps of a workflow. These were solved efficiently in case of a single eligible resource per atomic request, but often required several hours solving time when the number of resources was increased.

Thus, we can devise the following recommendations for using a mixed integer linear programming model to schedule co-reservations. First, for each atomic request only a single eligible resource should be considered. This requires a very efficient filtering in the matchmaking (cf. step (2) in Fig. 2). Second, the number of constraints should be kept small. Last, requests for complex applications requiring multiple resources should be scheduled individually.

## 5.    Related Work

Previous work provides means either for individual steps of the processing of requests (cf. Section 2) or implements a very specific application scenario. In contrast, we aim at a more generic approach which supports a wide variety of scenarios in terms of the structure of the applications, the types of the reservable resources and the means to specify constraints and objectives.

Resource discovery for the immediate execution of rigid (non-moldable) requests using static and current status information about the resources are implemented by Condor ClassAds [9]and many todays Grid resource brokers such as GridWay [5]and the EGEE Workload Management System [3]. Liu and Foster [7]applied constraint satisfaction techniques to extend Condor ClassAds. Naik et al. [8]developed an integer programming model for resource discovery.

Mechanisms for advance reservations require the prediction of the future state of resources (steps (3) and (4)). In [6], several techniques are explored for predicting the runtimes of applications and deriving the queuing time of a new compute job. In contrast, our mechanisms [10–11]for deriving the future state of resources not only provide a single value for a new job, but rather a set of probes over the range of start times and service levels. Each probe may contain multiple metrics used in the selection of co-reservations.

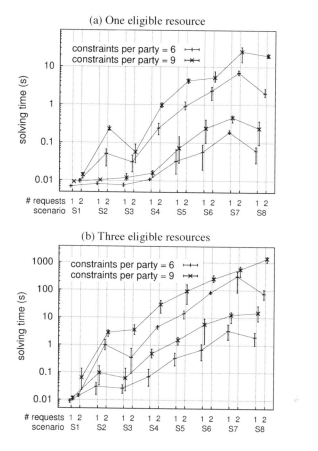

**Figure 5:** Solving time vs. the scenario and the number of requests for different numbers of eligible resources per request. The error bars show the average, minimum and maximum times measured for 3 runs. The lines connect the average values of experiments differing in the scenario only.

In [13], Wieczorek et al. present a taxonomy of the multi-criteria Grid workflow scheduling problem. However, none of the analyzed approaches supports all capabilities our generic model provides, i.e., multiple criteria, multiple workflows, advance reservation, moldable tasks and different types of requests (compute, network, storage, etc.).

The VIOLA meta-scheduler [12] schedules compute jobs to multiple resources by incrementally increasing the advance booking period until all jobs may be allocated. That is, it only supports one criteria – the earliest completion time.

Brandic et al. [1] propose a workflow engine which supports quality of service for web services. First, for each workflow activity, it contacts candidate services (cf. eligible resources in our model) and negotiates a single service level acknowledging the desired characteristics such as maximum execution time and maximum price. Second, it assigns each activity to a candidate service such that the utility function is maximized. The utility function is the weighted sum of the objectives of each activity and the overall workflow. The major differences to our approach are the single negotiated service level, the missing support for constraints and objectives of both the resources and the broker and the lack of temporal and spatial relationships among the activities.

In [14], Zeng et al. present a middleware for selecting web service instances to compose complex workflows. In particular, they propose a QoS model for atomic web services and for composite services. Based on this model, the middleware implements a QoS-aware selection of web services such that the user's satisfaction is maximized. The user's satisfaction is defined as the weighted sum of multiple criteria chosen by the user itself. The actual selection of the web services is implemented using *integer programming*. Besides constraints on each individual workflow activity, their implementation supports global constraints on the aggregated values of individual activities. For example, the total budget for executing a workflow or its total execution time may be limited. A side effect of constraining the execution time is the creation of a schedule, that is, a solution assigns a start time to each activity. In contrast, our model explicitly considers the start time as a variable. Additionally, our model supports moldable service levels and durations to optimize the user's satisfaction. Also, the resources (or web services) and the broker may specify constraints and objectives for each workflow activity. Moreover, our model provides rich capabilities for specifying temporal and spatial relationships and allows to define global constraints and objectives explicitly. In [2], Canfora et al. apply *genetic algorithms* to optimize the assignment of workflow activities to candidate services. Their approach supports user defined constraints and objectives for each activity. The objective of the whole workflow is constructed by aggregating the objectives of the individual activities. Canfora et al. describe different aggregation functions depending on the type of the objective (e.g., cost, time, availability, etc.) and the structural relationships among the activities (e.g., sequence, switch, loop, etc.). In our model, we only support the weighted sum as aggregation function. Moreover, we do not need to distinguish between different control flow elements of a workflow, since we assume that all activities must be executed. Because we use mixed integer linear programming, all constraints and objectives must be linear functions. In contrast, the use of genetic algorithms allows to use arbitrary functions. The major difference to our work is the single variable per activity. Our model supports flexible start times, service levels and durations. Of course, that flexibility comes at a high cost, namely, the size of the search space.

Table 2 summarizes the approaches and compares them against our model.

**Table 2:** Comparison of existing approaches to schedule multiple reservations in advance and to manage workflows. Symbols: **types of entities** (c - compute, n - network, d - data, l - license, ws - web services), **variables per assignment** (s - resource level, d - duration, q - service level, t - start time, A-any; lower left {method of specification}: I-implicitly; E-explicitly; lower right {properties}: variables $t, q, d$, A-arbitrary, L-linear, $=$-equality, $\geq$-inequality}; **objectives/OBJ** (upper left: cf. CON; upper right: cf. CON + optimization goal; lower left: cf. CON; lower right {functions / aggregation}: cf. CON / $\omega$-weighted sum, p-pareto set}, **temporal relationships** (ST - same time, SEQ - sequence, OL - partially overlapping), **spatial relationships** (net - network, nmt - non-network), **techniques** (GA - genetic algorithms, IP - integer programming, MILP - mixed integer linear programming, T&E - trial and error)

| approach | no. of co-requests | types of entities | variables p. assignment | request CON | request OBJ | resource CON | resource OBJ | broker CON | broker OBJ | temp. int.-rel. | spat. int.-rel. | global CON | global OBJ | applied technique(s) |
|---|---|---|---|---|---|---|---|---|---|---|---|---|---|---|
| | | | | *modeling of an atomic entity* | | | | | | *modeling of a co-reservation* | | | | |
| VIOLA [12] | 1 | any | $t$ | M $t,q,d$ / I $C_=$ | – | M A / I $C^\geq$ | – | – | – | ST | no | – | S min $t$ / E NL | T&E |
| *Reservation based Meta-Scheduling* | | | | | | | | | | | | | | |
| VGE [1] | 1 | ws | $s, t$ | M A / I $C^\geq$ | M max / E $L_\omega$ | M A / I $C_=$ | – | – | – | no | no | M A / I $C^\geq$ | M max / E $L_\omega$ | IP |
| *Workflow Management* | | | | | | | | | | | | | | |
| Zeng et al. [14] | 1 | ws | $s, t$ | M A / I $C^\geq$ | M A / E $C_\omega$ | M A / I $C_=$ | – | – | – | SEQ | no | M A / I $A^\geq$ | M A / I $C_\omega$ | IP |
| *Web Services Composition* | | | | | | | | | | | | | | |
| SeCSE [2] | 1 | ws | $s$ | M A / I $C^\geq$ | M max / E $C_{any}$ | M A / I $C_=$ | – | – | – | no | no | M A / I $A^\geq$ | M max / I $A_{any}$ | GA |
| *Our Approach* | | | | | | | | | | | | | | |
| this work | $\geq 1$ | any | $s, t, q, d$ | M A / E $L^\geq_=$ | M A / E $L_\omega$ | M A / E $L^\geq_=$ | – | M A / E $L^\geq_=$ | M A / E $L_\omega$ | SEQ, ST, OL | net nmt | M A / E $L^\geq_=$ | M A / E $L_\omega$ | MILP |

## 6.    Conclusion

In this paper, we studied the use of global optimization for scheduling multiple co-reservations in the Grid. We modeled the problem as mixed integer linear program (MILP). In particular, it supports flexible constraints and objectives of all involved parties – users submitting requests, providers of resources and the broker of a virtual organization. Furthermore, our approach supports the flexibility of requests in four dimensions – the resource to reserve, the start time, the service level and the duration. Dependencies among the parts of a distributed application are modeled by temporal and spatial relationships. We performed an extensive experimental evaluation using the standard solver CPLEX (version 10.1). The results of the evaluation showed that independent requests may be scheduled very efficiently. In contrast, many co-reservation requests are only efficiently processed if the number of eligible resources is very small.

In summary, we can devise the following recommendations for using a mixed integer linear programming model to schedule co-reservations. First, for each atomic request only a single eligible resource should be considered. This requires a very efficient filtering in the matchmaking (cf. step (2)). Second, the number of constraints should be kept small. Last, requests for complex applications requiring multiple resources should be scheduled individually.

## Acknowledgments

This work was partially funded by the German BMBF project AstroGrid-D (grant 01AK804C) and the EU Network of Excellence CoreGRID (contract IST-2002-004265). The author wants to thank Mikael Högqvist and Alexander Reinefeld for proof-reading.

## References

[1]  Ivona Brandic, Siegfried Benkner, Gerhard Engelbrecht, and Rainer Schmidt. Qos support for time-critical grid workflow applications. In *First International Conference on e-Science and Grid Technologies (e-Science 2005), 5-8 December 2005, Melbourne, Australia*, pages 108–115. IEEE Computer Society, 2005.

[2]  Gerardo Canfora, Massimiliano Di Penta, Raffaele Esposito, and Maria Luisa Villani. An approach for qos-aware service composition based on genetic algorithms. In *Genetic and Evolutionary Computation Conference, GECCO 2005, Washington DC, USA, June 25-29, 2005*, pages 1069–1075. ACM, 2005.

[3]  Enabling Grids for E-sciencE. http://www.eu-egee.org, March 2008.

[4]  AstroGrid-D project homepage. http://www.gac-grid.org/, March 2008.

[5]  Eduardo Huedo, Rubén S. Montero, and Ignacio Martín Llorente. The GridWay Framework for Adaptive Scheduling and Execution on Grids. *Scalable Computing: Practice and Experience*, 6(3):1–8, September 2005.

[6]  Hui Li, D. Groep, J. Templon, and L. Wolters. Predicting job start times on clusters. In *CCGRID '04: Proceedings of the 2004 IEEE International Symposium on Cluster*

*Computing and the Grid*, pages 301–308, Washington, DC, USA, 2004. IEEE Computer Society.

[7] Chuang Liu and Ian Foster. A constraint language approach to grid resource selection. Technical Report TR-2003-07, Department of Computer Science, University of Chicago, March 2003.

[8] Vijay K. Naik, Chuang Liu, Lingyun Yang, and Jonathan Wagner. On-line resource matching in a heterogeneous grid environment. In *Proceedings of the IEEE International Symposium on Cluster computing and Grid 2005 (CCGrid05), Cardiff, Wales, UK*, volume 2, pages 607–614, May 2005.

[9] Rajesh Raman, Miron Livny, and Marvin Solomon. Matchmaking: Distributed resource management for high throughput computing. In *Proceedings of the 7th IEEE International Symposium on High Performance Distributed Computing, Chicago, Illinois, USA*, pages 140–146. IEEE Computer Society Press, July 1998.

[10] Thomas Röblitz and Krzysztof Rzadca. On the Placement of Reservations into Job Schedules. In *12th International Euro-Par Conference 2006, Dresden, Germany*, pages 198–210, 2006.

[11] Thomas Röblitz, Florian Schintke, and Alexander Reinefeld. Resource Reservations with Fuzzy Requests. *Concurrency and Computation: Practice and Experience*, 18(13):1681–1703, November 2006.

[12] Oliver Wäldrich, Philipp Wieder, and Wolfgang Ziegler. A meta-scheduling service for co-allocating arbitrary types of resources. In *Proceedings of the 6th International Conference on Parallel Processing (PPAM 2005), Poznan, Poland*, volume 1, pages 782–791, September 2005.

[13] Marek Wieczorek, Radu Prodan, and Andreas Hoheisel. Taxonomies of the multi-criteria grid workflow scheduling problem. Technical Report TR-0106, Institute on Resource Management and Scheduling, CoreGRID - Network of Excellence, August 2007.

[14] Liangzhao Zeng, Boualem Benatallah, Anne H.H. Ngu, Marlon Dumas, Jayant Kalagnanam, and Henry Chang. Qos-aware middleware for web services composition. *IEEE Transactions on Software Engineering*, 30(5):311–327, 2004.

# LOAD INFORMATION SHARING POLICIES IN COMMUNICATION-INTENSIVE PARALLEL APPLICATIONS

Javier Bustos Jimenez
*Escuela de Ingenieria Informatica. Universidad Diego Portales*
*Av. Ejercito 441, Santiago, Chile.*
javier.bustos@inf.udp.cl


Denis Caromel, Mario Leyton
*INRIA Sophia-Antipolis, CNRS-I3S, UNSA.*
*2004, Route des Lucioles, BP 93,*
*F-06902 Sophia-Antipolis Cedex, France.*
Denis.Caromel@sophia.inria.fr, Mario.Leyton@sophia.inria.fr


Jose Miguel Piquer
*Departamento de Ciencias de la Computacion (DCC). Universidad de Chile.*
*Blanco Encalada 2120, Santiago, Chile.*
jpiquer@dcc.uchile.cl

**Abstract**    One usage of Grid infrastructures is to perform parallel computing of scientific applications, most of the time related to hard sciences (physics, chemistry, biology). To exploit parallelism most of these applications are intensive communicated in data and synchronisation messages. On this context, grid systems have to take in account to not interfering with the normal execution of applications. Starting from this idea, in this article we present a study of information sharing policies used by load-balancing algorithms developed for the middleware *ProActive*, analyzing the performance scalability of: *response time* (time of reaction against instabilities) and *bandwidth*, from a communication-intensive application context. We divided the policies into: *Centralized* or *Distributed* oriented; and *Eager* or *Lazy* load information sharing. Our experimental results show that *Eager Distributed* oriented policies have better performance (response time and bandwidth usage).

**Keywords:**    Dynamic load balancing, Communication-intensive parallel applications, Load information sharing policies, Load information collection.

## 1.    Introduction

*Load-balancing* is the process of distributing parallel application tasks on a set of processors while improving the performance and reducing the application response time. The decisions of *when*, *where* and *which* tasks have to be transferred are critical, and therefore the load information has to be accurate and up to date [9]. In *dynamic load-balance*, decisions depend on the information collected from the system. Load information can be shared among processors periodically or "on demand", using *Centralized* or *Distributed* information collectors [12]. When dealing with communication-intensive applications (parallel applications which transfer a large amount of data among processors), the information sharing policy influences not only the load-balancing decisions but also the communication itself. We studied this problem, because our results can be applied to optimise performance load-balancing algorithms for the middleware ProActive[2].

The performance of load-balancing algorithms for non-intensive communication applications has been studied in depth since the last years of the 80's [3, 11, 12] focusing on *stability* (ability of balancing the work only if that action improves the performance of the system) and *response time* (ability of reacting against instabilities). Casavant and Kuhl [3] show that a faster response-time is more important than stability for improving the performance of load-balancing algorithms.

This article describes experiments which measure the response time and bandwidth usage for different information sharing policies applied by well-known load-balancing algorithms. These policies are studied in a communication-intensive context and are defined as follows:

1 **Centralized Full Information**: Nodes share all their load information with a central server. Figure 1.a presents an example with three nodes: nodes A and C send their load information L to the server B periodically. The server collects that information and keeps the system balanced (in the figure, ordering A to balance with C). This policy is widely used on systems like Condor [6, 8] and middlewares like Legion [4]. Theoretical and practical studies report this policy as non scalable [3, 12].

2 **Centralized Partial Information** There is partial information sharing among the nodes through central server. Figure 1.b presents an example using three nodes which share information only when they are overloaded. A node A registers on the server B when it enters an "overloaded state" (that is, the "load metric" is above a given threshold), and node C unregisters from the server because it exits the "overloaded state". At the same time C asks the server for overloaded nodes, the server chooses one node from its registration table and starts the load-balancing between them.

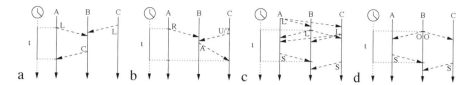

**Figure 1:** a) Centralized Full Info. b) Centralized Partial Info. c) Distributed Full Info. d) Distributed Partial Info.

3 **Distributed Full Information** Nodes share all their information using broadcast. Figure 1.c shows an example using three nodes: Each node broadcasts its load to the others periodically. The nodes use the information for load balancing [10]. Then, A and C realize they can share B's load and send the balance message S. The figure also shows the main problem of this policy: there is no control on the number of balance messages an overloaded node might receive. For our response time measurements, we considered only the first balance message (in the figure: the message from A).

4 **Distributed Partial Information** There is partial information sharing among the nodes using broadcast. Figure 1.d presents an example for the *overloaded* case noting that, unlike in the previous policy, only the reply from A is considered.

We studied the policies at the load balancing module of the middleware **ProActive** [2]. ProActive provides a strong deployment infrastructure, communication and active-object migration [5]. Using active-objects, communication-intensive parallel applications such as Jem3D [7] have been developed.

This article is organized as follows: Section 2 presents the load models and the policies simulated with ProActive. Section 3 summarizes the main results of this study. Section 4 shows the conclusions and discusses future work.

## 2. Model Overview and Definitions

This section provides the main definitions and a brief overview of the load-balancing algorithms and information sharing policies used in our analysis.

In this paper, each **node** represents a machine (virtual or real) which participates in the balancing. As in [12], we compare centralized and distributed algorithms, adding partial-information algorithms in our experiments. In ProActive, there is no notion of **tasks** like in parallel batch systems [8, 13]. We use the word **task** to refer to a **service** [2], and the word **job** for a **set** of services **served** by an active object. In the literature, the word **load** represents a metric such as the CPU queue length, the available memory, a linear combination of both, etc. In this paper, **load** represents the number of tasks in the CPU queue modelled with ProActive (see section 2.2). In our study, **response time** is the time since a node entering the *overloaded* state and the beginning of the load-balancing.

## 2.1    Load Model

Following the recommendations of [1, 3], we simulate the load of each node with a discrete-time population process with birth-rate $\lambda$ and death-rate $\mu$. The value of $\lambda$ represents the number of jobs which arrive every second to a node. The job size (in terms of number of tasks) follows an exponential distribution with mean 1. The death-rate $\mu$ represents the number of tasks served by a single node per second. In our experiments we use $\lambda = 1, 2, ..., 10$, and in order to maintain the system stable: $\mu = 10$. Note that this methodology simulates the load balance process and its communications. Simulation data will conclude whether the policies hinder intensive-communicated parallel applications. Our experiments have to be comparable for all policies and number of nodes. Therefore, we calculated the total number of incoming tasks every second (along a period of 60 seconds) for each value of $\lambda$. These precomputed values were used for all the experiments.

In our experiments, the nodes are labelled $0, ..., n$ and the value of $\lambda$ assigned to the node $i$ is $\lambda_i = 1 + i$ mod 10. Each node used the initial precomputed incoming rate $\lambda_i$, and after 60 seconds, the simulation was restarted again with the value of $\lambda_i$.

Several studies have shown that on a set of workstations (without load balancing), more than 80% of the workstations are idle during the day [8, 12]. The concept of *occupied* workstations and *overloaded* nodes are similar: processors which want to share work. Therefore, in our study, if no load balance was made, 20% of the nodes had to reach the overloaded state. To achieve this with the previously calculated values for $\lambda$, we used the convention: Underloaded Node means load $< 10$, Normal Node means $10 \leq$ load $< 15$, and Overloaded Node means load $\geq 15$.

## 2.2    Implementing the Information Sharing Policies

Since the information-sharing policies defined in section 1 can be *full* or *partial*, when unspecified we will be referring to *full* information sharing policies. In *full* information sharing policies, load information from overloaded and underloaded nodes is shared.

On the other hand, we will classify *partial* information policies into two groups: *eager* or *lazy*. *Eager* policies correspond to the ones where an *overloaded* node triggers the load-balancing, and therefore the partially shared information corresponds to the underloaded nodes. *Lazy* policies correspond to the ones where the *underloaded* node triggers the load-balancing, and therefore the partially shared information corresponds to the overloaded nodes.

Each node is modelled as an *active object* with three principal operations:

- `register`: registers on the communication channel (server, broadcast). This method starts the clock in our experiments.

- `loadBalance`: starts the load-balancing process, to stop the clock in our experiments, and to calculate the response time.

- `addLoad(x)`: adds $x$ tasks to the callee.

## Centralized

For this policy, one active object was chosen as a central server which collected and stored load-balance information of each node as: underloaded, normal or overloaded. The policy works as follows:

- Every second, the nodes call the remote `register` execution on the server. The *load server* processes incoming method calls. If the call originates from an overloaded node, the server randomly chooses an address of an underloaded node (if any) and calls the method `loadBalance` on the overloaded node with the chosen address.

- The overloaded node performs locally `addLoad(-myLoad/2)` (according to the recommendations of Berenbrink, Friedetzkyand Goldberg [1]) and the underloaded node (remotely) performs the execution of `addLoad(myLoad/2)`.

## Lazy Centralized

We studied this policy looking for a reduction of the information transmitted over the network. For this, we included an `unregister` method to the node model. This policy is described as follows:

- When a node reaches the overloaded state, it registers on the central server, and when a node leaves the overloaded state, it unregisters (removes its reference) from the server.

- Every second, if a node is underloaded it asks the server for overloaded nodes. When the server receives that query, it randomly chooses the address of an overloaded node (if any), and starts the load-balancing: ordering the overloaded node to balance with the node that originated the query.

## Eager Centralized

This policy is similar to the previous one, but underloaded nodes share their information instead of overloaded ones. The nodes register on the server when they reach the underloaded state and unregister when leaving it:

- When a node is in overloaded state, it asks the server for underloaded nodes once per second.

- Upon receiving the query, the server randomly chooses the address of an underloaded node (if any) and begins the load-balancing by ordering the overloaded node that sent the query to balance with the chosen underloaded node.

**Distributed**

The policy is similar to *Centralized*, but instead of sending the information to a central server, nodes broadcast their information.

**Lazy Distributed**

This policy is similar to *Lazy Centralized*, but in this case the information is shared through the multicast channel instead of a central server. We expected this policy to have similar time delay but use less bandwidth than the *Distributed* policy due to the reduction in the number of sent messages.

**Eager Distributed**

This policy is the broadcast version of *Eager Centralized*, and we expected a behavior similar to the *Lazy Distributed* policy.

## 2.3     Hardware and Software

We tested the policies on a heterogeneous network composed of: 3 Pentium II 0.4 GHz, 10 Pentium III 0.5 - 1.0 Ghz, 3 Pentium IV 3.4GHz and 4 Pentium XEON 2.0GHz for the nodes and a Pentium IV 3.4GHz for the server. We uniformly at random distribute the nodes (active objects) on the processors. For *response time* measurements we used the system clock, and for bandwidth measurements we used Ethereal software. The policy methods for nodes and servers were developed using the *ProActive* middleware on Java 2 Platform (Standard Edition) version 1.4.2.

## 3.     Results Analysis

We tested the policies on $20, 40, 80, 160, 320$ nodes distributed on 20 machines. For each case we took $1000$ samples of response times and the bandwidth reports from *Ethereal*. In this section we present the main results of this study. We will first discuss the *response-time*, and then the *bandwidth* analysis.

## 3.1     Response Time

Figure 2 shows *response-time* for all the policies. Following the recommendations of [9], response time should be less than the periodical update time, and in this study the update time was 1000 ms.

Using this reference, *Distributed* policies presented better response times than *Centralized* policies. Also, policies that sent underloaded information (*Eager* policies) had better performance than policies which shared overloaded information (*Lazy* policies). This happens because in the *Eager* policies, overloaded nodes generate the load balancing request, while in *Lazy* policies over-loaded nodes have to wait until an underloaded node contacts them.

Note that for the *Eager Distributed* policy, overloaded nodes obtain the information of underloaded ones before the balance process. Therefore, since the response time is near to zero, we decided not to show this algorithm in the figure. Also note that, the poor scalability of the *Lazy Centralized* policy, can be explained because the server is monothreaded. Using a multithreaded central server can increase the saturation threshold, but it is not scalable solution because new constraints like bandwith usage or mutual exclusion are generated.

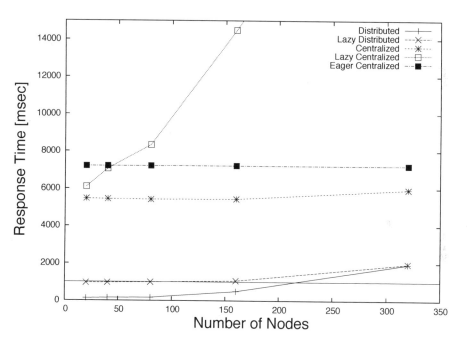

**Figure 2:** Mean response time for all policies

## 3.2   Bandwidth

In this section we tested the policies bandwidth usage. Unfortunately, the underlying implementations introduces an additional difference: TCP or UDP based communications (resp. *Centralized* and *Distributed* policies). To avoid having to interpret such bias, we compare performance between *full* and *partial* information policies, developed on *centralized* and *distributed* load-balancing algorithms.

Figure 3 shows the bandwidth used during the information sharing phase, counting only messages sent to the server:

1 *Centralized* policies use between 5 (*Eager Centralized*) and 40 times (*Centralized*) more bandwidth than distributed policies.

2 For *partial information* schemes with *centralized* policies: when overloaded nodes share their information, less than 20% of the total nodes (see section 2.1) will send register/unregister messages, and more than 80% of them will send queries for registered nodes (every second).

3 When underloaded nodes share their information, more than 80% of the total nodes will send register/unregister messages and less than 20% of them will send queries. This behavior causes the former approach to consume more bandwidth than the latter.

Figure 4 shows the total bandwidth used by our load model, including the loadBalance and addLoad messages:

1 *Eager* policies which share *partial* information of underloaded nodes have the lowest bandwidth usage for each case (*Centralized* and *Distributed*).

2 *Lazy* policies which share *partial* information of overloaded nodes generate a great increase of the bandwidth usage, because there is no control on how many underloaded nodes send loadBalance messages. In the *Lazy Centralized* policy, this behavior generates a saturation on the communication channel even though the number of messages is half of that of the *Centralized* policy. This happens because most of the messages are balance queries, and the server has to choose an overloaded node and send the loadBalance message to it.

3 When the service queue of a central server becomes saturated (over 300 nodes on our experiments), the response time increases and the bandwidth usage decreases, because the saturation will causes less messages to be sent over the network. As noted for the *response time* analysis (see 3.1), using a multithreaded central server it is not a scalable solution.

## 3.3    Testing a real application

We tested the impact of the policies with a real application: the calculus of a *Jacobi* matrix. This algorithm performs an iterative computation on a real-valued square matrix. On each iteration, the value of each element is computed using its own value and the value of its neighbors on the previous iteration. We divided a 3600x3600 matrix into 25 disjoint sub-matrices of equal size, each one managed by an active object called "*worker*" (implemented using ProActive). Each worker communicates only with its direct neighbors.

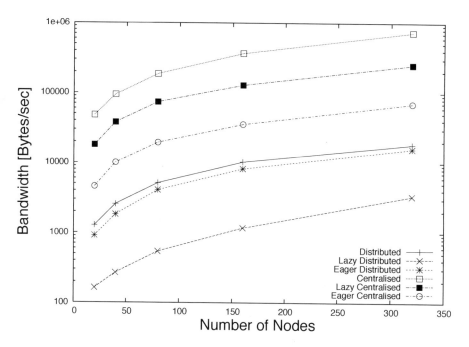

**Figure 3:** Bandwidth usage of coordination policies: Information sharing phase.

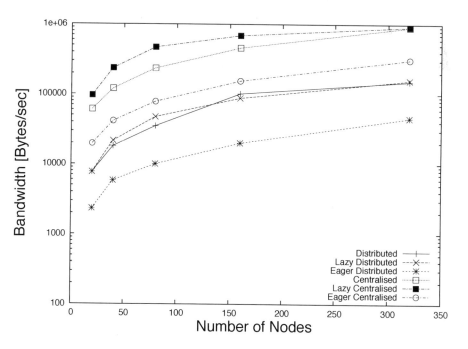

**Figure 4:** Bandwidth usage of coordination policies: Total.

As a reference, all the workers are randomly distributed among 15 machines, using at most two workers by machine. Using this distribution, we measured the mean execution time of performing 1000 sequential calculi of Jacobi matrices (first row of Table 1).

To determine the impact of the policies on the *Jacobi* application, we distributed 30 nodes among the 15 machines. We ran the application (placing one load server outside of the simulation machines), and measured the execution time of *Jacobi*. Separately for each policy we measured the CPU cost (in % of busy time) for the 15 machines. The results are in Table 1.

Table 1: Policy effects on execution time of a parallel Jacobi application

| Policy | Execution Time (sec) | % policy cost (time) | % policy cost (CPU) |
|---|---|---|---|
| None | 914.361 | — | — |
| Centralized | 1014.960 | 11.00% | 1.3% |
| Lazy Centralized | 995.873 | 8.91% | 1.1% |
| Eager Centralized | 972.621 | 6.37% | 1.1% |
| Distributed | 1004.800 | 9.89% | 10.7% |
| Lazy Distributed | 925.964 | 1.26% | 4.5% |
| Eager Distributed | 915.085 | 0.08% | 4.1% |

While *Centralized* policies use less CPU on the "client" side, they use more bandwidth than their distributed equivalents. A special case is the *Distributed* policy, which uses less bandwidth than the *Centralized* policies, but the largest CPU time consumption, and it produces almost 10% of time delay on the application. So, if this policy is used, the load balancing itself will produce overloading.

## 4. Conclusions and Future Work

In this study we presented a comparison between six communication policies for load-balancing algorithms developed into the middleware ProActive. We focused on two metrics: communication *bandwidth* usage and *response time*.

We conclude that *Distributed* oriented policies have the best performance using these metrics, and the best information-sharing protocol is to share information only from underloaded nodes (*Eager*). Therefore, for a load-balancing architecture for communication-intensive parallel applications developed with asynchronous communicated middlewares such as ProActive, we suggest using an *Eager Distributed* policy where overloaded nodes trigger the balancing using previously acquired information, thus avoiding the need of *Centralized* servers. Moreover, if the load index could be updated with a lower frequency than one per second and similar accuracy, the policy would use less coordination messages, producing less interference with parallel applications.

Our future goal is to optimize the selection of the best node candidate for the load-balancing process from a total or partial view of the network and considering different network topologies still aiming for the best performance in terms of *bandwidth usage*, *response time* and interference with parallel applications.

## Acknowledgments

This work was partially supported by NIC Labs and CoreGrid Network of Excellence.

## References

[1] Petra Berenbrink, Tom Friedetzky, and Leslie Ann Goldberg. The natural work-stealing algorithm is stable. In *IEEE Symposium on Foundations of Computer Science*, pages 178–187, 2001.

[2] Javier Bustos-Jimenez, Denis Caromel, Alexandre Di Costanzo, Mario Leyton, and Jose Piquer. Balancing active objects on a peer to peer infrastructure. In *Proceedings of XXV International Conference of SCCC, Valdivia, Chile*. IEEE CS Press, November 2005.

[3] T. L. Casavant and J. G. Kuhl. Effects of response and stability on scheduling in distributed computing systems. *IEEE Trans. Softw. Eng.*, 14(11):1578–1588, 1988.

[4] Steve J. Chapin, Dimitrios Katramatos, John Karpovich, and Andrew S. Grimshaw. The Legion resource management system. In Dror G. Feitelson and Larry Rudolph, editors, *Job Scheduling Strategies for Parallel Processing*, pages 162–178. Springer Verlag, 1999.

[5] Wilfired Klauser Denis Caromel and Julien Vayssiere. Towards seamless computing and metacomputing in java. *Concurrency Practice and Experience*, 1998.

[6] Elisa Heymann, Miquel A. Senar, Emilio Luque, and Miron Livny. Adaptive scheduling for master-worker applications on the computational grid. In *GRID*, pages 214–227, 2000.

[7] Fabrice Huet, Denis Caromel, and Henri Bal. A high performance java middleware with a real application. In *Proc. of High Performance Computing, Networking and Storage (SC2004), Pittsburgh, USA*, 2004.

[8] Miron Livny Michael Litzkow and Matt Mutka. Condor - a hunter of idle workstations. In *Proc. of 8th International Conference on Distribuited Computing Systems*, pages 104–111, 1998.

[9] M. Mitzenmacher. How useful is old information? *IEEE Transactions on Parallel and Distributed Systems*, 11(1):6–34, 2000.

[10] J.L. Bosque Orero, D. Gil Marco, and L. Pastor. Dynamic load balancing in heterogeneous clusters. In *Proc. of IASTED International Conference on Parallel and Distributed Computing and Networks*, 2004.

[11] Niranjan G. Shivaratri, Phillip Krueger, and Mukesh Singhal. Load distributing for locally distributed systems. *IEEE Computer*, 25(12):33–44, 1992.

[12] M. M. Theimer and K. A. Lantz. Finding idle machines in a workstation-based distributed system. *IEEE Trans. Softw. Eng.*, 15(11):1444–1458, 1989.

[13] W. Zhu, C. Steketee, and B. Muilwijk. Load balancing and workstation autonomy on amoeba. *Australian Computer Science Communications*, 17(1):588–597, 1995.

# A MARKOV MODEL FOR FAULT-TOLERANT TASK PARALLEL COMPUTATIONS *

Carlo Bertolli, Massimiliano Meneghin
*Department of Computer Science*
*Parallel and Distributed Research Group*
*University of Pisa*
*Largo Bruno Pontecorvo, 3, Pisa, 56125 Pisa, Italy*
bertolli@di.unipi.it
meneghin@di.unipi.it

Joaquim Gabarro
*Universitat Politècnica de Catalunya, ALBCOM Research Group*
*Edifici $\Omega$, Campus Nord Jordi Girona, 1-3, Barcelona 08034, Spain*
gabarro@lsi.upc.edu

**Abstract**     One of the main issues for Grid applications is to deal with frequent failures, due to the dynamic and distributed nature of Grid platforms. This issue becomes even more important if we want to exploit Grid platforms to support High-Performance applications. Our work starts from the choice of structured parallelism (e.g. skeletons) as programming model to attack this issue. We present our study of the performance impact of failures on the execution time of a specific class of structured parallel programs, namely task parallel computations. We introduce a Markov model for task parallel computations and we present a framework to study it. The result is an analytical tool for predicting the completion time of task parallel computations, in the case the number of tasks is known in advance. Otherwise such a number is unknown, we can still obtain the steady-state performance. We describe the framework and we present preliminar experimental results to validate it.

**Keywords:**     Parallel Computing, Fault Tolerance, High-Level Programming, Structured Parallel Programming, Performance Models

*All authors were partially supported by the FP6 Network of Excellence CoreGRID funded by the European Commission (Contract IST-2002-004265). Carlo Bertolli was also partially supported by the FIRB In.Sy.Eme. Project. Joaquim Gabarro was also partially supported by FET pro-active Integrated Project 15964 (AEOLUS) by Spanish projects TIN2005-09198-C02-02 (ASCE) and MEC-TIN2005-25859-E and TIN2007-66523 (FORMALISM).

## 1. Introduction

Grid computing platforms [5] have been exploited to support High-Performance applications as they can provide the required computing power. In general, the exploitation of grid platforms is made difficult by the high frequency of failures affecting the resources. As a consequence, in the specific case of High-Performance applications, it is difficult to ensure any kinds of Quality of Service (QoS), because of failures.

We face this issue by targeting structured parallel programming. A structured parallel program is composed of high-level parallel structures (e.g. *skeletons* [4]), for which there is some compile-time knowledge of the interactions between the parallel entities performing the computation. Along with other important properties, this knowledge allows to introduce simple fault tolerance strategies. In our study we introduce Markovian models of the computations, and related fault tolerance strategies, to obtain an analysis of the run-time impact of failures on the computation performance. Markovian models have been deeply studied in the context of parallel and distributed computing to analyze the impact of failures of the performance of computations. For instance, in [9] a markovian model is exploited to analyze the performance impact due to failures in the case of a two-level recovery scheme for fault tolerance. The computation model consists in a set of processes executing a distributed program, interacting through message-passing, and periodically taking consistent checkpoints. The recovery scheme is two-level in the sense that checkpointing is performed on both volatile and stable storage supports at different frequencies, and the recovery is different depending on the failures, and the availability of collected information. The developed markov model allows to prove that the two-level scheme enable higher resiliency degrees w.r.t. one-level schemes. In [10] the computation model consists of performing a set of independent task, supporting fault tolerance by checkpointing, i.e. partial execution of tasks is periodically checkpointed. The failure model considered includes software errors, i.e. the execution of a task can deliver an incorrect result. A Markow Reward Model is exploited to analyze the performance impact of checkpointing schemes based on task duplication. Parameters of the Markovian model are the average time intercurring between checkpoints, and the total average task execution time. The paper analyzes four different schemes for fault tolerance, mixing checkpointing, software replication techniques and forward recovery.

In this paper, we show the results of our study on the performance impact of failures for a specific class of structured parallel computations, namely *task parallel*. In [2–3] we have addressed this issue by introducing a formal Markov model for task parallel computations subject to failures. The Markov model describes how the completion time of task parallel computations behaves when the failure probability of Grid resources and the total number of tasks to be performed are known. Indeed, we obtained upper bounds of completion times for base cases (2 tasks performed on 2 resources being the most complex one), validated by experimental results [3]. We present our study on the Markov model for the general case of $n$ tasks performed on $m$ resources. The final result is a framework that allows to study the performance impact due to failures, which correctness is validated by experiments we performed on some interesting cases, characterized by values of $n$ larger than $m$.

The outline of the paper is the following. In Section 2 we recall the programming and computation model we target and its fault tolerance support. In Section 3 we describe the Markov model we introduced and we present a framework to study the recursive equation presented in [2]. Two fundmental items of this work, $T_{stay}$ and $T_{jump}$ representing the average time spent in a level of the Markov chain and the average time spent going from one level to the next one are introduced. In Section 4 we develop a worked example with $n = 4$ and $m = 2$. In Section 5 the value $N_a$ representing the average number of entries of a given state is is considered. In Section 6 we present a simplified framework to study the time needed to execute $n$ tasks on $m$ resources and we give experimental results to validate the approach. Finally, in Section 7, we give the conclusions of this paper.

## 2. Computation Model and Fault Tolerance

Our study on the run-time quantitative behavior of parallel computations is based on the muskel programming environment (see [1]). A muskel program is a macro data-flow graph composed of sequential and parallel modules, connected through streams, i.e. possibly unlimited sequences of typed elements. Parallel modules are expressed as *skeletons*[4], expressing well-known parallel structures, that can be nested in arbitrary hierarchies. Examples of skeletons that can be used to implement a parallel algorithm are farm and pipeline. Farm computations express a task parallel computation, where a set of *workers* performs the same program on different input data (obtained from an input stream), and delivering an output stream of results (one for each task). In a pipeline computation, each element received from an input stream is passed to a set of nested functions (e.g. $out = F_1(F_2(\ldots F_n(in)\ldots)))$, and the results are delivered to an output stream. Each function $F_i$ is implemented in a different *stage*, and the evaluation of two functions on different input elements are independent, and can happen in parallel.

The implementation of muskel is based on a *master-slave* strategy:

- A whole data-flow graph is mapped in each slave, that represents the unit of parallelism. The data-flow graph can be modeled as a function **F**, which application to an input data represents the *task* of the computation. A slave computation consists in iteratively: (1) receiving an input value from the master; (2) applying it as actual parameter of **F**, and producing a result; (3) returning the result to the master. This scheme is applied to a stream of input values (produced by the master), and it produces an output stream of results (consumed by the master).

- The master owns a local queue of tasks (i.e. the input data), and is responsible of coordinating slaves: it schedules to workers the input data, and it receives results back from slaves.

We define an abstract description of the implementation model of muskel , to introduce its mathematical formulation. The model consists in a set of n tasks performed on m resources. Each task is performed independently with each other. We assume that each task can be performed in an average execution time, denoted with the symbol $\delta$.

For what concern failure modeling, in this paper we target the fail-stop failure model [7] for slaves and we assume that the master cannot fail. Each slave fails independently of the other ones and with a known probability $q = 1 - p$, where $p$ is the probability of success. The failure of a slave corresponds with the lost of the computation related to the last received input element. We abstractly model this as the failure of the task execution (with probability $q$). When a slave fails, the master is notified of its failure by the low-level communication support. The fault tolerance support is based on re-scheduling of the failed tasks: whenever a slave fails, the master detects the failure, and it re-schedules the lost task to an available slave [3]. We also assume that failed slaves are eventually restarted by some sub-system, and they re-join the computation. The time needed to detect a failure, plus the one needed to restart a slave has a known average (denoted with $\Delta$) that is a parameter of our model.

In our previous study [2] we introduced a Markovian model of the computation to model fault-prone executions. The model exploits a Bulk-Synchronous Parallel (BSP)-like scheme, where the computation is composed of super-steps, each including a computation and communication phase. Supersteps are sequentialzed by synchronizing the parallel execution during the communication phase. In our model, at each super step:

- The master schedules an input element to each slave.

- The slaves perform the computation in parallel w.r.t. each other, and they either succeed (with probability $p$) or fail (with probability $q$).

- The master re-schedule the next set of tasks only *after* each slave either returned a result, or failed and restarted.

As highlighted in [3], we exploit this model to obtain an upper bound of the actual completion time, but not in the actual implementation of muskel . In muskel slaves are directly re-scheduled withtout waiting for all other ones

| Variable | Meaning |
|---|---|
| $n$ | number of tasks to be performed |
| $m$ | number of slaves |
| $p$ | probability of success of evaluation of **F** on an input value |
| $q = 1 - p$ | probability of failure of evaluation of **F** on an input value |
| $\delta$ | average task execution time |
| $\Delta$ | average time needed to detect a failure, and restart the a slave |
| $\mu$ | is the maximum between $\delta$ and $\Delta$ |

**Table 1:** Table of the notation used in the rest of the paper.

performed in parallel to either fail or succeed. We demand to the continuation of this work a full proof of the differences between the Markov model, and the implementation one. In the rest of the paper we exploit the notation described in table 1.

## 3. A General Markov Model for Fault Tolerance

In this section, we introduce and discuss a Markov model [6] describing the impact of failures on the computation completion time. Figure 1 is a graphical representation of the model. The states of the Markov chain are represented as black circles labeled with two indexes. The first index denotes the *level* (see below) at which we place the state, while the second one denotes the relative position inside the level. A state of the Markov chain represents a specific point in the computation we have reached and it can be formalized as the number of tasks that remain to be performed:

$$t(i,j) = \begin{cases} n & i = 0 \text{ and } j = 0 \\ n - ((i-1)m + j) & \text{oth.} \end{cases}$$

With the initial state $(0,0)$ we represent the fact that $n$ tasks have to be performed. Each level of the model includes exactly $m$ states. For simplicity, we assume that $n$ is a multiple of $m$. We define an initial level 0 that includes just the initial state $(0,0)$. Level 1 include states from $(1,1)$ to $(1,m)$, where: in $(1,1)$ we have performed a single tasks, and $n - ((1-1)m+1) = n-1$ are still to be performed. In $(1,m)$ we have performed $m$ tasks, and $n - ((1-1)m+m) = n - m$ are still to be performed. Below, for labeling the states, we sometimes exploit their $t(i,j)$ value, instead of the pair notation $(i,j)$.

Now consider the state $(0,0)$. Recall that we exploit exactly $m$ resources to perform tasks. We assign a task to each of the $m$ resources, and we can obtain 0 to $m$ failures. In the case we obtain $m$ failures, we remain in state $(0,0)$. In the case we obtain $m - 1$ failures, we have performed 1 task, and we transit

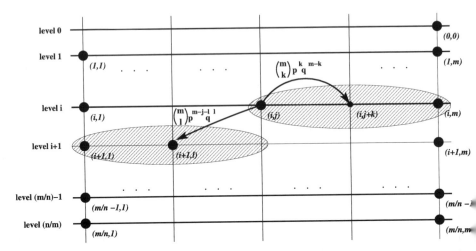

**Figure 1:** Representation of the Markov model of computation of $n$ tasks on $m$ resources (with $n >> m$), where each resource can fail with probability $q$.

in state $(1, 1)$, in the next level. If we obtain $0$ failures, we go directly down to state $(1, m)$. As the maximum degree of parallelism is $m$, we cannot obtain more than $m$ successes. Thus, we cannot go from level $0$ to level $2$ *with just one transition*. We have first to pass from at least one of the states belonging to level $1$. This is the general semantics behind the characterization in levels of the Markov model.

In a generic computation, we will transit in some states inside the same level. Next, we jump into a state in the next level. The transition probabilities and their weights are given by the general formula for $n \geq n$ introduced in [2]:

$$T_{n,m} = q^m (\Delta + T_{n,m}) + \sum_{k=1}^{m-1} \binom{m}{k} p^k q^{n-k} (\mu + T_{n-k,m}) + p^m (\delta + T_{n-m,m})$$

Consider the highlighted state $(i, j)$ in Fig. 1. We schedule $m$ tasks, and we can:

- Remain in $(i, j)$, if we obtain $m$ failures. This event has probability $q^m$ and it costs $\Delta$.

- Transit in a state at the right of $(i, j)$, if the number of successes is not sufficient to change level. For instance, we can transit in state $(i, j+k)$, if we obtain $k$ successes, and $m - k$ failures. This transition has probability $\binom{m}{k} p^k q^{m-k}$, and it has a weight of $\mu$ seconds.

- Transit down-left in a state $(i+1, j-l)$ in the next level. In this case, we obtain a number of successes sufficient to make us change level. In this specific case, the transition has probability $\binom{m}{l}p^{m-j-l}q^l$, and it costs $\mu$ seconds.

- Transit directly down, if we obtain $m$ successes. We take this transition with probability $p^m$, and it costs $\delta$ seconds, i.e. the average tasks execution time (as we perform all tasks in parallel).

It remains to consider the case $0 \leq n < m$. Of course, when $n = 0$ it holds $T_{0,m} = 0$. For $0 < n < m$, we have

$$T_{n,m} = q^n(\Delta + T_{n,m}) + \sum_{k=1}^{n-1}\binom{m}{k}p^kq^{n-k}(\mu + T_{n-k,m}) + p^n\delta$$

Note that, two types of transitions are not admitted in our model. Transitions to the left are forbidden. According to the fault tolerance model, we cannot loose results that we have performed in previous steps (see Sect. 2). Transition to the down-right are also forbidden. This happens because we can obtain up to $m$ successes for a transition. Going to the down-right means that we obtain more than $m$ successes.

Each computation features a different path in the computation states, but we can characterize a general behavior. Consider the level $k$: we transit in one of the states of level $k$, from a state of the level $k - 1$; we transit in one or more states (possibly all) of the level $k$, until we jump to one of the states at the next level $k + 1$. From a quantitative viewpoint, we can characterize each level with two quantities. $T_{stay}(k)$ is the *average time passed in level $k$* and $T_{jump}(k)$, the *average time needed to jump from level $k$ to level $k + 1$*. According to [9], $T_{stay}(k) = \sum_{a,b \in k} V_{a,b}Q_{a,b}N_a$, the sum is over all transitions $a \to b$ in level $k$, $V_{a,b}$ is the time needed in $a \to b$, $Q_{a,b}$ is the probability of $a \to b$ and $N_a$ and that is the average number of entries into state $a$. Similarly, we can compute the average time needed to jump from a level $k$, to its successor $k + 1$ by considering all the transitions from a state $a$ at level $k$ to the state $b$ at level $k + 1$: $T_{jump}(k) = \sum_{a \in k, b \in k+1} V_{a,b}Q_{a,b}N_a$. The expected time can be computed as

$$T_{n,m} = \sum_{0 \leq k \leq m/n} T_{stay}(k) + \sum_{0 \leq k < m/n} T_{jump}(k)$$

## 4. Example with 4 taks and 2 slaves

We develop the preceding approach in a small example with $m = 2$ and $n = 4$. Denoting $T_{k,2} = \tau_k$ for $0 \leq k \leq 4$ we have the equations

$$\tau_k = q^2(\tau_n + \Delta) + 2pq(\mu + \tau_{k-1}) + p^2(\delta + \tau_{k-2}) , \ 2 \leq k \leq 4$$
$$\tau_1 = q(\tau_1 + \Delta) + p\mu , \ \tau_0 = 0$$

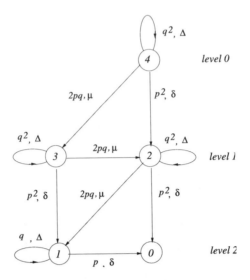

**Figure 2:** Markov model of computation of $n = 4$ tasks on $m = 2$ slaves, each slave can fail with probability $q$. State numbering denotes the number of pending tasks.

For $2 \leq k \leq 4$ the recurrence for $\tau_k$ follows the general formula given in Section 3. For $k = 1$ only one slave is needed because only one task need to be executed. Finally for $k = 0$, $\tau_0 = 0$ because there are no pending tasks. The Figure 2 is a rewriting of the recursive equations in terms of the absorbing Markov chain (the Figure 2 is a concrete example of Figure 1). States in Figure 2 are numbered by the number of pending tasks, 4 is the initial state and 0 is the final absorbing state.

In the following we use recurrence equations to find $T_{stay}(k)$ and $T_{jump}(k)$ for $0 \leq k \leq 2$. Starting from 4, the expected time before absorption verifies $\tau_4 = q^2(\tau_4 + \Delta) + 2pq(\mu + \tau_3) + p^2(\delta + \tau_2)$ and therefore $\tau_4 = \frac{q^2}{1-q^2}\Delta + \frac{2pq}{1-q^2}(\mu + \tau_3) + \frac{p^2}{1-q^2}(\delta + \tau_2)$. This equation give us directly $T_{stay}(0) = \frac{q^2}{1-q^2}\Delta$ and $T_{jump}(0) = \frac{2pq}{1-q^2}\mu + \frac{p^2}{1-q^2}\delta$. Using the notations given in Section 3

$$T_{stay}(0) = V_{4,4}Q_{4,4}N_4 = \Delta q^2 \frac{1}{1-q^2}$$

$$T_{jump}(0) = V_{4,3}Q_{4,3}N_4 + V_{4,2}Q_{4,2}N_4 = \mu 2pq\frac{1}{1-q^2} + \delta p^2\frac{1}{1-q^2}$$

where we can identify $N_4 = \frac{1}{1-q^2}$. From this point, we have to analyse the system from level 1 represented by the expression $\frac{2pq}{1-q^2}\tau_3 + \frac{p^2}{1-q^2}\tau_2$. Unfolding this equation an enough number of times we obtain

$$T_{stay}(1) \quad = \quad \frac{q^2}{1-q^2}\Delta + \left(\frac{2pq}{1-q^2}\right)^2\left(\mu + \frac{q^2}{1-q^2}\Delta\right)$$

The term $\frac{q^2}{1-q^2}\Delta$ is the expected time looping around states 3 and 4. The term $\left(\frac{2pq}{1-q^2}\right)^2\left(\mu + \frac{q^2}{1-q^2}\Delta\right)$ give us the probability to take transiton $(3,2)$ coming from 4 multiplied by the expected time going from 3 to 2 and looping in 2 before leaving. It can be rewriten as

$$
\begin{aligned}
T_{stay}(1) \quad &= \quad V_{3,3}Q_{3,3}N_3 + V_{3,2}Q_{3,2}N_3 + V_{2,2}Q_{2,2}N_2 \\
&= \quad \Delta q^2 \frac{2pq}{1-q^2}\frac{1}{1-q^2} + \mu 2pq\frac{2pq}{1-q^2}\frac{1}{1-q^2} + \\
&+ \quad \Delta q^2\left(\left(\frac{2pq}{1-q^2}\right)^2 + \frac{p^2}{1-q^2}\right)\frac{1}{1-q^2}
\end{aligned}
$$

We have $N_3 = \frac{2pq}{1-q^2}\frac{1}{1-q^2}$ and $N_2 = \left(\left(\frac{2pq}{1-q^2}\right)^2 + \frac{p^2}{1-q^2}\right)\frac{1}{1-q^2}$. Following this analysis we find

$$
\begin{aligned}
T_{jump}(1) \quad &= \quad \frac{2pq}{1-q^2}\mu\left(\left(\frac{2pq}{1-q^2}\right)^2 + \frac{p^2}{1-q^2}\right) + \frac{p^2}{1-q^2}\delta\left(\left(\frac{2pq}{1-q^2}\right)^2 + 1\right) \\
T_{stay}(2) \quad &= \quad \left(\left(\frac{2pq}{1-q^2}\right)^3 + 2\frac{pq}{1-q^2}\frac{p^2}{1-q^2}\right)\left(\delta + \frac{q}{1-q}\Delta\right)
\end{aligned}
$$

## 5. Computation of the Average Number of State Entries

Recall that we denote with $N_s$ the average number of entries in the state $s$ (where $s$ is the number of tasks that remain to be performed in that state). We want to estimate the value of $N_s$ for each non absorbing state $s$. When $s$ is different from the initial state, we have [9]:

$$N_s = \sum_{\{t|(t,s)\text{is an arc}\}} P_{t,s}N_t$$

where $P_{t,s}$ is the probability of taking the transition $t \to s$. When $s$ is the initial state we have $N_s = 1 + \sum_{\{t|(t,s)\text{is an arc}\}} P_{t,s}N_t$.

EXAMPLE 1 *Let us recompute $N_k$ for $4 \le k < 0$ for Figure 2. Using the equations*

$$N_4 = 1 + q^2N_4 \ , \quad N_3 = q^2N_3 + 2pqN_4 \ , \quad N_2 = q^2N_2 + 2pqN_3 + p^2N_4$$

*we reobtain $N_4, N_3$ and $N_2$. Finally $N_1 = qN_1 + 2pqN_2 + p^2 N_3$ and*

$$
\begin{aligned}
N_1 &= \frac{1}{1-q}2pqN_2 + \frac{1}{1-q^2}p^2 N_3 \\
&= \frac{1}{1-q}\Big(\frac{2pq}{1-q^2}\Big)^3 + 2\frac{1}{1-q}\frac{2pq}{1-q^2}\frac{p^2}{1-q^2}
\end{aligned}
$$

*We can check the correctness of the whole approach recomputing*

$$
\begin{aligned}
T_{jump}(1) &= \delta p^2 N_3 + \mu 2pqN_2 + \delta p^2 N_2 \\
T_{stay}(2) &= \Delta qN_1 + \delta pN_1
\end{aligned}
$$

Let us consider the general case. According to the Figure 1, $(0,0)$ corresponds to the inital state with $n$ tasks to be executed. As in the example we identify $(0,0)$ and $n$. As $N_n = 1 + q^m N_n$ we obtain $N_n = \frac{1}{1-q^m}$. Consider the state $(1,1)$ with $n-1$ tasks has to be executed, as $N_{n-1} = mpq^{m-1}N_n + q^m N_{n-1}$,

$$
N_{n-1} = m\frac{pq^{m-1}}{(1-q^m)^2}
$$

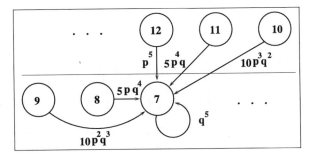

**Figure 3:** Snapshot of the graphical representation of markov models in the case of $m = 5$ and $n = 15$, to compute the average number of entries into state 5.

EXAMPLE 2 *Before to write the general case we consider the case $m = 5$ and $n = 15$. We want to compute the expected number of entries into state $s = 7$. Note that state 7 appears in the second level of the Markov chain. In Fig. 3 we show the representation of the portion of graph needed to compute $N_7$. We sum up all the contributions to enter 7 and we get*

$$
N_7 = \frac{1}{1-p^5}\Big(5pq^4 N_{s+1} + 10p^2q^3 N_{s+2} + 10p^3q^2 N_{s+3} + 5p^4q N_{s+4} + p^5 N_{s+5}\Big)
$$

We can now easily generalize this formula to the case of $m$ resources:

$$
\begin{aligned}
N_s &= p^m N_{s+m} + q^m N_s + \sum_{0<k<m} \binom{m}{k} p^k q^{m-k} N_{s+k} \\
&= \frac{1}{1-q^m}\left(p^m N_{s+m} + \sum_{0<k<m} \binom{m}{k} p^k q^{m-k} N_{s+k}\right)
\end{aligned}
$$

## 6. A Framework to Compute Approximate Values for $T_{n,m}$

As we have seen the values of $N_a$ are different for different nodes $a$. Next we study experimentally the possibility to replace all the different values by a unique average. We can apply the formula allowing to compute $N_s$ to concrete examples in order to get an idea of the behavior of this value. We have implemented a simple program that takes as input the quantities describe in Table 1, and produces the $N$ value for all states of the Markov chains. The results are shown in Tables 2, 3 4, and 5.

| $n$ | $m$ | $\delta$ | $\Delta$ | $p$ | $N_{avg}$ | $N_{var}$ |
|---|---|---|---|---|---|---|
| 500 | 5 | 10 | 5 | 0.9 | 0.223 | 0.0022 |
| 500 | 5 | 10 | 5 | 0.8 | 0.251 | 0.0015 |
| 500 | 5 | 10 | 5 | 0.5 | 0.401 | 0.001 |
| 1000 | 5 | 10 | 5 | 0.9 | 0.223 | 0.0011 |
| 1000 | 5 | 10 | 5 | 0.8 | 0.250 | 0.0007 |
| 1000 | 5 | 10 | 5 | 0.5 | 0.400 | 0.0004 |
| 2000 | 5 | 10 | 5 | 0.9 | 0.222 | 0.0006 |
| 2000 | 5 | 10 | 5 | 0.8 | 0.250 | 0.0004 |
| 2000 | 5 | 10 | 5 | 0.5 | 0.400 | 0.0002 |

**Table 2:** Evaluation of $N$ for $n = 5$, and $n = 10$.

From these numerical results, it seems a reasonable hypothesis to take the same average value $\overline{N}$. Therefore we assume the following:

**Working Hypotesis.** In the computation of $T_{stay}$ and $T_{jump}$ we replace all the values $N_a$ by an average value $\overline{N}$.

First consider the average time passed in the level $k$:

$$
\begin{aligned}
T_{stay} &= \sum_{a,b\in k} V_{a,b} Q_{a,b} N_a \approx \overline{N} \cdot \sum_{a,b\in k} V_{a,b} Q_{a,b} \\
&= \overline{N} \cdot \left[ m\Delta q^m + \sum_{0<k<m} (m-k)\mu \binom{m}{k} p^k q^{m-k} \right]
\end{aligned}
$$

| $n$ | $m$ | $\delta$ | $\Delta$ | p | $N_{avg}$ | $N_{var}$ |
|---|---|---|---|---|---|---|
| 500 | 10 | 10 | 5 | 0.9 | 0.112 | 0.0026 |
| 500 | 10 | 10 | 5 | 0.8 | 0.126 | 0.0020 |
| 500 | 10 | 10 | 5 | 0.5 | 0.201 | 0.0014 |
| 1000 | 10 | 10 | 5 | 0.9 | 0.112 | 0.0013 |
| 1000 | 10 | 10 | 5 | 0.8 | 0.125 | 0.0010 |
| 1000 | 10 | 10 | 5 | 0.5 | 0.200 | 0.0007 |
| 2000 | 10 | 10 | 5 | 0.9 | 0.111 | 0.0007 |
| 2000 | 10 | 10 | 5 | 0.8 | 0.125 | 0.0005 |
| 2000 | 10 | 10 | 5 | 0.5 | 0.200 | 0.0004 |

**Table 3:** Evaluation of $N$ for $n = 5$, and $n = 10$.

| n | m | $\delta$ | $\Delta$ | p | $N_{avg}$ | $N_{var}$ |
|---|---|---|---|---|---|---|
| 500 | 20 | 10 | 5 | 0.9 | 0.056 | 0.0030 |
| 500 | 20 | 10 | 5 | 0.8 | 0.063 | 0.0023 |
| 500 | 20 | 10 | 5 | 0.5 | 0.101 | 0.0018 |
| 1000 | 20 | 10 | 5 | 0.9 | 0.056 | 0.0015 |
| 1000 | 20 | 10 | 5 | 0.8 | 0.063 | 0.0011 |
| 1000 | 20 | 10 | 5 | 0.5 | 0.100 | 0.0009 |
| 2000 | 20 | 10 | 5 | 0.9 | 0.056 | 0.0007 |
| 2000 | 20 | 10 | 5 | 0.8 | 0.063 | 0.0006 |
| 2000 | 20 | 10 | 5 | 0.5 | 0.100 | 0.0004 |

**Table 4:** Evaluation of $N$ for $n = 5$, and $n = 10$.

| n | m | $\delta$ | $\Delta$ | p | $N_{avg}$ | $N_{var}$ |
|---|---|---|---|---|---|---|
| 510 | 30 | 10 | 5 | 0.9 | 0.038 | 0.0030 |
| 510 | 30 | 10 | 5 | 0.8 | 0.043 | 0.0023 |
| 510 | 30 | 10 | 5 | 0.5 | 0.068 | 0.0019 |
| 1020 | 30 | 10 | 5 | 0.9 | 0.037 | 0.0015 |
| 1020 | 30 | 10 | 5 | 0.8 | 0.042 | 0.0012 |
| 1020 | 30 | 10 | 5 | 0.5 | 0.067 | 0.0009 |
| 2010 | 30 | 10 | 5 | 0.9 | 0.037 | 0.0008 |
| 2010 | 30 | 10 | 5 | 0.8 | 0.042 | 0.0006 |
| 2010 | 30 | 10 | 5 | 0.5 | 0.067 | 0.0005 |

**Table 5:** Evaluation of $N$ for $n = 5$, and $n = 10$.

| n | p | $T_c$ exp. | $T_c$ th. | dev. (%) |
|---|---|---|---|---|
| 500 | 0.9 | 1014.695 | 1115.106 | 9% |
| 500 | 0.8 | 1025.893 | 1253.799 | 18% |
| 500 | 0.5 | 1648.587 | 1972.688 | 16.43% |
| 1000 | 0.9 | 2037.750 | 2226.211 | 8.47% |
| 1000 | 0.8 | 2057.511 | 2503.599 | 17.82% |
| 1000 | 0.5 | 2763.726 | 3941.438 | 29.88% |
| 2000 | 0.9 | 4047.495 | 4448.422 | 9.01% |
| 2000 | 0.8 | 4392.028 | 5003.199 | 12.22% |
| 2000 | 0.5 | 6559.243 | 7878.937 | 16.75% |

**Table 6:** Experimental results for $m = 5$.

We can similarly consider all the transitions from any states at a level $k$ to any states at level $k + 1$, and compute $T_{jump}$ as:

$$
T_{jump} = \sum_{a \in k, b \in k+1} V_{a,b} Q_{a,b} N_a \approx \overline{N} \cdot \sum_{a \in k, b \in k+1} V_{a,b} Q_{a,b} =
$$

$$
= \overline{N} \cdot \left[ m \Delta p^m + \sum_{0 < k < m} (m - k) \mu \binom{m}{k} p^{m-k} q^k \right]
$$

We have performed experiments exploiting the `muskel` support, as extension of the ones performed for simple cases (refer to [3] for a complete description of the simulation environment). We have chosen to test the cases for $m = 5$, and $m = 10$, with numbers of tasks equal to 500, 1000, and 2000, with $\delta = 10$, $\Delta = 5$, and $\mu = 10$. Tables 6 and 7 show the completion times we obtained from the experiments, the corresponding one computed according to the $T_{stay}$ and $T_{jump}$ quantities, and their deviation w.r.t. the theoretical value. Apart of some issues (that we do not discuss here for brevity), the deviation seems to increase with the probability of failure, that actually gives more uncertainty to the actual result. We demand to the future work extensive experiments.

## 7.   Conclusions

We have presented a study of a Markov model for task parallel computations subject to failures, with known probability quantities. The study resulted in a framework to evaluate the program completion time, instead of giving a direct solution, in the form of a formula, to the recurrence equation describing the Markov model. We have validated the theoretical results with experiments: we obtained that our approach provides an upper bound that, depending on the quantities in play, remains tight to the experiment results.

| n | p | $T_c$ exper. | $T_c$ theo. | dev. (%) |
|---|---|---|---|---|
| 500 | 0.9 | 513.856 | 560.056 | 8.25% |
| 500 | 0.8 | 595.157 | 629.500 | 5.46% |
| 500 | 0.5 | 851.208 | 1004.010 | 15.22% |
| 1000 | 0.9 | 1028.474 | 1115.611 | 7.81% |
| 1000 | 0.8 | 1036.899 | 1254.500 | 17.35% |
| 1000 | 0.5 | 1706.031 | 2003.521 | 14.85.77% |
| 2000 | 0.9 | 2062.921 | 2226.722 | 9.01% |
| 2000 | 0.8 | 2096.943 | 2504.500 | 12.22% |
| 2000 | 0.5 | 2165.239 | 4002.545 | 16.43% |

**Table 7:** Experimental results for $m = 10$.

# References

[1] M. Aldinucci and M. Danelutto. *Algorithmic skeletons meeting grids*. Par. Comp., 32(7-8):449–462, 2006.

[2] C. Bertolli and J. Gabarro. *On the cost of Task Re-Scheduling in Fault-Tolerant Task Parallel Computations*. CoreGRID Integr. Work. 2008. Poster Session, 2-4 April 2008 Crete.

[3] C. Bertolli and J. Gabarro. *On the cost of Task Re-Scheduling in Fault-Tolerant Task Parallel Computations*. CoreGRID REP 104 Tech. Rep., avail. at: http://www.coregrid.net/mambo/images/stories/REP/tr-coregrid.pdf

[4] M. Cole *Bringing skeletons out of the closet: a pragmatic manifesto for skeletal parallel programming* Par. Comp., 30(3): 389–406, Elsevier 2004.

[5] I. Foster and C. Kesselman, editors. *The grid: blueprint for a new computing infrastructure*. Morgan Kaufmann Pub. Inc., San Francisco, CA, USA, 1999.

[6] J. Kemeny and J. Snell; *Finite Markov Chains*. Springer,1976.

[7] R. D. Schlichting and F. B. Schneider. *Fail-stop processors: an approach to designing fault-tolerant computing systems*. ACM Trans. Comput. Syst., 1(3):222–238, 1983.

[8] K. S. Trivedi. *Probability and Statistics with Reliability, Queuing and Computer Science Applications*. John Wiley and Sons Ltd., 2002.

[9] N. H. Vaidya. *A Case for Two-Level Recovery Schemes*. In IEEE Trans. Comput., Vol. 47 Numb. 6, 1998. IEEE Comp. Soc., Washington, DC, USA.

[10] A. Ziv and J. Bruck. *Analysis of checkpointing schemes for multiprocessor systems* In Procs. of 13-th Symp. on Rel. and Distr. Systems., 1994. IEEE. Comp. Soc.

III

# SERVICE LEVEL AGREEMENT AND SELF-*

# TOWARDS SLA-BASED SOFTWARE LICENSES AND LICENSE MANAGEMENT IN GRID COMPUTING

Jiadao Li, Oliver Wäldrich, Wolfgang Ziegler
*Department of Bioinformatics*
*Fraunhofer Institute SCAI*
*53754 Sankt Augustin, Germany*
{jiadao.li, oliver.waeldrich, wolfgang.ziegler}@scai.fraunhofer.de

**Abstract**     Software protection and licensing are important topics for both the independent software vendors and software users. In Grid environments, the use of license protected applications is almost impossible and becomes a challenging task. The reasons are twofold: (i) there are no business models of the independent software vendors for the Grid and (ii) there is no licensing technology suitable for Grid environments. In this paper, the state of the art of license management in software industry as well as the current practice for managing the licenses in Grid computing is presented. The challenges and requirements of managing the software license in Grid environments are identified. Two general models developed in the European projects BEinGRID and SmartLM for managing the software licenses in Grid computing based on service level agreement (SLA) are presented.

**Keywords:**     Grid, license mechanisms, service level agreements

## 1.  Introduction

Grid computing is considered a cornerstone of next generation distributed computing, which is defined as "coordinated resource sharing and problem solving in dynamic, multi-institutional collaborations". Current Grid computing infrastructure is built in accordance with the service oriented architecture (SOA [17]) paradigm. A service-oriented architecture is one in which all entities are services. The services [33] may include both traditional resources (e.g., compute services offered, network bandwidth, or space on a storage system) and virtualized services (e.g., database, data transfer, simulation, licenses), which may differ in the functions they provide to users but are consistent in the manner in which they can deliver those functions across the network. In Grid computing, the co-allocation of different kinds of services (compute resources, memory capacity, applications, etc) usually belonging to different resource/service providers is needed in order to satisfy the needs of a complex job. Virtual organizations (VOs) are dynamically created according to the requirements of different jobs (users). The jobs will potentially be scheduled and relocated across the whole Grid, and users might have no knowledge about the places where their jobs are to be executed. The current practice of managing and using the software licenses is limited to the local administrative domain while Grid infrastructure is usually stretching across domains as we introduced before. As a result, the users often can not use Grid resources because the applications they need are not licensed on the remote resources.

To this end, software licenses become a major obstacle for the users to use Grid infrastructures. Moreover, if possible at all, using Grid resources with the current licensing and pricing models of the independent software vendors (ISVs) is most often more expensive than running the application locally. To leverage use of Grid resources for license protected applications flexible pricing and licensing models for the benefit of both the software vendors and users are needed [8], [31].

To better integrate licenses into Grid infrastructure software licenses should become schedulable and manageable services as other services. Service level agreements (SLAs) have turned out to be a valuable instrument for agreements on the terms of service usage and reservation in different administrative domains. We see a SLA-based license management approach as the appropriate solution to the licensing problem in the Grid. Two different, complimentary approaches will be briefly presented, which are currently under development in the European projects BEinGRID and SmartLM.

The rest of the paper is organised as follows: In Section 2 we briefly give an overview on existing technologies. Section 3 presents the existing models for licensing and pricing. Current work on two different, complimentary approaches is presented in Section 4 and Section 5 concludes the paper with an outlook.

## 2. Related Work

To the best of our knowledge currently there are no other approaches to overcome the licence problem in the Grid, except for the approaches for license scheduling described in Section 4. However, software protection and license management is an important topic for the software industry and under continuous discussion, e.g. SoftSummit [19] is an executive conference dedicated to strategies and best practices for software licensing, pricing as well as application packaging and license tracking. Within a single adminstration domain, the centralized license management paradigm is suitable and efficient to manage the licenses. To this end, there are many license management systems from different companies available, e.g., LUM from IBM [6], License asset manager from TeamEDA [9], iFOR/LS from HP [28], RLM [14] from reprise software, Open iT [12], license tracker [20], Sentinel software protection and licensing package from SafeNet Inc [16], FLEXnet manager from Macrovision [24, 23, 26, 25, 27]. The license management system should be in charge of the whole life cycle of the license use, which includes: demonstration licenses, evaluation licenses, full-production licenses, product updates, maintenance releases, etc. Most often used common license models supported by these license management toolkits are described below. Some of these mechanisms need the license servers and vendor daemons, while other mechanisms do not need them.

To this end, FLEXnet is a typical license management toolkit used by many ISVs. The FLEXnet manager provides numerous kinds of license models supporting different scenarios. The ISVs decide and offer the different license policies based on the currently available models in FLEXnet in order to satisfy the needs of their users while increasing the revenue at the same time. Today, we see limited incremental progress towards more flexible licensing solutions on the side of the companies providing the licensing technology, and even less progress on the side of the ISVs. It must also be mentioned that the price for both licensing solutions leveraging flexibility of the end-user and pricing of the ISVs increases with degree of flexibility, which clearly is a show-stopper for usage of commercial applications in Grids.

## 3. Current license and pricing models

In this section we give an overview on current models. We use licensing models (and terminology) of FLEXnet, as this is the technology for software licensing most often used by ISVs and the other licensing technology providers offer either subsets of models supported by FLEXnet or quite similar models.

## 3.1    Typical License Models

The basic license models provided by FLEXnet [24, 23, 26, 25, 27] presented next can be combined to create new license models.

**Node-locked licenses:** Node-locking means the software can only be used on one machine or a set of machines. There are two types of node-locked licenses: uncounted and counted. For the counted node locked licenses, a license server and a vendor daemon are necessary.

**Floating (concurrent) licenses:** Anyone on the network can use the licensed application, up to the limit specified in the license file (also referred to as concurrent usage or network licensing).

**Mixed node-locked and floating licenses:** Uncounted node-locked and concurrent usage licenses can be mixed in the same license file, therefore more flexible usage models can be derived.

**Demo licenses/evaluation licenses:** Properties of an evaluation license may include: (i) Limited product functionalities or features, (ii) Limited number of uses, (iii) Expiration date.

**Usage-based licensing:** A quite important license strategy in which the actual usage patterns are monitored by the license management system, and billing or auditing are based on the actual usage data. FLEXnet Licensing supports several usage-based models, e.g: *Overdraft*: allowing the ISV to specify a number of additional licenses which customers are allowed to use in addition to the licenses purchased; *Pay-per-use*: allowing the customers to pay for the effective usage of the licenses, which can be audited based on time, the number of transactions, etc.

**Mobile licensing:** Used when users want to run an application on a machine that does not have a *continuous* connection to a license server system. These situations can include:

- Working on a laptop; or using a computer both at work and at home or off-site; or working from several different computers not connected to a license server system

- Fulfilled from a prepaid license pool: The license is fulfilled from a prepaid number of license-days for the usage period.

- Node-locked to a user name: If a license is to be used exclusively by one user on different machines, that license can be node-locked to the user¡⁻s user name.

- License rehosting: if an end-user want to move a license without using one of the other mobile licensing methods. In this model, a new node-locked license certificate for each new machine should be generated.

- Hard-mobile: Mobile license usage is controlled by a FLEXid. If the FLEXid is attached to a license server system, then the use floats on the network. To temporarily transfer the license, the user moves the FLEXid from the server to a standalone machine.

- Soft-mobile: Licenses are temporarily transferred to a license server system on the mobile laptop. The FLEXenabled product uses an encrypted local file, placed there by the license server system, to do checkouts during the usage period.

- License borrowing: A license can be borrowed from a license server system via a special checkout and used later to run an application on a computer that is no longer connected to the license server.

## 3.2    Current Business and Pricing Models

ISVs usually define different licensing policies with respect to their different products and target customers, e.g., some software vendors will provide the enterprise software, while others provide non-enterprise business software or consumer software. For some software products ISVs may expect a large number of customers, while the use of other products is limited to a specific user group. The open source software model also has great impact on the software licensing and pricing. To fully understand the models it is important to realise that the ISVs do not sell software but the right to use a certain software under dedicated conditions, which on the other hand implies that the customer only buys the right for limited usage of the software governed by the model he is willing to pay for. With the current move to multicore CPU technologies with tens or hundreds of cores in one CPU, we expect strong impact on the CPU based models. In the yearly license usage report [8] published by Macrovision [10], Softsummit [19], and the Centralized Enterprise Licensing User Group (CELUG) [3], etc, a general view of typical license and business models is given and analyzed and compared in the viewpoint of the ISVs and enterprises. It is evident, that the interests of software vendors and the enterprises are conflicting. For example, the per seat model is one of the most preferred pricing models for ISVs; while the enterprises will prefer the concurrent user model.

In the following, typical business/pricing models for licensing the software [8] are introduced.

**Subscription:** Licenses are paid for with a recurring (often annual) fee to continue using the software. If the fee is not paid, the software stops working.

**Perpetual:** Licenses are paid for on a one-time basis, giving the user the right to run the program as long as he/she chooses. It does not imply a right to upgrades, which are typically sold separately as part of a maintenance agreement or on a per-upgrade basis. Some vendors sell perpetual licenses on a term basis, which on the surface appears to be subscription based because the payments are spread out over time.

**Concurrent User:** Software is licensed based on how many users may access the software simultaneously. Such license models are often used for business/enterprise software.

**Seat (per machine/per server):** The software usage is restricted to a specific machine or server.

**Per CPU or per CPU-core:** The software will be licensed to run on a specific CPU. With the wide adoption of the multi-core CPU technologies, the ISVs will make different license policies, that is, they will license the software per CPU or per CPU-core. Usually the enterprises will prefer the per CPU model.

**Usage metric/pay-per-use;** The users will pay according to the real usage of their license.

**Seat (named user):** In this model, each software license and corresponding usage rights are assigned to a specific person.

**Financial metric based licensing:** License models that are based on varying business, usage or financial metrics, such as revenue, budgets, or cost of goods sold.

**Custom contract:** For some business sectors, e.g., Electronic Design Automation (EDA) software, there is no price list, prices will be agreed upon individually in the customer contracts.

Similar to the licensing models the individual business/pricing models can be combined. There will be different business models with respect to different versions of the business software. e.g., Oracle is charging differently depending on different versions [29]. There are some new trends for the software license using and pricing according to the yearly license usage report [8], e.g., the subscription model will become more and more predominant method to license the software. The ISVs expect that the subscription model will increase their revenue in the future and their software will be more widely adopted.

## 3.3    Software as a Service

Software as a service (SaaS) is a rapidly growing business model of software usage and in consequence software licensing. In contrast to traditional models where users buy a perpetual-use license, SaaS users buy a subscription from the service publisher. Whereas traditional ISVs typically release new product features as part of new versions of software once in a few years, publishers using SaaS have an incentive to release new features as soon as they are completed. There are several key characteristics of software delivered by SaaS which are identified in the report of IDC [38], including:

- Network-based access to and management of commercially available software

- Activities that are managed from central locations rather than at each customer's site, enabling customers to access applications remotely via the Web

- Application delivery that typically is closer to a one-to-many model (single instance, multi-tenant architecture) than to a one-to-one model, including architecture, pricing, partnering, and management characteristics

- Centralized feature updating, which obviates the need for downloadable patches and upgrades.

The property of the software as a service [32] licensing model leads to greater investment in product development under most conditions. This increased investment leads to higher software quality in equilibrium under SaaS compared to perpetual licensing. However, there are some weaknesses in this model, e.g., the prerequisite of accessing the software is the internet connection, and also sensitive information of the users will probably be stored at the SaaS provider side, thus a trust relationship has to be established. According to the predictions of Gartner [5], by 2012, at least one-third of business application software spending will be as service subscription instead of as product license. All leading business applications vendors (Oracle, SAP, Microsoft) and many web technology leaders (Google, Amazon) will promote this model, and the SaaS model of deployment and distribution of software services will become the mainstream use during the next five years. There are some companies which are adopting the SaaS models, e.g., NetSuite [11] offers subscription-based access to its enterprise resource planning (ERP), CRM, business intelligence software which is targeted toward small and medium-sized businesses. Salesforce.com [15] as one of the pioneers in deploying the SaaS, it provides the on demand customer relationship management solutions built on its infrastructure and the services will be delivered directly to users over the internet. The SaaS model is mostly attractive for smaller businesses because they are less willing to invest in large, expensive systems that they have to maintain.

## 3.4    License Scheduler

If the number of available licenses available for an enterprise is limited, e.g., due to the cost factor, it is necessary that these licenses are efficiently managed and highly utilised since even if an enterprise can apply for additional licenses from the ISV, it has to pay for the extra licenses. A local license scheduler could help scheduling the licenses of a site efficiently. However, while in most cases the local license management system provides information on the licenses already in use and still available there are no built-in queuing or reservation mechanisms. While an external scheduler might create an efficient schedule for the available licenses based on the users' requests, monitoring the use of the licenses and enforcing the schedule is difficult due to the usually encrypted communication between license server and application. Co-operations between license technology providers and license scheduler implementations could be a way to overcome this limitation. For instance, platform computing offers a product called LSF license scheduler [13] which is a local license scheduler restricted in a single administration domain and manages the license tokens instead of controlling the licenses directly. The current available number of licenses can be obtained by the FLEXnet manager. There are several license scheduling polices provided, e.g., fairshare, round robin, preemption. The licenses can also be checked out for the non-LSF jobs. In this way, the licenses can be scheduled and co-allocated with other resources/services. Dong et al. [34] developed a software sharing system in the grid environment which is not restricted to a single domain. The system adopts the constellation model for resource management and combines the sharing and scheduling of both hardware and software license resources. However, there is no support for SLAs and QoS in this system.

## 4.    SLA Based Software Licenses and License Management

As introduced before, license management in Grid context is challenging. In the following sub-sections we will analyse the requirements and challenges for license management and present two solutions developed in European projects.

### 4.1    Requirements and challenges for license usage and license management in Grids

The different business/pricing models introduced before can be leveraged in Grid environments, however, the requirements and usage mode in the Grids should be considered. Obviously, the license models in Grids should be evolutionized in order to allow a smooth transition from the current practice dealing with the challenges from both technical and business/pricing aspects. The following list identifies these aspects in detail:

**Different administrative domains:** License management may involve more than a single administrative domain. Therefore, issues like e.g., firewalls, remote usage control should be considered. Also, different usage policies might be defined for different administrative domains.

**Transparent management:** Licenses should be transparently managed as part of the Gird job management.

**Co-allocation of different resources:** Co-allocation of computing resources and software licenses should be supported. Software licenses should be co-scheduled together with other kinds of services or resources.

**Remote license enforcement** Jobs may be executed remotely while the validity of the licenses has to be guaranteed at the same time.

**Virtual organizations (VOs):** In the Grid VOs are often dynamically created and their members need temporal access rights for specific software suites from different domains, so flexible means of obtaining the temporal licenses should be provided.

**Dynamicity:** The ability to suspend, preempt and resume the license use should be supported.

**Interoperability:** License management should be integrated with the common Grid middlewares, e.g.,GT4 [35], glite [4], UNICORE [21]. Licenses and license management should be built on standards instead of proprietary solutions.

**Costs:** The scalability of the Grid influences the costs using the existing license models. Models like paying per-CPU, per-Seat, per-Job may quickly become expensive in Grid environments, concurrent floating licenses across the Grid are also too expensive for the software users [31]. Moreover, even if the price can be agreed upon, some issues remain, e.g., how the license usage will be audited and instrumented.

**Support for workflows:** With the adoption of web services, service oriented architectures and BPEL, complex applications often are composed as workflows, which makes the license management more difficult. For instance, when executing a workflow, different applications may be used in different phases of the workflow. How to retrieve and reserve the right licenses for the applications in advance is one of the issues that need to be addressed.

**Support for virtualization:** Licenses and license management for environments with virtualised resources or based on multicore technology is required.

**Software is a service:** SaaS and on demand use as well as the utility pricing mechanisms should be considered both for the license models and license management in Grid environments.

Considering the requirements for Grid environments, according to the 451 report [31], most of the enterprises want to have more flexible license models from the ISVs. It will be a great advantage for the enterprise if the licenses can be dynamically moved and managed in the global Grid. E.g., the EDA software licenses are bounded to some specific CPUs, machines today, while the enterprises hope that the ISVs of EDA software will support the Grid-wide licenses models so that the companies can run the software anywhere. However, the EDA vendors are reluctant to do so until today. Some major pharmaceutical ISVs also do not want to change their ways of licensing softwares. On the other hand, pharmaceutical companies may immediately benefit from using Grid resources to increase ther computational power since many of the applications of the pharmaceutical sector are embarrassingly parallel and well suited for distributed environments with only best-effort network connectivity.

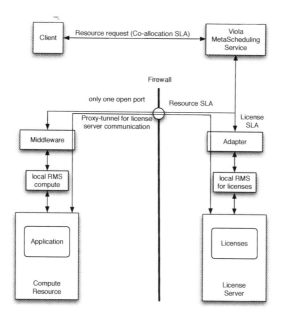

**Figure 1:** Basic approach of the BEinGRID project.

## 4.2 SLA-based Licenses and License Management

Recent R&D in two European projects [2, 18] shows that most of the requirements and challenges for licenses and license management in Grid computing can be tackled using a SLA based approach. In the preparatory process of defining the policies for software usage, which are governed by individual SLAs later, the polices and conflicts between the software vendors and the software users can be observed and reconciled. Negotiation is the preferred approach to create the SLAs between the license server and the user or the software entity acting on behalf of the user. These negotiation processes should be automatically executed based on a job description using JSDL and license description language (LDL) considering the large scale of the transactions and the scalability of the Grid infrastructures [33, 36]. WS-Agreement [30] and WS-Negotiation [22] are considered as the best suited existing or evolving negotiation protocols to create the SLAs between the respective resource management systems, license management systems and the end users [37]. The definition of the term language used to represent and manage the licenses is currently under definition in the SmartLM project. The Job Submission Description Language [7] is already used in agreements as a term language for computational resources. The LDL describing license requirements is defined as an extension of JSDL. Such LDL includes terms like *life time of the license agreement, hardware environment the license might be used in, software features available through the license,*

*license model and pricing model, compensation policies if the agreement is not fulfilled.*

## 4.3 Current Approaches to SLA-based License Management

On a European level currently two projects funded by the European Commission are addressing license issues in the Grid

- the BEinGRID project (Business Experiments in GRID) deals with licenses issues through a dedicated horizontal activity in one of its service clusters

- the SmartLM project that is in total focussing on a general solution for Grid-frienly software licensing for location independent application execution.

**BEinGRID.** Figure 1 shows the initial basic idea of the solution implemented in BEinGRID [1]. A meta-scheduling service (MSS) [39] is responsible for the negotiation of reservations of computational services and license services. A local license resource management system is in charge of supporting flexible license models and polices. This component also supports the reservation of licenses for later use and allows queries about reservations made and current license usage. The adapter will connects to the local license resource management system implementing the API of the system on one end while supporting the WS-Agreement based negotiation with the MSS. Thus the MSS is able to negotiate agreements for the reservation of the required compute services and the appropriate license required for the execution of the protected application.

Other than the SmartLM solution, BEinGRID is targeting on enabling use of existing license technologies for Grids without addressing new license mechanisms or new business models. The approach is based on a proxy solution that transparently tunnels the communication between the remotely executed application and the FLEXnet server while at the same time making the FLEXnet server believe that it is talking to an application running locally. The current BEinGRID implementations differs from the initial approach since the MSS is not used for the negotiation of the co-allocation bit the co-allocation is done manually by the user. However, the BEinGRID implementation provides additional services like improved security features, accounting and interfaces for billing. In addition to UNICORE and Globus Toolkit 4 the BEinGRID solution also supports the GRIA middleware environment.

**SmartLM.** In contrast to BEinGRID, SmartLM [18] is focussing on developing both licensing technology suitable for the use in distributed environments like Grid *and* - together with ISVs - new business models for the use of licensed

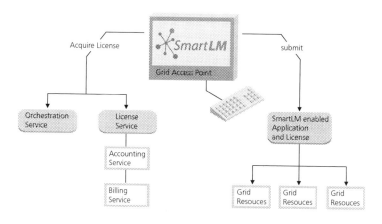

SmartLM's distributed architecture

**Figure 2:** Basic approach of the SmartLM project.

software in Grid or SOA environments. These new business models are also relevant for environments where application service provides start delivering their compute resources to their customers through virtualisation. Similar, the growing number of clouds where service providers offer a completely virtualised computation environment may benefit from the developments since the classic license mechanisms and the related business models will not work anymore. The project starts with adapting codes of the three participating ISVs; ANSYS, INTES and LMS. In the second phase the project aims to attract other ISVs through its extensive dissemination and marketing activities.

Figure 2 depicts the general idea of the SmartLM solution. A grid scheduler (MSS) is retrieving the Grid resources required by the user as described in his job. Once the appropriate resources have been identified, the local license service managing all licenses of a site is contacted to negotiate a SLA for the remote use of a license protected application. If both the requested compute resources and the license(s) are available they are reserved for the use by the requesting user. Like in the BEinGRID approach, a local license resource management system is in charge of the reservation of the licenses.

As said before, SmartLM is devoted to implement existing or evolving standards thus WS-Agreement is used for the creation of the SLAs and the project is contributing to the current work in the GRAAP-WG of the OGF on WS-Agreement-Negotiation. The resulting SLA is defining the terms of the application usage based on the local policies and the privileges of the user. This SLA is then bundled by the orchestration service with the SLA for accessing the remote resources and transferred to the remote site where the job is executed. Since no communication is required between application and license server at run-time and the license SLA is created at the site of the user firewalls do not cause a problem. Moreover, the application may be migrated to another machine if the license SLA is migrated as well.

The application may run without any internet connection to the license server during run-time. However, if there is - at least temporarily - a connection to the site hosting the license server additional functionality of the new license mechanisms may be used, e.g. re-negotiation of the period the license is valid in case the application needs more time than foreseen by the user. Or, freeing a license that is no longer needed.

## 5.  Conclusion

Software licensing and pricing is an important problem to be solved for a better acceptance of Grid infrastructures in productive environments with commercial applications. We present the state of art of software licensing and typical licensing and business and pricing models for managing software are analyzed. Further we identify requirements and challenges for using license protected software in the Grid. Ongoing work in two European projects aiming to overcome the limitations of existing license mechanisms in the Grid has been presented. The approach implemented in the BEinGRID project will become available in spring 2008 through the projects Gridipedia site. A prototype of the SmartLM solution including both new business models and the enabling technology for distributed environments will be available begin of 2009.

## 6.  Acknowledgment

This paper includes work carried out jointly within the CoreGRID Network of Excellence funded by the European Commission's IST programme under grant #004265.

## References

[1] BEinGRID Open Source Grid Software Repository. http://www.gridipedia.eu/index.php?id=702.

[2] BEinGRID Project. http://www.beingrid.eu, 2008.02.

[3] Centralized Enterprise Licensing User Group. http://www.celug.com/, 2008.01.

[4] Egee glite project. http://glite.web.cern.ch/glite/, 2008.02.

[5] Gartner's top 10 IT predictions. http://www.pcwelt.de/it-profi/englishnews/Hardware/145606/.

[6] IBM License Management. http://www-306.ibm.com/software/awdtools/lum/sys-requirements.html, 2007.06.

[7] Job Submission Description Language WG (JSDL-WG). http://www.ogf.org/gf/group_info/view.php?group=jsdl-wg, 2007.3.

[8] Key Trends In Software Pricing and Licensing (2006-07). http://www.softsummit.com/softsummit_knowledge_library_industry_reports.shtml.

[9] License Asset Manager. http://www.teameda.com/licenseassetmanager.html, 2008.02.

[10] Macrovison WebSite. http://www.macrovision.com/.

[11] NetSuite Software. http://www.netsuite.com/portal/home.shtml.

[12] Open iT License Management Software. http://www.openit.com/, 2008.01.

[13] Platform LSF License Scheduler. http://www.platform.com/Products/Platform.LSF. Family/Platform.LSF.License.Scheduler/, 2007.06.

[14] Reprise License Manager (RLM). http://www.reprisesoftware.com/rlm.htm, 2008.01.

[15] Salesforce SaaS CRM Software. http://www.salesforce.com/de/, 2008.02.

[16] Sentinel RMS. http://www.safenet-inc.com/products/sentinel/software_protection.asp, 2008.02.

[17] Service Oriented Architecture. http://en.wikipedia.org/wiki/Service-oriented_architecture, 2008.02.

[18] SmartLM project web pages. http://www.smartlm.eu, 2008.02.

[19] Softsummit Conference. http://www.softsummit.com/index.shtml, 02.2008.

[20] The license tracker. http://www.licensetracker.ca/index.htm, 2008.01.

[21] Unicore Open Source. http://www.unicore.org, 2008.02.

[22] Web Services Agreement Negotiation Specification. http://www.ogf.org/gf/group_info/view.php?-group=graap-wg, 2006.11.

[23] *Flexnet Licensing 11.4 Programming and Preference Guide for Trusted Storage-Based Licensing*. Macrovision, 2006.

[24] *Flexnet Licensing End User Guide*. Macrovision, 2006. Product Version 11.4, Document Revision 01.

[25] *Flexnet Licensing for Java Programming Guide*. Macrovision, 2006. Product Version 11.4, Document Revision 01.

[26] *Flexnet Licensing Programming and Reference Guide for License File-Based Licensing*. Macrovision, 2006.

[27] *Getting Started With the Licensing Toolkit for License File-based Licensing*. Macrovision, 2006. Product Version 11.4, Document Revision 01.

[28] *iFOR/LS Quick Start Guide*. HP, 2006. HP Part No, B2355-90108, June 1996.

[29] Oracle software investment guide. Technical report, Oracel Corporation, 2007. http://www.oracle.com/corporate/pricing/sig.pdf.

[30] Web Services Agreement Specification, 03 2007. http://www.ogf.org/gf/group_info/view.php?group=graap-wg.

[31] Grid computing - the impact of software licensing. Technical report, The 451 Group, March, 2005.

[32] Vidyanand Choudhary. Software as a service: Implications for investment in software development. *hicss*, 0:209a, 2007.

[33] K. Czajkowski, I. Foster, and C. Kesselman. Agreement-based resource management. *Proceedings of the IEEE*, 93(3):631–643, 03 2005.

[34] Xiaoshe Dong, Yinfeng Wang, Fang Zheng, Zhongsheng Qin, Hua Guo, and Guofu Feng. Key techniques of software sharing for on demand service-oriented computing. In Yeh-Ching Chung and José E. Moreira, editors, *GPC*, volume 3947 of *Lecture Notes in Computer Science*, pages 557–566. Springer, 2006.

[35] I. Foster and C. Kesselman. Globus: A Metacomputing Infrastructure Toolkit. *The International Journal of Supercomputer Applications and High Performance Computing*, 11(2):115–128, 1997.

[36] J. Li. *Strategic Negotiation Models for Grid Scheduling*. PhD thesis, Universität Dortmund, Informationstechnik, 2007.

[37] Jan Seidel, Oliver Wäldrich, Philipp Wieder, Ramin Yahyapour, and Wolfgang Ziegler. Using sla for resource management and scheduling - a survey. In Domenico Thalia, Ramin Yahyapour, and Wolfgang Ziegler, editors, *Grid Middleware and Services - Challenges and Solutions*, volume 8 of *CoreGRID Series*. Springer, 2008.

[38] Erin Traudt and Amy Konary. Software as a service taxonomy and research guide. Technical report, IDC, 06 2005.

[39] Oliver Wäldrich, Philipp Wieder, and Wolfgang Ziegler. A meta-scheduling service for co-allocating arbitrary types of resources. In Roman Wyrzykowski, Jack Dongarra, Norbert Meyer, and Jerzy Wasniewski, editors, *PPAM*, volume 3911 of *Lecture Notes in Computer Science*, pages 782–791. Springer, 2005.

# USING SLA BASED APPROACH TO HANDLE SABOTAGE TOLERANCE IN THE GRIDS

Syed Naqvi, Stephane Mouton, Philippe Massonet
*Centre of Excellence in Information and Communication Technologies, Belgium*
{syed.naqvi, stephane.mouton, philippe.massonet}@cetic.be


Gheorghe Cosmin Silaghi
*Babeş-Bolyai University of Cluj-Napoca, Romania*
gheorghe.silaghi@econ.ubbcluj.ro


Dominic Battré and Matthias Hovestadt
*Technische Universität Berlin, Germany*
dominic.battre@tu-berlin.de
maho@cs.tu-berlin.de


Karim Djemame
*University of Leeds, United Kingdom*
karim@comp.leeds.ac.uk

**Abstract**     This work explores the potential of employing service level agreements to make grids sabotage tolerant. The complex nature of the grid requires comprehensive security and trust solutions that can encompass different aspects of their operational environments. In this paper, we argue that the use of service level agreement (SLA) based exchange of information (negotiations of SLA contracts) can enhance the efficiency of the grid security architecture by providing a sabotage tolerant system design. The use of an SLA-based approach covers nearly the entire spectrum of the grid applications and grid based systems, where sabotage tolerance is an essential requirement, especially in the case when the grid spans the organizational border, moving under the collaborative control of potential competing stakeholders.

**Keywords:**     Grid Computing, Sabotage Tolerance, Service Level Agreement (SLA), Security Negotiations, Trust parameters

## 1.    Introduction

A range of new security threats and vulnerabilities are coming to the fore with the broadening scope of grid computing [5]. Introduction of grids in the commercial sector has open up new ventures in the business arena [4]. However, unlike the pioneer grid applications of the particle physics domain, the contemporary grid application domains require many protections from malicious entities. These applications and their underlying infrastructure have to protect the critical information about its stakeholders; provide safeguards to the economic interests of the enterprises using it; and win the confidence of the society which is already skeptical of the digital data processing [8].

In this work, we present the cohesion of two important areas of security assurances in contemporary grid security solutions. They are Sabotage Tolerance and Service Level Agreements (SLA). We explore the potential of employing service level agreements to make the grids sabotage tolerant. We have considered several scenarios for the sabotage tolerance techniques particularly the Desktop Grids. We have identified the areas of sabotage tolerance where SLA(s) can leverage the overall efficiency of the security architecture.

This paper is organized as follows: Section 2 provides an overview of the sabotage tolerance techniques in the grids. The use of service level agreements is elaborated in section 3. In section 4, we present our vision of employing SLA based approach for sabotage tolerance. We give a concise description of our future directions in section 5. Finally the paper is concluded in section 6.

## 2.    Sabotage Tolerance in Grids

Sabotage tolerance is gaining importance in grid environments notably in the situation where different grid domains have conflicting interests. The term *sabotage tolerance* was originally coined in the specific area of Desktop Grids, where voluntarily Internet users contribute to the grid with computing cycles. Because everyone can take part in such a grid, the environment started loosing its trustworthiness. Since computations run in an open and un-trustable environment, it is necessary to protect the integrity of data and validate the computation results. Sabotage tolerance techniques need to be employed mainly for the detection of malicious users who may submit erroneous results.

In a classical grid, sabotage tolerance is not an issue because the grid environment is trustable, in the sense that someone controls strictly the grid resources and their ownership. When a grid resource is malfunctioning, the grid owner is notified who has necessary tools to resurrect it. However, if the grid scales at the size of Internet or spans over multiple administrative domains without a hierarchical subordination of control and ownership, sabotage tolerance becomes mandatory, for the protection of both the grid users and other grid contributors.

Sabotage tolerance techniques are applied in grid systems that employ the master-worker computational model [16]. This grid model is not restrictive and maps well on the wide variety of grids. This model can be summarised as a server (referred further as the master) that distributes work units of an application to grid nodes (workers). A result error is any result returned by a worker that is not the correct value or within the correct range of values [10]. Sabotage-tolerance techniques imply detecting result errors, which are very important as they can undermine long computations that have been executing during weeks or even months by several workers [6]. The *error rate* $\epsilon$ is defined as the ratio of bad results or errors among the final results accepted at the end of the computation. Thus, for a batch of $N$ work units with error rate $\epsilon$, the master expects to receive $\epsilon N$ errors. For every application, the master employs some sabotage-tolerance mechanism for obtaining an acceptable error rate $\epsilon_{acc}$ with regard to its application. If a grid user comes with an application divided on a big number of tasks (e.g. 10 batches of 100 work units each) and it requires a global error rate of $10^{-2}$, the sabotage tolerance technique should provide with a work unit error rate of about $10^{-5}$ [10]. Many applications, especially the ones from computational biology and physics require bounds on the error rates, as the correctness of the computed results is essential for making accurate scientific conclusions.

Sabotage tolerance techniques for Desktop Grids can be classified in three big classes [6]: replication with voting, sampling and checkpoint-based verification. Here, we provide a short overview for the principal sabotage tolerance techniques in Desktop Grids. The reader may refer to [6] for a more detailed discussion.

Replication with majority voting [16] is widely used in the BOINC Desktop Grid platform [1]. The master distributes $2m - 1$ replicas of a workunit to workers and when it collects $m$ similar results, it accepts that result as being the correct one. Each collected result is seen as a vote in a voting pool with $2m - 1$ voters and with majority agreement being the decision criteria. The error rate of this method is determined by the number of identical results required $(m)$, which is a measure of redundancy. High levels of redundancy provide very low error rates (less than $10^{-5}$). The main benefit of the method is its simplicity, while the big drawback is the fact that it wastes a lot of resources.

Sampling-based techniques are developed to overcome limitations of replication, especially redundancy. Within sampling, the master determines the trustworthiness of the workers by verifying them only on a few samples of their results. The basic sampling is the naïve one [7], where the master sends probes with verifiable results to workers. If workers respond well to the probes, they are considered trustworthy. The main drawback is the workers can easily recognize the probes and respond well to them, while cheating on the ordinary workunits. Quizzes [20] are an improvement to basic probing. With this method, the master sends to workers batches with workunits and it places the probes inside of those batches. Given the actual required error rate, the master can compute the number of quizzes to place inside a batch. A drawback of probing is the fact the master should possess some heuristic in order to generate the probes and make them to resemble with the real workunits. Because this is a difficult task, the master can use actual workunits as probes [16]. The master verifies (using replication) only a sample of results and if a worker is caught cheating all its previous results are invalidated.

Checkpoint based verification addresses the problems with sequential computations that can be broken in multiple temporal segments $(S_{t_1}, S_{t_2}, \ldots, S_{t_n})$. At the end of each segment a checkpoint is submitted to a stable storage. The checkpoints are stored locally to allow recovering the long tasks from faults. After finishing a task, the worker sends back the result along with a list of hashes for the checkpoints. In the basic checkpoint verification [12], the master randomly selects a checkpoint time $S_{t_i}$ for a task and asks the worker to deliver its local checkpoint $C(S_{t_i})$. Then the master computes the task from $S_{t_i}$ up to the next checkpoint and compares the results with the hash value submitted by the worker for $C(S_{t_{i+1}})$. If the hash verification succeeds, then the worker passed the verification. In the distributed version of the checkpoint verification, the master selects a third worker for verification purposes and let the verifier to compute the checkpoint verification. The distributed version has the advantage of not overloading the master with a lot of verification tasks. The error rate of this method strongly depends on the number of verified checkpoints - i.e. a high percentage of verified checkpoints yield a low error rate, for the cost of increased computation (redundancy) and bandwidth.

## 3. Use of Service Level Agreements

Service Level Agreements (SLAs) form a contract between two parties. WS-Agreement [3] defines the roles "*agreement initiator*" and "*agreement responder*" to distinguish the parties participating in the agreement where each role can be filled by individuals or organizations. This assignment strongly focuses on the technical way of addressing the parties of an SLA. In real life, the two parties included in an SLA usually are service provider and service consumer, e.g. a resource provider operating high performance compute resources and a end-user who wants to use these resources for the computation of his job.

Even if such a provider usually plays the service provider role in such an SLA contract, he is not fixed in that. If he uses the Grid environment for migrating local jobs to other resource providers, this provider plays the service consumer role, requesting the Grid for suitable Grid resources. The same holds valid for the role of a Grid broker. Such a broker service is acting as a service intermediate between the service consumer and the service provider. Hence, there are two SLAs negotiated: one between the end-user and the broker, and one between the broker and the resource provider.

As SLAs have a legal character, it is important that the negotiating parties authenticate themselves during the negotiation phase and sign all messages to be sent. This ensures that nobody can pretend to be somebody else (i.e. agree a contract on behalf of somebody else) and that nobody can claim to have received a different message (i.e. claim in the case of a dispute that something different was agreed). Both aspects are crucial for sabotage tolerance in Grids. WS-SecureConversation [2] and SAML [9] provide means for authentication and signing messages. If only authenticated users can negotiate SLAs this provides a very important step for sabotage tolerance.

The body of an agreement defines the terms that the parties agree upon. This comprises functional and non-functional terms, rewards for compliance, and penalties for violations. First of all, the service to be delivered needs to be described. Then guarantees about the quality of service are specified. These guarantees can be either invariant or conditional to something; e.g. during weekends other guarantees might be given than during weekdays. Guarantees need to be monitorable and a penalty and reward is attached to each guarantee for violation or compliance. These can range from monetary payments to being pilloried. WS-Agreement provides a framework for the description of such SLAs. While WS-Agreement sets the framework, the actual description of the service and guarantees are domain specific. WS-Agreement defines a very simple protocol to establish agreements. More sophisticated negotiation protocols [11] can precede this request/reply protocol that allows to actually negotiate on the price or other features of the agreement.

The SLA-negotiation is the first step in the lifecycle of SLA-bound jobs. Here, service customer and service provider agree on the terms of the SLA, i.e. all obligations and expectations within the business relationship. Thanks to this negotiation, to use flat security profiles is no longer mandatory. In such a flat profile the provider defines his internal security policies, defining the handling of all incoming user jobs. Usually, this profile is not communicated to the outside world, so that the user has no knowledge about the technical details. It underlines the asymmetry in security management in classical systems: the customer has to trust the resource while the resource distrusts the customer job.

SLA negotiations provide means to describe terms of the security policy to be applied. In a provider driven market it is the provider who describes internal security policies at this place. In a customer driven market it is the customer who demands from the provider that a specific set of security policies has to be enforced.

The agreement partner evaluates these policies comply vis-a-vis his security requirements. If, for example, the provider allows negotiation on security aspects, the customer can define his own requirements, e.g. the establishment of micro-firewalls for isolating the used compute resources from the outside world, or the application of active sabotage tolerance mechanisms. SLA deployment requires incentives that have to be awarded to the provider for his participation and the installation of appropriate security and sabotage tolerance mechanisms. A major incentive is the access to specific user communities i.e. closed communities with strong financial background or high reputation for the provider. Similar incentives already drive companies to apply for certifications like ISO9001.

Fault tolerance mechanisms are mandatory for providers to provide SLA-compliant services. Such mechanisms have been developed in the EC-funded projects AssessGrid [13] and HPC4U [14]. Planning based SLA-aware resource management and periodic checkpointing of running applications are major building blocks of these fault tolerance mechanisms. A job is checkpointed in periodic intervals and therefore a resource provider can take a checkpoint of a running application, redundantly resuming its execution on other resources. The provider can either execute both applications until their end, then comparing their results, or to execute until the next checkpoint has to be generated, then comparing the checkpoints (cf. section 2). If the result of original job and redundantly executed job differ, this is a clear indication that one of his resources may be sabotaged, e.g. by viruses or rootkits.

Planning based resource management is predestined to support this sabotage tolerance since knowledge is available about both present and future resource usage. New scheduling strategies have to be developed, e.g. using external waste for executing redundant execution, minimizing the impact on the overall machine and ensuring the SLA-compliant execution of all other jobs despite of the overhead caused by redundant execution.

The project AssessGrid introduced the concept of a confidence service at the grid broker level. This element realizes reputation management, using the knowledge available at broker level about the performance of providers to evaluate the probability of failure in SLA offerings. This estimate enables the users to rate the offering in the light of provider's reputation rather than blindly trust him [17]. Knowledge of sabotage at provider level can be obtained by a broker by executing a specific percentage of all jobs in a redundant manner, then comparing the results of both jobs. Since the provider himself does not know if the broker executed a specific job redundantly or not, he generally runs in danger if sabotaging a given job. If the broker detects sabotage of the provider, he logs this in its internal experience databases, informing future users about potential sabotage problems. Hence, on the long term a sabotage provider can be identified by the confidence service, dissuading users from selecting this provider.

# 4. Perspectives of Using SLA based Approach for Sabotage Tolerance

Service level agreement (SLA) is emerging as an effective and standard way of negotiating a contract among the collaborating parties. SLA has the potential of providing adequate support for the various sabotage tolerance methodologies presented in this paper. Significance of sabotage tolerance techniques in Desktop Grids in particular is highlighted in the section 2. In this section, we argue that the use of SLA based exchange of information (negotiations of SLA contracts) can enhance the grid with efficiency provided by a sabotage tolerant system design.

The use of SLA based approach covers nearly the entire spectrum of the grid applications and grid based systems, where sabotage tolerance is an essential requirement, especially in the case when the grid spans the organizational border, moving the grid under the collaborative control of (possible) competing stakeholders. In this section we explore the sabotage tolerance support for a virtual organizations enhanced operating system.

## 4.1 Operating System Support for Virtual Organizations

Virtual Organizations (VOs) are the sum and substance of Grid technology. They facilitate dynamic collaborations through sharing of computing and storage resources. There are several different ways of defining support for the creation, functioning, and conclusion of VOs such as resource management, security and trust issues, etc. These supports are traditionally managed by the middleware services. Middleware consist of tools and services that coordinate between the applications and the operating system. In the recent past, the European Commission funded a project, called XtreemOS, for the development of Linux-based operating system to support virtual organizations for the next generation Grids [15].

XtreemOS is meant to provide native support for the virtual organizations. The challenges for this quest of the project include interoperability with diverse VO frameworks and security models [19]. Besides the scope of the XtreemOS security concerns, there are implications of reputation-based trust system on several components of the XtreemOS architecture [18], as a method to mitigate the uncertainty over the entities' behavior. This approach stipulates that an incentive-based mechanism be designed to make entities aware about their role in the VO and to facilitate the participation of entities to the social network by providing feedback for third parties. The incentive mechanism includes both rewards and penalties. Rewards are for the entities that delivered the agreed quality of service (QoS) for a contract; penalties for the ones that failed to deliver the agreed QoS.

With an incentive-based approach, the reputation management system can be seen as a method for sabotage tolerance in the operating system for grids. The dynamicity of the SLA contracts (starting and closing of the contracts with the negotiation parameters) can leverage the QoS of a grid operating system and make it sabotage tolerant.

## 4.2  Adapting SLAs for sabotage tolerance support in grid resource management

But, even in virtual organizations, reputation lists are not enough to decisively enhance sabotage tolerance. A common attack against the reputation mechanisms is the one when an individual behaves well for a long period of time, especially fulfilling low value transactions, and, when a high value important transaction comes to the execution; the individual cheats and go away after. In such a case, sabotage tolerance techniques selected from the one presented in section 2 are mandatory.

SLAs become important when some grid entity takes the role of brokering between the user requests and resource providers. This brokering role can happen in strong structured grids, with long-lasting VOs inside the VO boundaries or can happen in volatile grid environments, with very dynamic VOs, that changes their very often competence and that can appear and disappear with high probability. In this second scenario, which is very close with the grid design adopted by the XtreemOS project [19], we consider that is mandatory for VO manager to use sabotage tolerance techniques in order to assure the soft security protection of the user.

If the user is able to define its acceptable error rate and the reward it will pay for having the job done, then, including the error rate besides the rewards in the SLA will allow the VO manager (i) to select proper entities as part of the VO, based on the existing reputation lists and (ii) to select a proper sabotage tolerance method. We should notice from section 2 that a sabotage tolerance method usually produces smaller error rates with higher computational costs, measured in terms of redundancy. Therefore, given the requested error rate and reward the customer is willing to pay, the VO manager can select one sabotage tolerance technique and assess its associated costs. Therefore, the VO manager can further negotiate with the customer a bigger reward or a higher error rate, if the previous ones can not be accomplished within the newly formed VO with a sabotage tolerance technique.

## 5.  Future Directions

This work explores the potential of fostering logical interactions between two important areas of grid computing sabotage tolerance and the formulation of standard contracts among the participating parties. The composite security model is meant to tap the potential of SLA to assure sabotage tolerance in the grid environments (applications as well as systems). We plan to add new fields in the existing WS-Agreement based SLA contracts so that sabotage tolerant systems can be developed. As performance factors are very crucial in the deployment of highly scalable and dynamic environments like grids, we plan to carryout a comprehensive performance analysis of the proposed SLA extension to validate the design.

This work brings together the researchers from two European funded projects CoreGRID and AssessGrid. The former project has developed expertises in the domain of sabotage tolerance techniques; whereas the later has developed expertises in the domain of risks management and service level agreements. We aim to harness these competencies to assure the sustainability of the excellences developed under the umbrella of these projects.

## 6. Conclusions

In this paper, we identified the use of service level agreement (SLA) to handle the sabotage tolerance in the grids. SLA provides a standard mechanism of exchanging contracts and facilitates negotiations among the potential collaborating entities. We are using this standardised way of negotiations in the sabotage tolerance techniques where specific information is exchanged to determine whether or not an attacker was successful in jeopardising the integrity of the grid resources.

This work provides an opportunity to the researchers of these ostensibly different areas to work together and bring forward practical results by implementing the SLA based negotiations techniques for the sabotage tolerance. This initiative will also bring the researchers of Grid based operating system (XtreemOS) to contribute for the implementation of the SLA based grid resource management scenario.

## Acknowledgments

This research work is supported by: the European Network of Excellence CoreGRID (project number 004265), the European Specific Targeted Project AssessGrid (project number 031772) and the Romanian Authority for Scientific Research (project code IDEI_573).

## References

[1] David P. Anderson. Boinc: A system for public-resource computing and storage. In *GRID '04: The Fifth IEEE/ACM International Workshop on Grid Computing*, pages 4–10, Washington, DC, USA, 2004. IEEE Computer Society.

[2] Steve Anderson et al. Web services secure conversation language (WS-SecureConversation), September, 2005.

[3]   A. Andrieux, K. Czajkowski, A. Dan, K. Keahey, H. Ludwig, J. Pruyne, J. Rofrano, S. Tuecke, and Ming Xu. Web services agreement specification (WS-Agreement), September 20, 2005.

[4]   Commercial grid solutions. *Grid Computing Planet*, December 18, 2006. available at http://www.gridcomputingplanet.com/resources/article.php/933781.

[5]   Y. Demchenko, L. Gommans, C. de Laat, and B. Oudenaarde. Web services and grid security vulnerabilities and threats analysis and model. In *GRID '05: The 6th IEEE/ACM International Workshop on Grid Computing*, pages 262–267, Washington, DC, USA, 2005. IEEE Computer Society.

[6]   P. Domingues, B. Sousa, and L.M. Silva. Sabotage-tolerance and trust management in Desktop Grid computing. *Future Gener. Comput. Syst.*, 23(7):904–912, 2007.

[7]   Wenliang Du, Jing Jia, M. Mangal, and M. Murugesan. Uncheatable grid computing. In *ICDCS '04: The 24th International Conference on Distributed Computing Systems (ICDCS'04)*, pages 4–11, Washington, DC, USA, 2004. IEEE Computer Society.

[8]   J. Ermisch and D. Gambetta. People's trust: The design of a survey-based experiment. IZA Discussion Papers 2216, Institute for the Study of Labor (IZA), 2006. available at http://ideas.repec.org/p/iza/izadps/dp2216.html.

[9]   J. Hughes et al. Technical overview of the oasis security assertion markup language (SAML), v1.1. OASIS, May, 2004.

[10]  D. Kondo, F. Araujo, P. Malecot, P. Domingues, L.M. Silva, G. Fedak, and F. Cappello. Characterizing result errors in Internet Desktop Grids. In *Euro-Par 2007, 13th International Euro-Par Conference on Parallel Processing, Rennes, France, 2007*, vol. 4641 of *LNCS*, pages 361–371. Springer.

[11]  J. Li, R. Yahyapour. Negotiation strategies for grid scheduling. In *1st International Conference on Grid and Pervasive Computing, 2006*, vol. 3947 of *LNCS*. Springer.

[12]  F. Monrose, P. Wyckoff, and A.D. Rubin. Distributed execution with remote audit. In *The Network and Distributed System Security Symposium, NDSS 1999, San Diego, California, USA*. The Internet Society.

[13]  Project ASSESSGRID. http://www.assessgrid.eu.

[14]  Project HPC4U. http://www.hpc4u.org.

[15]  Project XtreemOS. http://www.xtreemos.eu.

[16]  Luis F. G. Sarmenta. Sabotage-tolerance mechanisms for volunteer computing systems. *Future Gener. Comput. Syst.*, 18(4):561–572, 2002.

[17]  K. Tserpes, D. Kyriazisa, A. Menychtasa and T. Varvarigoua. A novel mechanism for provisioning of high-level quality of service information in grid environments. In *European Journal of Operational Research*, Article in press, Corrected proof, 2007, Elsevier

[18]  XtreemOS.   First   draft   specification   of   security   services,   project   deliverable   D3.5.3.   http://www.xtreemos.eu/publications/project-deliverables/d3-5-3-firstspecofsecurityservices_vfinal.pdf, 2007.

[19]  E.Y. Yang, B. Matthews, A. Lakhani, Y. Jégou et. al. Virtual organization management in XtreemOS: an overview. In *Towards Next Generation Grids, Proc. of the CoreGRID Symposium, Rennes, France, 2007*. Springer.

[20]  S. Zhao, V. Lo, and C. GauthierDickey. Result verification and trust-based scheduling in peer-to-peer grids. In *P2P '05: The 5th IEEE International Conference on Peer-to-Peer Computing (P2P'05)*, pages 31–38, Washington, DC, USA, 2005. IEEE Computer Society.

# ENABLING SELF-MANAGEMENT OF COMPONENT BASED DISTRIBUTED APPLICATIONS *

Ahmad Al-Shishtawy,[1] Joel Höglund,[2] Konstantin Popov,[2]
Nikos Parlavantzas,[3] Vladimir Vlassov,[1] and Per Brand[2]

[1]*Royal Institute of Technology (KTH), Stockholm, Sweden*
{ahmadas,vladv}@kth.se

[2]*Swedish Institute of Computer Science (SICS), Stockholm, Sweden*
{kost,joel,perbrand}@sics.se

[3]*INRIA, Grenoble, France*
nikolaos.parlavantzas@inria.fr

**Abstract**     Deploying and managing distributed applications in dynamic Grid environments requires a high degree of autonomous management. Programming autonomous management in turn requires programming environment support and higher level abstractions to become feasible. We present a framework for programming self-managing component-based distributed applications. The framework enables the separation of application's functional and non-functional (self-*) parts. The framework extends the Fractal component model by the component group abstraction and one-to-any and one-to-all bindings between components and groups. The framework supports a network-transparent view of system architecture simplifying designing application self-* code. The framework provides a concise and expressive API for self-* code. The implementation of the framework relies on scalability and robustness of the Niche structured p2p overlay network. We have also developed a distributed file storage service to illustrate and evaluate our framework.

**Keywords:**   self-management, autonomic computing, component-based applications, P2P, Grid

*This research is supported by the FP6 Project Grid4All funded by the European Commission (Contract IST-2006-034567) and by the FP6 Network of Excellence CoreGRID funded by the European Commission (Contract IST-2002-004265).

# 1.    Introduction

Deployment and run-time management of applications constitute a large part of software's total cost of ownership. These costs increase dramatically for distributed applications that are deployed in dynamic environments such as unreliable networks aggregating heterogeneous, poorly managed resources.

The autonomic computing initiative [11] advocates self-configuring, self-healing, self-optimizing and self-protecting (self-* thereafter) systems as a way to reduce the management costs of such applications. Architecture-based self-* management [10] of component-based applications [5] have been shown useful for self-repair of applications running on clusters [3].

We present a design of a component management platform supporting self-* applications for community-based Grids, and illustrate it with an application. Community-based Grids are envisioned to fill the gap between high-quality Grid environments deployed for large-scale scientific and business applications, and existing peer-to-peer systems which are limited to a single application. Our application, a storage service, is intentionally simple from the functional point of view, but it can self-heal, self-configure and self-optimize itself.

Our framework separates application functional and self-* code. We provide a programming model and a matching API for developing application-specific self-* behaviours. The self-* code is organized as a network of *management elements* (MEs) interacting through events. The self-* code *senses* changes in the environment by means of events generated by the management platform or by application specific sensors. The MEs can *actuate* changes in the architecture – add, remove and reconfigure components and bindings between them. Applications using our framework rely on external resource management providing discovery and allocation services.

Our framework supports an extension of the Fractal component model [5]. We introduce the concept of component groups and bindings to groups. This results in "one-to-all" and "one-to-any" communication patterns, which support scalable, fault-tolerant and self-healing applications [4]. For functional code, a group of components acts as a single entity. Group membership management is provided by the self-* code and is transparent to the functional code. With a one-to-any binding, a component can communicate with a component randomly chosen at run-time from a certain group. With a one-to-all binding, it will communicate with all elements of the group. In either case, the content of the group can change dynamically (e.g. because of churn) affecting neither the source component nor other elements of the destination's group.

The management platform is self-organizing and self-healing upon churn. It is implemented on the Niche overlay network [4] providing for reliable communication and lookup, and for sensing behaviours provided to self-* code.

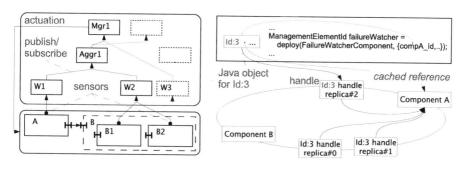

**Figure 1:** Application Architecture.          **Figure 2:** Ids and Handlers.

Our first contribution is a simple yet expressive self-* management frame-work. The framework supports a network-transparent view of system architec-ture, which simplifies reasoning about and designing application self-* code. In particular, it facilitates migration of components and management elements caused by resource churn. Our second contribution is the implementation model for our churn-tolerant management platform that leverages the self-* properties of a structured overlay network.

We do not aim at a general model for ensuring coherency and convergence of distributed self-* management. We believe, however, that our framework is general enough for arbitrary self-management control loops. Our example application demonstrates also that these properties are attainable in practice.

## 2. The Management Framework

An application in the framework consists of a component-based implemen-tation of the application's functional specification (the lower part of Fig. 1), and an implementation of the application's self-* behaviors (the upper part). The management platform provides for component deployment and communi-cation, and supports sensing of component status.

Self-* code in our management framework consists of *management elements* (MEs), which we subdivide into watchers (W1, W2 .. on Fig. 1), aggregators (Aggr1) and managers (Mgr1), depending on their roles in the self-* code. MEs are stateful entities that subscribe to and receive events from *sensors* and other MEs. Sensors are either component-specific and developed by the pro-grammer, or provided by the management framework itself such as component failure sensors. MEs can manipulate the architecture using the management *ac-tuation* API [3] implemented by the framework. The API provides in particular functions to deploy and interconnect components.

Elements of the architecture – components, bindings, MEs, subscriptions, etc. – are identified by unique *identifiers* (IDs). Information about an architec-

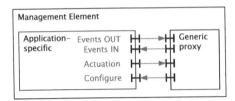     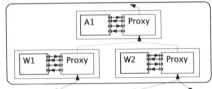

**Figure 3:** Structure of MEs.          **Figure 4:** Composition of MEs.

ture element is kept in a *handle* that is unique for the given ID, see Fig. 2. The actuation API is defined in terms of IDs. IDs are introduced by DCMS API calls that deploy components, construct bindings between components and subscriptions between MEs. IDs are specified when operations are to be performed on architecture elements, like deallocating a component. Handles are destroyed (become invalid) as a side effect of destruction operation of their architecture elements. Handles to architecture elements are implemented by *sets of network references* described below. Within a ME, handles are represented by an object that can cache information from the handle. On Fig. 2, handle object for id:3 used by the deploy actuation API call caches the location of id:3.

An ME consists of an application-specific component and an instance of the generic proxy component, see Fig. 3. ME proxies provide for communication between MEs, see Fig. 4, and enable the programmer to control the management architecture transparently to individual MEs. Sensors have a similar two-part structure.

The management framework enables the developer of self-* code to control location of MEs. For every management element the developer can specify a *container* where that element should reside. A container is a first-class entity which sole purpose is to ensure that entities in the container reside on the same physical node. This eliminates network communication latencies between co-located MEs. The container's location can be explicitly defined by a location of a resource that is used to host elements of the architecture, thus eliminating the communication latency and overhead between architecture elements and managers handling them.

A **Set of Network References**, SNR [4], is a primitive data abstraction that is used to associate a *name* with a set of *references*. SNRs are stored under their names on the structured overlay network. SNR references are used to access elements in the system and can be either direct or indirect. Direct references contain the location of an entity, and indirect references refer to other SNRs by names and need to be resolved before use. SNRs can be cached by clients improving access time. The framework recognizes out-of-date references and refreshes cache contents when needed.

Groups are implemented using SNRs containing multiple references. A "one-to-any" or "one-to-all" binding to a group means that when a message is sent through the binding, the group name is resolved to its SNR, and one or more of the group references are used to send the message depending on the type of the binding. SNRs also enable mobility of elements pointed to by the references. MEs can move components between resources, and by updating their references other elements can still find the components by name. A group can grow or shrink transparently from group user point of view. Finally SNRs are used to support sensing through associating watchers with SNRs. Adding a watcher to an SNR will result in sensors being deployed for each element associated with the SNR. Changing the references of an SNR will transparently deploy/undeploy sensors for the corresponding elements.

SNRs can be replicated providing for reliable storage of application architecture. The SRN replication provides eventual consistency of SNR replicas, but transient inconsistencies are allowed. Similarly to handling of SNR caching, the framework recognizes out-of-date SNR references and repeats SNR access whenever necessary.

## 3. Implementation and evaluation

We have designed and developed YASS – "yet another storage service" – as a way to refine the requirements of the management framework, to evaluate it and to illustrate its functionality. Our application stores, reads and deletes files on a set of distributed resources. The service replicates files for the sake of robustness and scalability. We target the service for dynamic Grid environments, where resources can join, gracefully leave or fail at any time. YASS automatically maintains the file replication factor upon resource churn, and scales itself based on the load on the service.

## 3.1 Application functional design

A YASS instance consists out of *front-end components* which are deployed on user machines and *storage components* Fig. 5. Storage components are composed of *file components* representing files. The ovals in Fig. 5 represent resources contributed to a Virtual Organization (VO). Some of the resources are used to deploy storage components, shown as rectangles.

A user store request is sent to an arbitrary storage component (one-to-any binding) that will find some $r$ different storage components, where $r$ is the file's replication degree, with enough free space to store a file replica. These replicas together will form a *file group* containing the $r$ dynamically created new file components. The user will then use a one-to-all binding to send the file in parallel to the $r$ replicas in the file group. Read requests can be sent to any of

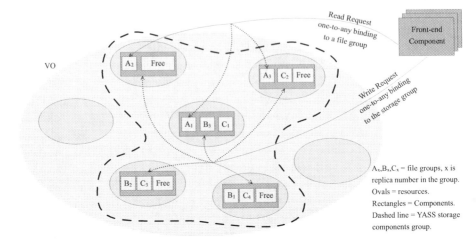

**Figure 5:** YASS Functional Part

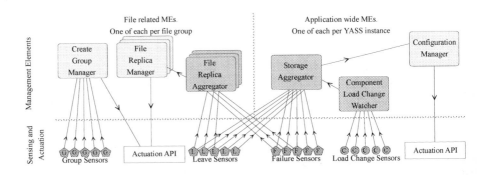

**Figure 6:** YASS Non-Functional Part

the $r$ file components in the group using the one-to-any binding between the front-end and the file group.

## 3.2    Application non-functional design

**Configuration of application self-management.** The Fig. 6 shows the architecture of the watchers, aggregators and managers used by the application.

Associated with the group of storage components is a system-wide Storage-aggregator created at service deployment time, which is subscribed to leave- and failure-events which involve any of the storage components. It is also subscribed to a Load-watcher which triggers events in case of high system load. The Storage-aggregator can trigger StorageAvailabilityChange-events, which the Configuration-manager is subscribed to.

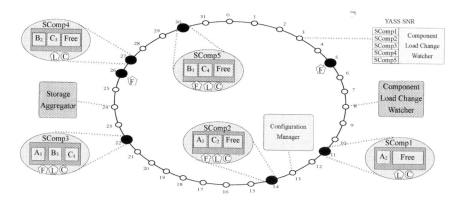

**Figure 7:** Parts of the YASS application deployed on the management infrastructure.

When new file-groups are formed by the functional part of the application, the management infrastructure propagates group-creation events to the Create-Group-manager which initiates a FileReplica-aggregator and a FileReplica-manager for the new group. The new FileReplica-aggregator is subscribed to resource leave- and resource fail-events of the resources associated with the new file group.

## 3.3    Test-cases and initial evaluation

The infrastructure has been initially tested by deploying a YASS instance on a set of nodes. Using one front-end a number of files are stored and replicated. Thereafter a node is stopped, generating one fail-event which is propagated to the Storage-aggregator and to the FileReplica-aggregators of all files present on the stopped node. Below is explained in detail how the self-management acts on these events to restore desired system state.

Fig. 7 shows the management elements associated with the group of storage components. The black circles represent physical nodes in the P2P overlay Id space. Architectural entities (e.g. SNR and MEs) are mapped to ids. Each physical node is responsible for Ids between its predecessor and itself including itself. As there is always a physical node responsible for an id, each entity will be mapped to one of the nodes in the system. For instance the *Configuration Manager* is mapped to id 13, which is the responsibility of the node with id 14 which means it will be executed there.

**Application Self-healing.** Self-healing is concerned with maintaining the desired replica degree for each stored item. This is achieved as follows for resource leaves and failures:

*Resource leave.* An infrastructure sensor signals that a resource is about to leave. For each file stored at the leaving resource, the associated FileReplica-aggregator is notified and issues a replicaChange-event which is forwarded to the FileReplica-manager. The FileReplica-manager uses the one-to-any binding of the file-group to issue a FindNewReplica-event to any of the components in the group.

*Resource failure.* On a resource failure, the FileGroup-aggregator will check if the failed resource previously signaled a ResourceLeave (but did not wait long enough to let the restore replica operation finish). In that case the aggregator will do nothing, since it has already issued a replicaChange event. Otherwise a failure is handled the same way as a leave.

**Application Self-configuration.** With self-configuration we mean the ability to adapt the system in the face of dynamism, thereby maintaining its capability to meet functional requirements. This is achieved by monitoring the total amount of allocated storage. The Storage-aggregator is initialized with the amount of available resources at deployment time and updates the state in case of resource leaves or failures. If the total amount of allocated resources drops below given requirements, the Storage-aggregator issues a storageAvailabilityChange-event which is processed by the Configuration-manager. The Configuration-manager will try to find an unused resource (via the external resource management service) to deploy a new storage component, which is added to the group of components. Parts of the Storage-aggregator and Configuration-manager pseudocode is shown in Listing 12.1, demonstrating how the stateful information is kept by the aggregator and updated through sensing events, while the actuation commands are initiated by the manager.

**Application Self-optimization.** In addition to the two above described testcases we have also designed but not fully tested application self-optimization. With self-optimization we mean the ability to adapt the system so that it, besides meeting functional requirements, also meets additional non-functional requirements such as efficiency. This is achieved by using the ComponentLoad-watcher to gather information on the total system load, in terms of used storage. The storage components report their load changes, using application specific load sensors. These load-change events are delivered to the Storage-aggregator. The aggregator will be able to determine when the total utilization is critically high, in which case a StorageAvailabilityChange-event is generated and processed by the Configuration-manager in the same way as described in the self-configuration section. If utilization drops below a given threshold, and the amount of allocated resources is above initial requirements, a storageAvailabilityChange-event is generated. In this case the event indicates that the availability is higher than needed, which will cause the Configuration-manager to query the ComponentLoad-watcher for the least loaded storage component, and instruct it to deallocate itself, thereby freeing the resource. Parts of

**Listing 12.1:** Pseudocode for parts of the Storage-aggregator

```
upon event ResourceFailure(resource_id) do
    amount_to_subtract = allocated_resources(resource_id)
    total_storage = total_amount - amount_to_subtract
    current_load = update(current_load, total_storage)
    if total_amount < initial_requirement or current_load > high_limit then
        trigger(availabilityChangeEvent(total_storage, current_load))
end
```

**Listing 12.2:** Pseudocode for parts of the Configuration-manager

```
upon event availabilityChangeEvent(total_storage, new_load) do
    if total_storage < initial_requirement or new_load > high_limit then
        new_resource = resource_discover(component_requirements, compare_criteria)
        new_resource = allocate(new_resource, preferences)
        new_component = deploy(storage_component_description, new_resource)
        add_to_group(new_component, component_group)
    elseif total_storage > initial_requirement and new_load < low_limit then
        least_loaded_component = component_load_watcher.get_least_loaded()
        least_loaded_resource = least_loaded_component.get_resource()
        trigger(resourceLeaveEvent(least_loaded_resource))
end
```

the Configuration-manager pseudocode is shown in Listing 12.2, demonstrating how the number of storage components can be adjusted upon need.

# 4. Related Work

Our work builds on the technical work on the Jade component-management system [3]. Jade utilizes the Java RMI, and is limited to cluster environments as it relies on small and bounded communication latencies between nodes.

As the work here suggests a particular implementation model for distributed component based programming, relevant related work can be found in research dealing specifically with autonomic computing in general and in research about component and programming models for distributed systems.

*Autonomic Management.* The vision of autonomic management as presented in [11] has given rise to a number of proposed solutions to aspects of the problem. Many solutions adds self-management support through the actions of a centralized self-manager. One suggested system which tries to add some support for the self-management of the management system itself is Unity [6]. Following the model proposed by Unity, self-healing and self-configuration are enabled by building applications where each system component is a autonomic element, responsible for its own self-management. Unity assumes cluster-like environments where the application nodes might fail, but the project only partly addresses the issue of self-management of the management infrastructure itself.

Relevant complementary work include work on checkpointing in distributed environments. Here recent work on Cliques [8]can be mentioned, where worker nodes help store checkpoints in a distributed fashion to reduce load on managers which then only deal with group management. Such methods could be introduced in our framework to support stateful applications.

*Component Models.* Among the proposed component models which target building distributed systems, the traditional ones, such as the Corba Component Model or the standard Enterprise JavaBeans were designed for client-server relationships assuming highly available resources. They provide very limited support for dynamic reconfiguration. Other component models, such as Open-COM [7], allow dynamic flexibility, but their associated infrastructure lacks support for operation in dynamic environments.

The Grid Component Model, GCM [9], is a recent component model that specifically targets grid programming. GCM is defined as an extension of Fractal and its features include many-to-many communications with various semantics and autonomic components.

GCM defines simple "autonomic managers" that embody autonomic behaviours and expose generic operations to execute autonomic operations, accept QoS contracts, and to signal QoS violations. However, GCM does not prescribe a particular implementation model and mechanisms to ensure the efficient operation of self-* code in large-scale environments. Thus, GCM can be seen as largely complementary to our work and thanks to the common ancestor, we believe that our results can be exploited within a future GCM implementation. *Behavioural skeletons* [1] aim to model recurring patterns of component assemblies equipped with correct and effective self-management schemes. Behavioural skeletons are being implemented using GCM, but the concept of reusable, domain-specific, self-management structures can be equally applied using our component framework.

GCM also defines collective communications by introducing new kinds of cardinalities for component interfaces: multicast, and gathercast [2]. This enables one-to-n and n-to-one communication. However GCM does not define groups as a first class entities, but only implicitly through bindings, so groups can not be shared and reused. GCM also does not mention how to handle failures and dynamism (churn) and who is responsible to maintain the group. Our one-to-all binding can utilise the multicast service, provided by the underlying P2P overlay, to provide more scalable and efficient implementation in case of large groups. Also our model supports mobility so members of the group can change their location without affecting the group.

A component model designed specifically for structured overlay networks and wide scale deployment is p2pCM [13], which extends the DERMI [12] object middleware platform. The model provides replication of component instances, component lifecycle management and group communication, including anycall functionality to communicate with the closest instance of a component. The model does not offer higher level abstractions such as watchers and event handlers, and the support for self-healing and issues of consistency are only partially addressed.

## 5. Future Work

Currently we are working on the management element wrapper abstraction. This abstraction adds fault-tolerance to the self-* code by enabling ME replication. The goal of the management element wrapper is to provide consistency between the replicated ME in a transparent way and to restore the replication degree if one of the replicas fails. Without this support from the framework, the user can still have self-* fault-tolerance by explicitly implementing it as a part of the application's non-functional code. The basic idea is that the management element wrapper adds a consistency layer between the replicated ME from one side and the sensors/actuators from the other side. This layer provides a uniform view of the events/actions for both sides.

Currently the we use a simple architecture description language (ADL) only covering application functional behaviours. We hope to extend this to also cover non-functional aspects.

We are also evaluating different aspects of our framework such as the overhead of our management framework in terms of network traffic and the time need execute self-* code. Another important aspect is to analyse the effect of churn on the self-* code.

Finally we would like to evaluate our framework using applications with more complex self-* behaviours.

## 6. Conclusions

The proposed management framework enables development of distributed component based applications with self-* behaviours which are independent from application's functional code, yet can interact with it when necessary. The framework provides a small set of abstractions that facilitate fault-tolerant application management. The framework leverages the self-* properties of the structured overlay network which it is built upon. We used our component management framework to design a self-managing application to be used in dynamic Grid environments. Our implementation shows the feasibility of the framework.

## References

[1] M. Aldinucci, S. Campa, M. Danelutto, M. Vanneschi, P. Kilpatrick, P. Dazzi, D. Laforenza, and N. Tonellotto. Behavioural skeletons in GCM: Autonomic management of grid components. In *PDP '08: Proceedings of the 16th Euromicro Conference*

*on Parallel, Distributed and Network-Based Processing (PDP 2008)*, pages 54–63. IEEE Computer Society, 2008.

[2] Francoise Baude, Denis Caromel, Ludovic Henrio, and Matthieu Morel. Collective interfaces for distributed components. In *CCGRID '07: Proceedings of the Seventh IEEE International Symposium on Cluster Computing and the Grid*, pages 599–610, Washington, DC, USA, 2007. IEEE Computer Society.

[3] S. Bouchenak, F. Boyer, S. Krakowiak, D. Hagimont, A. Mos, J.-B. Stefani, N. de Palma, and V. Quema. Architecture-based autonomous repair management: An application to J2EE clusters. In *SRDS '05: Proceedings of the 24th IEEE Symposium on Reliable Distributed Systems (SRDS'05)*, pages 13–24, Orlando, Florida, October 2005. IEEE.

[4] P. Brand, J. Höglund, K. Popov, N. de Palma, F. Boyer, N. Parlavantzas, V. Vlassov, and A. Al-Shishtawy. The role of overlay services in a self-managing framework for dynamic virtual organizations. In *CoreGRID Workshop, Crete, Greece*, June 2007.

[5] E. Bruneton, T. Coupaye, and J.-B. Stefani. The fractal component model. Technical report, France Telecom R&D and INRIA, February 5 2004.

[6] D. Chess, A. Segal, I. Whalley, and S. White. Unity: Experiences with a prototype autonomic computing system. *Proc. of Autonomic Computing*, pages 140–147, May 2004.

[7] G. Coulson, G. Blair, P. Grace, A. Joolia, K. Lee, and J. Ueyama. A component model for building systems software. In *Proceedings of IASTED Software Engineering and Applications (SEA'04)*, Cambridge MA, USA, November 2004.

[8] D. Kondo F. Araujo, P. Domingues and L. Moura Silva. Using cliques of nodes to store desktop grid checkpoints. In *Proceedings of CoreGRID Integration Workshop 2008*, pages 15–26, 2008.

[9] Basic features of the Grid component model. CoreGRID Deliverable D.PM.04, CoreGRID, EU NoE project FP6-004265, March 2007.

[10] J. Hanson, I. Whalley, D. Chess, and J. Kephart. An architectural approach to autonomic computing. In *ICAC '04: Proceedings of the First International Conference on Autonomic Computing (ICAC'04)*, pages 2–9, Washington, DC, USA, 2004. IEEE Computer Society.

[11] P. Horn. Autonomic computing: IBM's perspective on the state of information technology, October 15 2001.

[12] C. Pairot, P. García, and A. Gómez-Skarmeta. Dermi: A new distributed hash table-based middleware framework. *IEEE Internet Computing*, 08(3):74–84, 2004.

[13] C. Pairot, P. García, R. Mondéjar, and A. Gómez-Skarmeta. p2pCM: A structured peer-to-peer Grid component model. In *International Conference on Computational Science*, pages 246–249, 2005.

# SELF-OPTIMIZING CLASSIFIERS: FORMALIZATION AND DESIGN PATTERN*

Marco Pasquali, Patrizio Dazzi
*IMT (Lucca Institute for Advanced Studies) - Lucca - Italy*
*ISTI/CNR – Pisa – Italy & CoreGRID Programming Model Institute*
m.pasquali@isti.cnr.it, p.dazzi@isti.cnr.it


Antonio Panciatici
*Engineering PhD School "Leonardo da Vinci" – Pisa – Italy*
antonio.panciatici@iet.unipi.it


Ranieri Baraglia
*ISTI/CNR – Pisa – Italy & CoreGRID Resource Management and Scheduling Institute*
r.baraglia@isti.cnr.it

**Abstract**    In this paper we propose a design pattern for self-optimizing classification systems, i.e. classifiers able to adapt their behavior to the system changes. First, we provide a formalization of a self-optimizing classifier we use to derive the design pattern. Then, we describe the pattern classes, their interactions, and validate our approach applying the proposed pattern to a real scenario. Finally, to evaluate the proposed solution we compare the behavior of the self-optimizing classifier with a not self-optimizing one. Experimental results demonstrate the approach effectiveness.

**Keywords:**    Self-Optimizing Systems, Classification Systems, Heuristics Driven Systems

*This research is carried out under the FP6 Network of Excellence CoreGRID and the FP6 GridCOMP project funded by the European Commission (Contract IST-2002-004265 and FP6-034442).

## 1.    Introduction

*Autonomic Computing* is an initiative started by IBM in 2001 (aka ACI [11]), its aim is to create self-managing computer systems to overcome their rapidly growing complexity, and to enable their further growth. ACI focuses on the definition of foundations for autonomic systems, and in particular, on the definition of fundamental elements to make computing system autonomous, i.e. self-optimizing, self-configuring, self-healing, and self-protecting.

In this paper we propose a design pattern that drives programmers in implementing self-optimizing classification systems, i.e. classifiers able to adapt their behavior to system changes. Classification systems are used to classify items according to a rule or a heuristics defined by the system administrator. The heuristics defines the classifier behavior, and it is used to mark items with a priority value representing their relevance. A self-optimizing classifier must be able to face up system changes in order to obey a given classification policy.

In order to define our design pattern, we formalize a general classifier that does not adapt itself to system changes pointing out its main functions and their interactions. Afterwards, we extend the classifier formalization introducing elements needed to define a self-optimizing classifier (Section 2). In Section 3, we enrich the classifier formalization with the concept of *polytope*. Section 4 describes the design pattern we defined starting from the formal model. In Section 5, we describe a case study used to validate our approach. Section 6 describes the conducted experiments and the obtained results. In Section 7 related works are described. Finally, in Section 8 conclusions and future work are presented.

## 2.    Formalization of Priority Classification Systems

A priority classification system $S$ can be formally described according to the following higher-order function:

$$f_S \; : \; I \times F_{strategy} \longrightarrow O \tag{1}$$

where $I$ is the set of all possible items that need to be classified, $F_{strategy}$ is the set of all the possible strategy-functions, and $O \subset \mathbb{N}$ is a finite set of output values. A strategy-function $f_{strategy} \in F_{strategy}$ is defined as:

$$f_{strategy} : I \to O$$

The system $S$ applies $f_{strategy}$ to each input $i \in I$ in order to assign it an input item priority value $p \in O$. A priority classifier system can be defined self-optimizing when it is able to adapt its behaviour according to input values to compute valid classifications. From our perspective, a priority classifier behaves correctly when it is able to satisfy two requirements:

- the priority value assigned to each input item is well-proportioned to the item relevance (e.g. important items must obtain high priorities),

- the distribution of the priorities assigned by the classifier must be coherent with a target policy.

To model the classifier self-optimization mechanism, we need to enrich the definition of the strategy-function based classification systems, by defining how the *strategy-function* can be modified to enhance the classification precision. For this purpose we introduced three new entities: *evaluator, historical data* and *reconfigurator*. The *evaluator* evaluates the data previously evaluated by the classifier (*historical data*), and if needed it changes the strategy-function by using the *reconfigurator*.

Formally, the reconfiguration and evaluation activities can be modeled by using the two following functions:

$$F_{eval} \quad : \quad H \times C \longrightarrow C \tag{2}$$
$$F_{reconf} \quad : \quad C \longrightarrow F_{strategy} \tag{3}$$

$H$ is the power set of all possible historical data values and $C$ is the set of all possible configurations used by $F_{reconf}$ to select an appropriated strategy-function among the available ones.

Moreover, we introduce $h_{current}$ – the actual set of the classifier historical data, $d_{current}$ – the distribution of priorities in $h_{current}$, and $d_{target}$ – the target priorities distribution.

Every time a new item comes into the classifier, $F_{eval}$ analyzes the historical data $h_{current} \in H$ and computes the priorities distribution $d_{current} \in H$. If there is an incoherence between the $d_{current}$ priority distribution, and the target one ($d_{target}$), $F_{eval}$ generates a new configuration $c \in C$. If $F_{eval}$ does not recognize any incongruence, it simply returns as new configuration the current one. When a new configuration is available, $F_{reconf}$ uses this configuration in order to select a different, more appropriate, $f_{strategy}$ in the $F_{strategy}$ set.

## 3. Polytope

In the proposed formalization, the self-optimizing classification system can access to an unlimited set of historical data, and it generates a new strategy function if $F_{eval}$ recognized differences between $d_{current}$ and $d_{target}$. However, more realistic systems can only access to a finite set of historical data, and their reconfiguration mechanisms do not generate a new strategy function every time the classifier does not carry out the expected result. Indeed, in a real scenario, the evaluation mechanism should trigger strategy function changes only when the current behavior of the classifier is considered quite different with respect to the expected one. In order to formalize that, we exploited the concept of polytope.

Let be the output of $F_{eval}$ a point in a geometric space (i.e. the range of values) in which the classifier is free to move without implying a reconfiguration of the strategy-function. Such geometric space represents a *polytope*.

We can define the polytope $P$ of a strategy-function $S$, the set $C$ of the $F_{eval}$ outputs that does not trigger the strategy-function reconfiguration. Formally:

$$P = \{S_c \mid Acceptance_S(S_c)\}$$

where $Acceptance_S$ is a Boolean function that returns true if the strategy-function behavior is acceptable.

From a formal point of view, in order to consider the polytope, the $F_{eval}$ function must be changed. Indeed, it has to generate a new $f_{strategy}$ configuration only if $d_{current}$ does not belong to $P$:

$$F_{eval} : H \times C \times P \longrightarrow C$$

## 4.    Self-Optimizing Design Pattern for Priority Classification Systems

We exploited the presented formalization to propose a self-optimizing design pattern in order to provide a general repeatable design solution easing the implementation of self-optimizing classifier.

According to our formalization, a classification system can be seen made up of three entities: INPUTSTREAM, CLASSIFIER and OUTPUTSTREAM.

- INPUTSTREAM: a stream of independent elements $I$ among which there are not dependencies.

- CLASSIFIER: a classification function ($f$) applied to each element of $I$.

- OUTPUTSTREAM: a stream of elements $O$ such that each element is $e_i' = f(e_i)$ with $e_i \in I$ and $e_i' \in O$.

CLASSIFIER retrieves an input element (or item) from INPUTSTREAM, classifies the element, and sends it to OUTPUTSTREAM.

CLASSIFIER is, in turn, made up of four entities. Its main entity, called STRATEGY, is devoted to classify incoming items, to evaluate itself, and if needed, it changes its own behavior accordingly to some rules. To perform these tasks STRATEGY uses three entities: DATAREPOSITORY, EVALUATOR and RECONFIGURATOR.

- DATAREPOSITORY: holds up to a finite number of past input elements coupled with the respective computed outputs.

- EVALUATOR: suggests a STRATEGY reconfiguration. It takes as input the current configuration of STRATEGY, and using the data stored in DATAREPOSITORY, suggests a change in STRATEGY behavior.

- RECONFIGURATOR: takes as input the STRATEGY and the output of EVALUATOR. It is able to reconfigure STRATEGY, acting onto its specific tuning parameters, in order to optimize its performance.

CLASSIFIER forwards the items retrieved from INPUTSTREAM directly to STRATEGY. Before to classify the items, STRATEGY evaluates its own configuration by invoking EVALUATOR. EVALUATOR reads the past input/output from DATAREPOSITORY and then evaluates the adherence of the classifier behavior w.r.t. the expected classification policy. If the behavior is different from the expected one, EVALUATOR suggests a change in STRATEGY configuration. If a reconfiguration is needed, STRATEGY invokes RECONFIGURATOR passing it, as parameters, the reconfiguration suggested by EVALUATOR and the pointer to the STRATEGY object. RECONFIGURATOR retrieves the tuning parameters of the STRATEGY object, it changes the STRATEGY configuration, and as a consequence, the behavior of STRATEGY. After the reconfiguration, STRATEGY computes the output values according to its new configuration, and stores both the input and the computed output into DATAREPOSITORY. Finally, STRATEGY sends the computed output back to CLASSIFIER, which in turn sends it to OUTPUTSTREAM. Figure 1 depicts the UML schema of our self-optimizing design pattern.

In Table, 1 we point out how the abstract model of our classifier can be mapped into the defined design pattern.

| Abstract Model Functions | Design Pattern Components |
|---|---|
| I | INPUTSTREAM |
| $f_{strategy}$ | STRATEGY |
| $F_{eval}$ | EVALUATOR |
| $F_{reconf}$ | RECONFIGURATOR |
| H | DATAREPOSITORY |
| O | OUTPUTSTREAM |

**Table 1:** Abstract Model - Design Pattern mapping

## 5.    Case study

To validate our approach we applied it to a real scenario. It concerns to a Grid job scheduler. The scheduler is made up of two parts: a classifier, and a scheduler. The former assigns priorities to jobs evaluating their deadline, i.e. the time at which the execution of a job has to be finished. The latter is basically a Backfilling-based scheduler. Jobs are ordered in the backfilling queue according to their priorities. To assign priorities the classifier exploits the DeadLine heuristics (see below), which is able to recognize the relevance of each

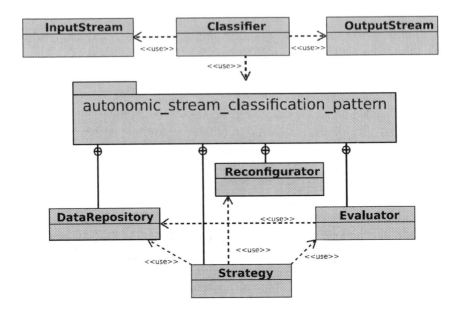

**Figure 1:** UML schema of the proposed autonomic strategy pattern.

job, exploiting only the job deadline parameter. The conducted experiments aim to demonstrate that the provided formalization, and the derived pattern makes easier the development of a self-optimizing classifier able to recognize its own bad behaviors and to fix them.

## 5.1    Static DeadLine Heuristics

The first version of Deadline has been proposed in [13]. It is a heuristics for job priorities assignment, which behaviour can be configured by the system administrator, who can specify a classification policy. Such policy can be used to express the heuristics required behavior [6], i.e. the priorty distribution the administrator defines as optimal. As target priorities distribution we chose the exponential one, i.e. a distribution in which the number of jobs with priority $p$ is equal to $\theta$-times number of jobs with priority $p - 1$. Where $\theta$ is the distribution *rate parameter*. This permits the system to strongly limit the number of jobs characterized by the highest priority value and, as a consequance, to increase the probability that jobs with high priorities will match their deadline.

The DeadLine heuristics computes each job priority considering a value called *Margin*. It represents the maximum time, expressed in simulator time units, the system can delay the job execution without missing the job deadline.

In order to compute the job *Margin* three values are needed: *job estimated execution time* – an estimation of the time requested to compute the job, *job submission time* – the time at which the job has been submitted to the system, and *job deadline* – the time at which the job has to be completed. *Margin* is computed subtracting from the *job deadline* the sum of *job estimated execution time* and *job submission time*.

To compute the priority value of a job $i$, i.e. $P_i$, DeadLine computes the average margin value, $E[Margin]$, as:

$$E[Margin] = \frac{\sum_{i=1}^{|N|} Margin_i}{N}. \tag{4}$$

where $N$ specifies the number of jobs elaborated by the heuristics before $i$. Such jobs contribute to compute the average margin ($E[Margin]$).

To compute $P_i$, DeadLine considers the double value of average margin ($2 \times E[Margin]$). This value can be considered as a separator between jobs with close deadlines, and the others. The interval $[0; 2 \times E[Margin]]$ is subdivided

**Figure 2:** Graphical representation of *Margin*, *job submission time*, *job estimated execution time*, and *job deadline*.

in a number of subintervals equals to the number of admitted priorities according to the following formula:

$$interval_{(max-k)} = [S_k, S_{k+1}] \text{ with } k = 0, ..., max$$

where $max$ is the highest priority value assignable to a job, and where:

$$\begin{cases} S_0 = 0 \\ S_k = S_{k-1} + MinUnity \cdot 2^k \end{cases}$$

where $MinUnity$ is

$$MinUnity = \frac{2 * E[Margin]}{\sum_{k=1}^{max} 2^k} \tag{5}$$

DeadLine assigns to jobs with a *Margin* value grater than $E[Margin] * 2$ the minimum priority value. This rule has been introduced for completeness.

In this way, Deadlines is able to assign priorities whatever the job Margins are. Even jobs with a longtime deadline can be classsified with a low relevance.

## 5.2    Self-Optimizing DeadLine Heuristics

The static DeadLine heuristics does not compute profitable classification when the job input stream ($js$) is made of job sub-streams ($js_1, js_2, ...$), each of which characterized with a $Margin$ different from the ones characterizing neighbouring substreams. As an example, let we define a stream constituted by two substreams. The first one, made up of jobs characterized by small margin values, and the second one made up of large values. In this case, in the boundary region between the two substreams, with high probability Deadline will assign the lowest priority value to each job belonging to the second substream, violating the target distribution policy. Note that this problem occurs only in the boundary region because the DeadLine heuristics, even in its static form, computes priorities taking its standings on the average $Margin$ value computed considering the last $k$ elapsed jobs. Where $k$ is a configurable parameters.

To avoid this phenomenon, we designed a DeadLine heuristics-based self-optimizing classifier. Such classifier is able to change the item classification according to the past assigned priorities, in order to address the target priority distribution. We enriched the static Deadline heuristics, introducing the $base$ parameter. Acting on the parameter it is possible to change the DeadLine behavior. In particular, we modify the expression (5) as:

$$MinUnity = \frac{2 * E[Margin]}{\sum_{k=1}^{max} base^k}$$

This cause a different partitioning of the $[0, 2 * E[Margin]]$ interval. In particular, higher values of $base$ increase the number of subintervals for low values of $Margin$, whereas values of $base$ belonging to the $(0, 1)$ interval increase the number of subintervals for high values of $Margin$. In order to design our self-optimizing classifier, we exploited the design pattern we propose. We mapped our classifier in the pattern classes organization depicted in Figure 1. The input and output job stream have been mapped respectively with INPUTSTREAM and OUTPUTSTREAM classes. RECONFIGURATOR, DATAREPOSITORY and EVALUATOR classes have been implemented with $Reconf$, $Data$ and $Eval$, respectively. $Data$ contains the classifier historical data about the past jobs. $Eval$ analyzes the priority values contained in $Data$ and returns a new value for the $base$ parameter. $Reconf$ uses the output of $Eval$ to produce a new $[0, 2 * E[Margin]]$ interval partitioning. We developed $Eval$ according to the polytope definition. Our polytope is defined in the vector space $D$ with $P$ dimensions, where $P$ is the number of possible priority values. Each priority distribution, obtained from $h \in H$, is represented with a vector $d = (d_1, ..d_k, .., d_P)$. Each component $d_k$ of $d$ is a value grater than or equal to zero and less than

| #Jobs | Margin Range |
|-------|--------------|
| 2000  | 0-200        |

| #Jobs | Margin Range |
|-------|--------------|
| 400   | 2000-4000    |
| 550   | 0-200        |
| 350   | 2000-4000    |
| 700   | 100-200      |

| #Jobs | Margin Range |
|-------|--------------|
| 500   | 3000-4000    |
| 500   | 100-200      |
| 500   | 500-700      |
| 500   | 100-200      |

First Stream                          Second Stream                          Third Stream

**Figure 3:** Job Streams details

or equal to one ($0 \leq d_k \leq 1 \ \forall_{k=1,...,P}$). It represents the percentage of jobs belongings to historical data $h$ to which the system has assigned the priority $k \in P$. Since each component $d_k$ is a percentage grater than zero and less than one, the sum of all $d_k$ must be equal to one ($\sum_{k=1}^{P} d_k = 1$). We enforce this last constraint by using the Norm ($\|.\|_1$). The polytope is defined as:

$$P = \{d : \|d - d_{target}\|_2 \leq \delta\}$$

It defines a circular region with a radius $\delta$ containing all the priority distributions, which are far from the $d_{target}$ less than $\delta$. The measure of the distance is performed using the Euclidean Norm ($\|.\|_2$). In other words, if $d_{current}$ belongs to the polytope $P$ it means that the distance between $d_{current}$ and $d_{target}$ is less than the fixed radius $\delta$, hence $f_{strategy}$ does not need to be reconfigured, otherwise a new configuration is returned.

## 6.    Experiments

We conducted some tests in order to evaluate the goodness of the Self-Optimizing DeadLine Heuristics (ADH). We applied the classification algorithm to three different job streams. Each one with a different distribution of the $Margin$ value. In the first stream $Margin$ was distributed according to a uniform distribution, whereas in the second and third streams according to a non-uniform one. In particular, both the second and the third streams were characterized by four interleaved sub-streams each of which has a different margin distribution. All tests have been performed using an event-driven simulator. Each simulation step includes: (i) selection and classification of new jobs, (ii) update of the system and heuristics state, (iii) check for correct behavior of the system and (iv) system adaptation. Figure 3 reports the three different streams of jobs we used to tests. Figure 4 reports the results of the first simulation. It's easy to see that the result of both the static heuristics and the self-optimizing heuristics are identical. That is because, the $Margin$ distribution of the stream does not change enough to trigger the ADH intervention. Figures 5 and 6 reports the results of the tests conducted using the second and third streams, respectively. In both the cases, ADH performs better than the original Dead-

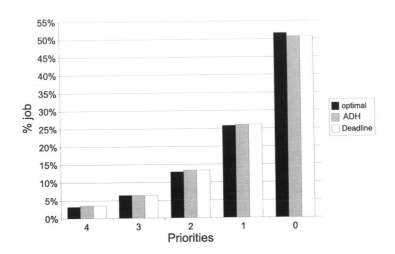

**Figure 4:** Deadline and ADH performances processing the first stream of jobs

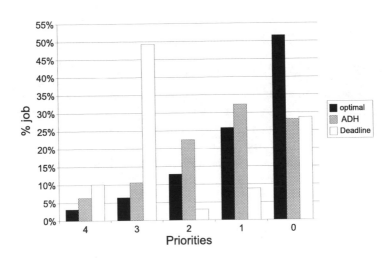

**Figure 5:** Deadline and ADH performances processing the second stream of jobs

Line. Indeed, in most cases the ADH bar is closer to the "optimal" than the Deadline bar. This is because, the original DeadLine heuristics is not able per se to handle rapid and significant changes in the $Margin$ distribution.

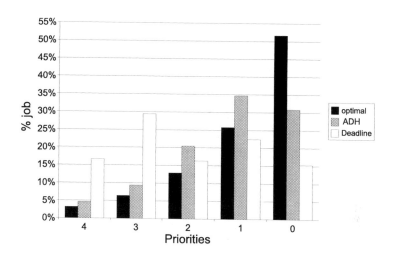

**Figure 6:** Deadline and ADH performances processing the third stream of jobs

# 7.    Related work

Adaptive performance tuning has only recently become conceivable, so only few papers address it directly. Diao et al. [7] analyze how to choose certain parameters of the Apache web server in order to keep CPU and memory usage near a pre-set parameter. The authors make the assumption that there is an optimal setting for those parameters, and make no claim that the parameters impact the performance of the web server in a known way. Bahati et al. define a policy as a notation to express required behavior of systems and applications. In [3], they describe how policies are exploited and how they are realized as actions driving autonomic performance management of an Apache Web server. In [15], Warren e al. describe mechanisms used to realize dynamic reconfiguration respecting a number of fundamental issues when making run-time changes. Their work concerns with preserving an application's integrity during periods of runtime change.They suggest that such mechanisms have to behave according to: (1) the dynamic reconfiguration capability should not compromise applications *integrity/correctness*, (2) the run-time *overhead* introduced by a reconfiguration management facility should be acceptable, (3) the dynamic reconfiguration should be *transparent* to application developers. Their work are particularly concerned with preserving the application integrity during periods of runtime change. They have extended OpenRec (a framework for managing reconfiguration of component-based applications [10]) with functionality, which automatically verifies the structure of an application during periods of dynamic reconfiguration.

Other approaches optimize performance maintaining a fixed level of service [1,5,9]. Abdelzaher et al. [1] outline a system that maintains multiple complete content trees, each with a different quality setting. As workload increases, quality can be decreased in order to satisfy the maximum number of users. Additionally, Cohen et al. [5] use Tree-Augmented Naive Bayesian Networks to correlate system statistics to a high-level performance metric (compliance or non-compliance with required service levels). Unlike our work, this work relies on a specialized instrumentation layer.

Hellerstien et al. [9] analyze the performance of a system over large spans of time with statistical models. In this way they can determine when unexpected behaviors occurred, and they can reconfigure the system. Other works within the field of autonomic computing focus on: file system organization [12], adaptive branch prediction [8], autonomous network creation [4], installation and configuration analysis [2] and utility function optimization [14].

## 8.    Conclusions and Future Works

In this paper we modeled a classification system, and we proposed a new design pattern to implement self-optimizing classifiers. We presented the components, and their interactions that programmers have to implement when designing a self-optimizing classifier. Furthermore, we exploited our design pattern to implement a classifier as a case study. We showed the way our classifier adapts itself to different situations, and we evaluate the proposed solution by comparing its resulting classifications to those computed by a not adapting classifier, elaborating the same job streams. As future works we plan to investigate the feasibility of our solution to complex and real scenarios.

## References

[1]  Tarek F. Abdelzaher, Kang G. Shin, and Nina Bhatti. Performance guarantees for Web server end-systems: A control-theoretical approach. *IEEE Transactions on Parallel and Distributed Systems*, 2002.

[2]  Gagan Aggarwal. On identifying stable ways to configure systems. In *ICAC '04: Proceedings of the First International Conference on Autonomic Computing (ICAC'04)*, pages 148–153, Washington, DC, USA, 2004. IEEE Computer Society.

[3]  Raphael M. Bahati, Michael A. Bauer, and Elvis M. Vieira. Mapping policies into autonomic management actions. *icas*, 0:38, 2006.

[4]  Yu-Han Chang, Tracey Ho, and Leslie Pack Kaelbling. Mobilized ad-hoc networks: A reinforcement learning approach. *icac*, 00:240–247, 2004.

[5]  Ira Cohen, Jeffrey S. Chase, Moisés Goldszmidt, Terence Kelly, and Julie Symons. Correlating instrumentation data to system states: A building block for automated diagnosis and control. In *OSDI*, pages 231–244, 2004.

[6] Patrizio Dazzi, Francesco Nidito, and Marco Pasquali. New perspectives in autonomic design patterns for stream-classification-systems. In *WRASQ '07: Proceedings of the 2007 workshop on Automating service quality*, pages 34–37, New York, NY, USA, 2007. ACM.

[7] Y. Diao, J. L. Hellerstein, S. Parekh, and J. P. Bigus. Managing web server performance with autotune agents. *IBM Syst. J.*, 42(1):136–149, 2003.

[8] Alan Fern, Robert Givan, Babak Falsafi, and T. N. Vijaykumar. Dynamic feature selection for hardware prediction. *J. Syst. Archit.*, 52(4):213–234, 2006.

[9] Joseph L. Hellerstein, Fan Zhang, and Perwez Shahabuddin. Characterizing normal operation of a web server: Application to workload forecasting and problem determination. In *Int. CMG Conference*, pages 150–160, 1998.

[10] J. Hillman and I. Warren. An open framework for dynamic reconfiguration. *ICSE '04: Proceedings of the 26th International Conference on Software Engineering*, page 594–603, 2004.

[11] IBM. Autonomic Computing Initiative. www.ibm.com/autonomic.

[12] Michael Mesnier, Eno Thereska, Gregory R. Ganger, and Daniel Ellard. File classification in self-* storage systems. In *ICAC '04: Proceedings of the First International Conference on Autonomic Computing (ICAC'04)*, pages 44–51, Washington, DC, USA, 2004. IEEE Computer Society.

[13] Marco Pasquali, Ranieri Baraglia, Gabriele Capannini, Laura Ricci, and Domenico Laforenza. A two-level scheduler to dynamically schedule a stream of batch jobs in large-scale grids. In *Proceedings of the 17th HPDC: ACM/IEEE International Symposium on High Performance Distributed Computing*, 2008. Accepted as a Poster.

[14] W. E. Walsh, G. Tesauro, J. O. Kephart, and R. Das. Utility functions in autonomic systems. In *In Proceedings of the 1st International Conference on Autonomic Computing*, May 2004.

[15] Ian Warren, Jing Sun, Sanjev Krishnamohan, and Thiranjith Weerasinghe. An automated formal approach to managing dynamic reconfiguration. In *ASE '06: Proceedings of the 21st IEEE International Conference on Automated Software Engineering (ASE'06)*, pages 37–46, Washington, DC, USA, 2006. IEEE Computer Society.

IV

# GRID MIDDLEWARE

# A TRACE-BASED INVESTIGATION OF THE CHARACTERISTICS OF GRID WORKFLOWS

Simon Ostermann, Radu Prodan, and Thomas Fahringer
*University of Innsbruck, AT*
simon@dps.uibk.ac.at
radu@dps.uibk.ac.at
tf@dps.uibk.ac.at


Alexandru Iosup and Dick Epema
*Delft University of Technology, NL*
A.Iosup@tudelft.nl
D.H.J.Epema@tudelft.nl

**Abstract**    Grid computing promises to enable a reliable and easy-to-use computational infrastructure for e-Science. To materialize this promise, grids need to provide full automation from the experiment design to the final result. Often, this automation relies on the execution of workflows, that is, of jobs comprising many inter-related computing and data transfer tasks. While several grid workflow execution tools already exist, not much is known about their workload. This lack of knowledge hampers the development of new workflow scheduling algorithms, and slows the tuning of existing ones. To address this situation, in this work we present an analysis of two workflow-based workload traces from the Austrian Grid. We introduce a method for analyzing such traces, focused on the intrinsic and on the environment-related characteristics of the workflows. Then, we analyze the workflows executed in the Austrian Grid over the last two years. Finally, we identify six categories of workflows based on their intrinsic workflow characteristics. We show that the six categories exhibit distinctive environment-related characteristics, and identify the categories that are difficult to execute for common workflow schedulers.

**Keywords:**    grid, workload traces, workflow execution, workflow characteristics, statistic analysis

## 1.    Introduction

The grid computing vision aims for an simple useable, dependable, and efficient computing architecture and structure. For this vision to become reality, grids must fully automate the process that starts with experiment design and ends with analysis results. In turn, the full automation necessarily involves the execution of workflows, that is, of jobs with a task graph structure and comprising computing and data transfer tasks [12–13]. While several grid workflow execution engines have recently emerged [17], not much is known about their demand, impacting adversely the evolution of old and new workflow engines. To address this situation, in this work we analyze the workflow-based e-Science applications executed in the Austrian Grid for the past two years.

Currently, there are no publicly available traces of workflow-based grid workloads, that is, of grid workloads that include workflows. This lack of information hampers the testing and the tuning of existing workflow engines, and the study and evolution of new workflow scheduling algorithms. Without proper testing workloads, workflow engines may fail when facing high load or border cases of workload characteristics. Without detailed workload knowledge, tuning lacks focus and leads to under-performing solutions. Without an understanding of real workloads, current research studies use synthetically generated workflows, and are limited in scope and applicability. Moreover, evolution lacks real problems, and may lead to impractical solutions. Understanding the characteristics of existing grid workloads is key to alleviating all these issues. As a first step towards understanding grid workflows, we study two long-term workload traces from the Austrian Grid. The goal of this work is the analysis of the traces and not comparison of their underlaying environment. However, the data alone are insufficient: there is a need for new methods to extract and analyze the workflow characteristics from the workload traces. Furthermore, there is a need to identify the class(es) of workflows for which the execution environment yields distinctively poor performance. Our contribution is threefold:

1  We propose a method for analyzing the intrinsic and the environment-related characteristics of workflow-based grid workloads;

2  We apply the proposed method on two long-term grid workload traces taken from the Austrian Grid;

3  Based on the results of the analysis, we identify six classes of workflows with distinct properties, facilitating the identification of the classes which the execution environments can handle the worst to identify improvement possibilities.

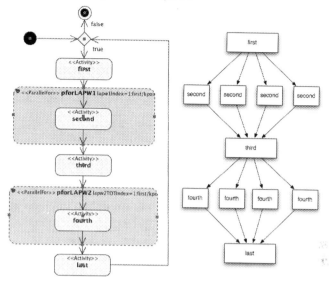

**Figure 1:** A sample workflow: Wien2k [1]. (*left*) in AGWL. (*right*) a possible DAG.

## 2. Background

In this section we present the background information necessary for following this work. We first introduce the workload model used throughout this work. Then, we present DEE and EE2, the workflow engines that executed the workflows investigated in this work.

### 2.1 A Workflow Model

We use for grid workflows the model introduced by Coffman and Graham [12]. Formally, a workflow is a directed graph $G$ in which nodes are computational tasks, and the directed edges represent communication; we denote the number of nodes and edges by $N$ and $E$ respectively. To begin a task, all its predecessor tasks and all communication with that task as the sink must be finished. For simplicity, we consider only directed acyclic graphs (DAGs), that is, there does not exist a loop in the directed graph which may require loop unrolling. We call *root* a node without predecessors; a DAG may have several roots. We further define *a node's level*, derived from breadth-first traversal of the task graph from its roots [2], as the minimal size of a path from the top to this node (in number of edges); the level of a root is 0. Finally, we call the maximum level of a leaf in the graph the *graph level*, which we denote by $L-1$; we denote by $L$ the *graph traversal height*. Note that parameter sweeps and other batches of jobs [10] may be considered as degenerate workflows with $L = 1$, and that master-worker applications can be seen as workflows with $L = 3$ (including a final task to assemble the worker results).

Figure 1 (left) shows a sample workflow from ASKALON [4], defined by the user in the Abstract Grid Workflow Language (AGWL) [5]. Figure 1 (right) depicts an instance of this example that has one iteration of the outermost while loop. The number of nodes $N$ is 11, the number of edges $E$ is 16, and the graph traversal height $L$ is 5.

## 2.2    The ASKALON Workflow Engine

The ASKALON grid middleware [14] can execute via its workflow execution engine workflows specified in AGWL. While execution, this abstract specification is instantiated, that is, the tasks are annotated with details concerning the used resources. ASKALON's workflow execution engine features a fine grain event system which is implemented as WSRF service and allows event-forwarding even through NAT or firewalls. An overview of this and other grid workflow systems can be found in the taxonomy of workflowsystems [17].

In the past two years, the ASKALON workflow execution engine evolved in two major steps. The first version, DEE [3], focused on functionality. DEE's primary shortcomings were the internal loop unrolling from the workflow specification, and the complete scheduling at the start of the execution. To improve on scalability and on adaptability to highly dynamic grid environments, the second generation engine EE2 was developed [16]. The EE2 uses internally a structure that is kept close to the AGWL specification and better scales for the execution of large workflows. Each job that is ready for execution will dynamically be send to the best available grid site at this moment.

## 3.    A Method for Workflow-based Grid Workloads Analysis

In this section we introduce a method for analyzing workflow-based grid workloads. The goal of our analysis is to establish the main characteristics of the workload such that building a workflow-based grid workload model is greatly facilitated. For our method to be applicable, the analyzed traces need to be long-term (i.e. at least a month) and to provide sufficient statistical confidence (i.e., to include at least several hundreds of workflows each). From a technical point of view, we extract for each workflow characteristic a comprehensive set of statistical properties (i.e. min, max, average, std. deviation and quantiles). We also compute the empirical distribution of the characteristics. For an overview of these statistical tools we refer to Jain's classical text [11].

Our method divides the characteristics into two classes, workflow-intrinsic and environment-related. We first analyze the intrinsic workflow characteristics in Section 3.1, which allows us to identify the workflow classes that may have different environment-related characteristics. Then, we analyze the environment-related characteristics for the complete workload data and per class in Section 3.2.

## 3.1 Intrinsic Workflow Characteristics

The intrinsic workflow characteristics refer to the size and the structure of the workflows, and to their arrival pattern. We assume that users are not influenced by the system properties (e.g. size) when defining their workload, and that the submission of the workflows is independent from the state of the system (though the submission of the tasks to the grid by the workflow engine may not be).

To characterize the workflow size and graph structure, we employ the following characteristics (listed in the chronological order of their analysis within our method):

**Number of nodes (N), Number of edges (E), Graph level (L)** ;

**Branching Factor (BF)** defined as the ratio between the number of edges $E$ and the number of nodes $N$. The branching factor may have a high impact on the graph execution time: the higher the branching factor, the higher the probability that a task's execution is delayed due to waiting for its predecessors.

**Work Size** defined as task runtime of a task on a base platform. To compute the task work size we face the problem of data coming from a heterogeneous environment: the same task may take different runtime when executed by different resources. To compute the work size, we normalize the task runtime logged in the workload trace with the ratio between the performance of the resource on which the task is executed and that of a base resource. Following the example of CERN's WLCG, at over 50,000 computing resources the largest grid that publishes size information, we express the resource performance in SPECInt2000 values. SPECInt2000 is a collection of twelve benchmarks representative for industrial and scientific applications [7].

The choice of using the SPECInt2000 values is based on the implicit assumption that this benchmark is representative for the applications executed in the studied workload trace.

**Variability of the work size inside a workflow (WSV)** defined as the ratio between the runtime of the longest and of the shortest task. The higher the variability, the more difficult it is for a task or workflow runtime predictor [18] to operate, leading to potentially low performance for the workflow scheduler.

**Sequential execution path** defined for a workflow as the sum of the work sizes of its tasks;

| Trace | Source | Duration | Number of WFs | Number of Tasks | CPUdays. |
|-------|--------|----------|---------------|-----------------|----------|
| T1 | DEE | 09/06-10/07 | 4,113 | 122k | 152 |
| T2 | EE2 | 05/07-11/07 | 1,030 | 46k | 41 |

**Table 1:** Workflow-based traces analyzed for this work.

**Critical execution path** defined for the longest execution path in the workflow graph. Any delay of a task on this path will result in a delay of the total executions end. [2].

## 3.2 Environment-Related Workflow Characteristics

The environment-related workflow characteristics are time-related (e.g., wait, run, and makespan), scheduler-related (e.g., makespan vs. critical path), and failure-related (e.g., amount of failures).

We employ the following performance metrics:

**Makespan** defined for a workflow as the time elapsed between the workflow's entering and exiting the system.

**Speedup (S)** defined as the ratio between a workflow's makespan and its sequential execution path size.

**Normalized Schedule Length (NSL)** [13], defined as the ratio between a workflow's makespan and its critical path size.

**Success Rate (SR)** defined for a workflow as the percentage of tasks that finished correctly from the workflow tasks.

## 4. The Results

In this section we describe the long-term trace data collected from the Austrian Grid, and the results obtained when applying the method described in the previous section to these data.

## 4.1 The Workload Traces

In this work we use two traces collected from the Austrian Grid over a period of more than one year. The T1 (T2) trace was collected from the system using the DEE (the EE2) as workflow engine (see Section 2.2). Table 1 summarizes the characteristics of the traces used in this work. Each of the traces contains information about more than a thousand workflows, satisfying our analysis method's input requirements.

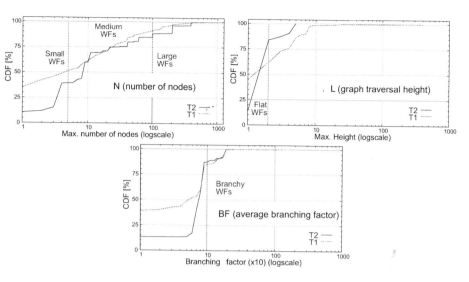

**Figure 2:** The workflow structure for T1 and T2. (*top left*) number of nodes. (*top right*) graph traversal height. (*bottom*) average branching factor.

The collected traces consist mostly of workflow test runs, albeit often of production workflows, done by the developers of the system in order to find bugs and drive development. Thus, the results presented in this section should be regarded as guiding, but not definitive, in establishing the characteristics of the grid workflows.

## 4.2 The Intrinsic Workflow Characteristics

Figure 2[1] shows the graph size and structure of the workflows from both studied traces. The average number of tasks per workflow is $30\pm70$[2] for T1 and $44\pm91$ for T2. The fact that the average is much higher than third quartile (25 and 31 for T1 and T2, respectively) indicates a skewed distribution, confirmed by Figure 2(bottom). For both traces, 75% of the workflows have fewer than 40 tasks, and 95% of the workflows have fewer than 200 tasks. The average branching factor is $0.64\pm0.67$ for T1 and $0.86\pm0.46$ for T2. This indicates that users prefer to submit loosely-coupled tasks, that is, tasks that do not depend on many previous results. Thus, the properties of $N$ and those of $E$ are very similar (we have also validated this finding separately). The graph level is $3.73\pm14.04$ for T1 and $2.25\pm1.0$ for T2, indicating that the new engine is mostly used for

---

[1] All CDF graphs in this paper are discrete as they map real values to their integral part before the accumulation.
[2] We use throughout this work the notation $\mu \pm \sigma$ to denote a set of values with the average $\mu$ and the standard deviation $\sigma$. Note that in some cases the values below or equal to zero are not meaningful, e.g., for the number of tasks in the workflow.

| Class | N | L | BF |
|---|---|---|---|
| Small | <5 | - | - |
| Medium | 5–100 | - | - |
| Large | >100 | - | - |
| Branchy | - | - | ≥1.0 |
| Flat | - | ≤2 | - |

**Table 2:** Classes of workflows based on their size and structure properties.

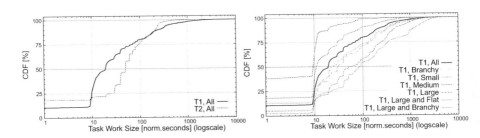

**Figure 3:** The distribution of the work sizes of the workflow tasks. (*left*) overall. (*right*) per workflow class.

graphs with little depth. For T2, slightly over 80% of the workflows have at most two levels.

Based on the results for the graph size and structure and experience from [10], we define the workflow classes summarized in Table 2; mixed classes can also be formed. The Small, Medium, and Large classes refer to the workflow size. The Branchy class contains workflows with more edges than usual. The Flat class contains workflows with at most two levels. Throughout the rest of this work we focus on the following classes: Small/Medium/Large(all the size-related classes), Branchy, Large and Flat, and Large and Branchy.

Figure 3 shows the CDF of the workflow tasks' Work Size, in normalized seconds (the runtime on a machine with a speed of 1000 SPECInt2000). While over 75% of the tasks take less than 100 seconds, the other 25% can take up to 4 hours (half an hour) for T1 (T2). Around 25% of the large and flat tasks took over 350 seconds while only 2% of the small tasks takes longer then 80 seconds. The medium runs have an overall lower task work size compared to the total (all), while the large a higher size.

Figure 4 shows the CDF of the workflow tasks' Work Size variability (see Section 3.1). More than 75% of the workflows have a Work Size variability below an order of magnitude of the task runtime variability. The maximum variability is over 3000 (150) for T1 (T2). Around 95% of the small workflows

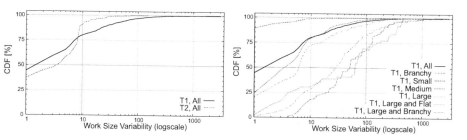

**Figure 4:** The distribution of the work size variability of the workflow tasks. (*left*) overall. (*right*) per workflow class.

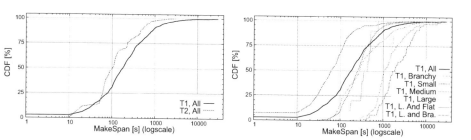

**Figure 5:** The distribution of the makespan of the workflows. (*left*) overall. (*right*) per workflow class.

have a variability smaller then 5 while approximately 20% of all the large workflows have a variability lower then 5.

## 4.3 The Environment-Related Workflow Characteristics

Figure 5 shows the CDF of the workflow makespan. Less than 5% of the T1 workflows take more than one hour; none of the T2 workflows reach one hour. Over 50% of the workflows take less than 4 minutes. As expected large workflows have a higher makespan than short ones.

Figure 6 shows the CDF of the workflow speedup. The average speed-up is 2.54±4.92 for T1 and 8.21±11.11 for T2; the median is 1.15 for T1 and 4.61 for T2. The first quartile value is 0.41 for T1 and 1.70 for T2. This means that for T1 the benefit of executing workflows is in general reduced; also for T1, 25% of the workflows are slowed down by being executed as workflows as opposed to being executed sequentially on a single processor. For T2, the benefits of grid workflow execution are much more visible, with quantile Q1, the median, and the average well above 1. Over 75% of the large and flat workflows were able to achieve a speed up higher then 15. About 50% of the large workflow runs gained a speedup of 9 and higher.

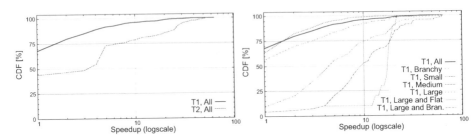

**Figure 6:** The distribution of the speed-up of the workflows. (*left*) overall. (*right*) per workflow class.

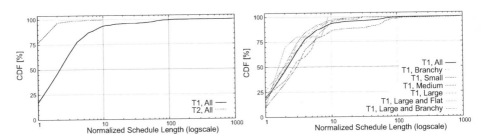

**Figure 7:** The distribution of the normalized schedule length of the workflows. (*left*) overall. (*right*) per workflow class.

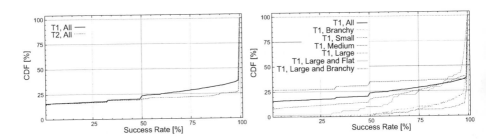

**Figure 8:** The distribution of the success rate of the workflow tasks. (*left*) overall. (*right*) per workflow class.

Figure 7 shows the CDF of the workflow normalized schedule length. The NSL values confirm the findings regarding the speedup (given the high correlation between the number of nodes and the number of edges). The average NSL is 1.72 for T1 and 1.58 for T2. This shows that the system used for T2 has less overheads in total and will be able to execute workflows on the grid more efficient. In the per class view, the large and flat workflows show special behavior as there where runs with short tasks where the overheads account more and longer runs where the total time could compensate the overheads.

Figure 8 shows the CDF of the workflow success rate. The percentage of workflows with a higher success rate then 98% are 65%, respectively 75% for trace T1 and T2. The large and branchy workflows for T1 have reached a success rate of 97% for even 89% of their runs while the large and flat only get more then 95% success rate for 60% of the traced workflows.

## 5. Related Work

There exists a lot work related to workload analysis and modeling for testing, tuning, and resource management design purposes [6, 13, 15, 14, 9, 8, 10].

Following the seminal work of Feitelson [6], several models for workloads of large computing environments have emerged [15, 14]; a comparative analysis of the characteristics of workloads from production grid environments is first presented in [8]. However, none of these research results is targetting workflows. Iosup et al. [10] present an investigation of the properties of batches of jobs (a degenerate case of workflows that is popular in today's grids) in grids.

Synthetic workloads have been used to test functionality in real and simulated environments; most of workflow engines have been tested with such workloads. Workflows from the Standard Task Graphs online archive have been reportedly used to test the ability of a multi-cluster grid to execute workflow workloads [9].

Closest to our work, Kwok and Ahmad propose four models of workflows used for testing in simulation traditional workflow scheduling algorihtms [13]. From these models, one model consists of pathological cases identified by scientists for the purpose of stressing their algorithms, two are synthetic models, and only one is extracted from real workloads. The latter models the flow of two parallel applications. Our analysis presents results that complement this latter model with a much broader application selection base (the real workload traces), and for which we can show the environment-related characteristics of executing these workloads in a real heterogeneous environment (including failures). We also add the workflow task work size as a parameter to model.

## 6. Conclusion and Ongoing Work

Realistic data concerning the characteristics of workflow-based grid workloads is key to the adoption and the evolution of grids, but is not readily available to scientists. To address this issue, in this work we present the characteristics of two long-term traces from the Austrian Grid, a grid environment in which workflows are common.

We introduce a method for analyzing such traces, then apply the method to the two Austrian Grid traces. The method identifies two broad classes of workflow characteristics, intrinsic and environment-related. Based on the observed values for the former, we devise six classes of workflows with distinct properties. The analysis of environment-related characteristics reveals that from the six classes several can be considered classes of "problem-workflows", which exhibit one or all of high variability of the work size of their tasks, high makespan, poor scalability, and higher than normal failure rate. Overall, we find that the workflow speedup is highly dependent on the system used for execution, and that the current task success rate requires more fault tolerance mechanisms, especially for large workflows.

We plan to extend our work with the analysis of other traces. In particular, we hope to find traces that include mostly production workflows submitted by real users. Based on these traces, we will be able to design a model for workflow-based grid workloads. We conclude by addressing the whole grid community with a request for making available their (workflow-based) grid workload traces to other researchers.

## Availability

The traces analyzed in this work are publicly available as part of the Grid Workloads Archive at: `http://gwa.ewi.tudelft.nl/`

## Acknowledgements

This work is supported by the European Union through IST-004265 and IST-2002-004265 CoreGRID and partially carried out in the context of Virtual Laboratory for e-Science project (`www.vl-e.nl`), supported by a BSIK grant from the Dutch Ministry of Education, Culture and Science, and which is part of the ICT innovation program Affairs. This work is co-funded by the European Commission through the EGEE-II project INFSO-RI-031688.

## References

[1] P. Blaha, K. Schwarz, and J. Luitz. WIEN2k, a full potential linearized augmented plane wave package for calculating crystal properties. Austria 1999. ISBN 3-9501031-1-2.

[2] T. H. Cormen, C. E. Leiserson, and R. L. Rivest. *Introduction to Algorithms*. The MIT Press and McGraw-Hill Book Company, 1989.

[3] R. Duan, R. Prodan, and T. Fahringer. Dee: A distributed fault tolerant workflow enactment engine for grid computing. In *HPCC*, volume 3726 of *LNCS*, pages 704–716. Springer-Verlag, 2005.

[4] T. Fahringer, A. Jugravu, S. Pllana, R. Prodan, C. S. Jr., and H. L. Truong. ASKALON: a tool set for cluster and grid computing. *CP&E*, 17(2-4):143–169, 2005.

[5] T. Fahringer, J. Qin, and S. Hainzer. Specification of grid workflow applications with agwl: an abstract grid workflow language. In *CCGrid*, pages 676–685. IEEE CS, 2005.

[6] D. G. Feitelson and L. Rudolph. Metrics and benchmarking for parallel job scheduling. In *JSSPP*, volume 1459 of *LNCS*, pages 1–24. Springer, 1998.

[7] J. L. Henning. Spec cpu2000: Measuring cpu performance in the new millennium. *IEEE Computer*, 33(7):28–35, 2000.

[8] A. Iosup, C. Dumitrescu, D. Epema, H. Li, and L. Wolters. How are real grids used? the analysis of four grid traces and its implications. In *GRID*, pages 262–269. IEEE CS, 2006.

[9] A. Iosup and D. H. J. Epema. Grenchmark: A framework for analyzing, testing, and comparing grids. In *CCGrid*, pages 313–320. IEEE CS, 2006.

[10] A. Iosup, M. Jan, O. Sonmez, and D. Epema. The characteristics and performance of groups of jobs in grids. In *Euro-Par*, LNCS. Springer-Verlag, August 2007.

[11] R. Jain. *The Art of Computer Systems Performance Analysis: Techniques for Experimental Design, Measurement, Simulation, and Modeling,.* May 1991.

[12] E. G. C. Jr. and R. L. Graham. Optimal scheduling for two-processor systems. *Acta Inf.*, 1972.

[13] Y.-K. Kwok and I. Ahmad. Benchmarking and comparison of the task graph scheduling algorithms. *J. PDC*, 59(3):381–422, 1999.

[14] H. Li, D. L. Groep, and L. Wolters. Workload characteristics of a multi-cluster supercomputer. In *JSSPP*, volume 3277 of *LNCS*, pages 176–193. Springer-Verlag, 2004.

[15] U. Lublin and D. G. Feitelson. The workload on parallel supercomputers: modeling the characteristics of rigid jobs. *J. PDC*, 63(11):1105–1122, 2003.

[16] K. Plankensteiner. EE2: A high performance execution engine for scientific workflows on Clusters and the Grid. U.Innsbruck, Master Thesis, 2008.

[17] J. Yu and R. Buyya. A taxonomy of scientific workflow systems for grid computing. *ACM SIGMOD Rec.*, 34(3):44–49, 2005.

[18] F. Nadeem, R. Prodan, and T. Fahringer. Optimizing Performance of Automatic Training Phase for Application Performance Prediction in the Grid. In *HPCC*, pages 309–321, 2007.

# CORE SERVICES FOR GRID MARKETS

Pablo Chacin*, Xavier Leon, Rene Brunner, Felix Freitag and Leandro Navarro
{pchacin,xleon,rbrunner,felix,leandro}@ac.upc.edu
*Computer Architecture Department,*
*Technical University of Catalonia, Spain*

**Abstract**     Markets are a powerful model for the coordination of distributed systems and, in particular, in the face of incomplete information and changing environments. The application of markets for the resource allocation in grid systems has recently been researched as an alternative to traditional approaches. However, the proper implementation of sophisticated markets capable of handling diverse trading models (various auctions types, bargaining) and structures (direct negotiation, brokering, etc.) requires a set of supporting services to provide participants a proper environment to engage in negotiations. Grid Market Middleware (GMM) is a framework that aims to ease the development of market based grid systems. In this paper we present its architecture, the services it provides and describe how they can be used to implement diverse market models. We also discuss our experience with the implementation of prototypes for various core services.

**Keywords:**     Grid Market, Economic Models, Middleware.

---
*Corresponding author. Phone:+34(93)405 40 59, Fax:+34(93)401 70 55

# 1.　Introduction

Markets are decentralized, goal-oriented mechanisms for allocating resources among competing interests while meeting some general goal, like the global utility of the users. A distributed system set up along market rules can adapt to changes in the environment, variations in the demand or supply of resource, or disturbances to individual members [10]. Therefor, many projects have explored market approaches for resource allocation (See [24] for a recent survey).

Despite of this interest, there is a significant absence of general-purpose frameworks to develop market oriented systems. Most of the proposed frameworks are specific of a market model (e.g. a specific type of auctions) or problem domain (e.g. logistic optimization, robotics), or are not suited for large scale fully decentralized deployments.

The intent of the Grid Market Middleware project (GMM)[1] is to provide such a generic framework. More specifically, the GMM aims to address the problems of a general infrastructure for decentralized markets, a scalable architecture and a high level programming abstractions independent of the market model. This work is based on our experience implementing market based resource allocation middleware for Application Layer Networks and its integration with grid applications [5, 13], and in our ongoing effort to implement the foundations for a grid market in the context of the SORMA[2] and Grid4All[3] European projects.

In this paper we present the design of the GMM's core services and how they can be used to implement diverse market models. The document is organized as follows: section 2 presents the general model of a GMM based grid market. Section 3 presents the general architecture and introduces its main components. Section 4 shows how diverse market models can be implemented using the GMM. Finally, section 5 presents some related work and 6 presents our conclusions and future work.

# 2.　Model

The general model of a GMM based grid market can be seen in figure 1. In this model, we differentiate three main components: (a) participants, which engage in economic exchanges to sell/buy/allocate resources, (b) the Economically Enhanced Resource Managers (EERM), which manage those resources and (c) Core Services that provides generic support functionalities for market oriented systems and a programming interface that facilitates the implementation of the participants and the EERM.

---

[1] http://recerca.ac.upc.edu/gmm
[2] http://www.sorma-project.eu
[3] http://www.grid4all.eu

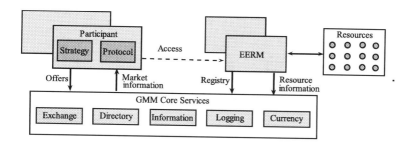

**Figure 1:** Model for a GMM based grid market.

Participants are agents (in the general sense) that act on behalf of resource providers, resource consumers, or mediate between them. Participants are responsible for gathering and evaluating market information and deciding their strategies to sell/buy (e.g. pricing). GMM does not make any special distinction among sellers and buyers. This is important to allow a participant to become an intermediary, buying resources and then reselling them and behave as a mediator (broker, arbiter) or a market maker which improves the scalability of the market and improves its liquidity [4].

Markets require a resource allocation mechanism [11], a protocol to allocate resources among participants. This mechanism can be embedded in the buyers and sellers themselves (when they use direct bargaining or single side auctions for trading) or might also be run as a separate participant (when auctioneers are used). GMM does not enforce any mechanism, but it does enforce the primitive messages on which such mechanisms could be implemented. This unifies the programming interface for agents and allows the application of policies at the middleware level, such as content based routing and filtering.

The EERM provides the capabilities to access grid resources from the grid market. It registers resources in the market and provides information about its availability and relevant performance metrics, which is integrated with the market information. EERM also serves as a gateway to access resources, verifying that the intended access are backed by a previous agreement between the parties (provider and consumer). The EERM is in large part platform dependent and is therefore not provided by the GMM. However, the interfaces to integrate it into the market are provided by the GMM.

## 3. Architecture

GMM's architecture has been designed under two guiding principles: (a) integrate under a common framework the services related to information gathering and dissemination in decentralized market and (b) take advantage of the functionalities provided by P2P overlays to organize a distributed system and

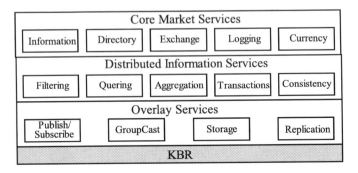

**Figure 2:** Architecture of the GMM

allow efficient communications and decentralization. The resulting architecture is arranged in four main layers:

- **Core Market Services:** market specific services that supports the development of participants, enabling them to engage in negotiations for resources.

- **Distributed Information Services:** generic services that allows an efficient management of information in fully decentralized deployments. Offers services for processing queries and their responses, filtering messages, aggregating information and ensuring consistency and transactional access to critical data.

- **Overlay Services:** provides sophisticated communication and cooperation mechanisms like publish/subscribe, group casting, distributed storage of data items (DHT), and replication of critical elements .

- **KBR:** offers a Key Based Routing mechanism to communicate different nodes based on logical, location independent keys [7].

In this paper we focus on the components of the Core Services Layer, which are explained below:

**Exchange Service.** Provides a trading infrastructure designed to support different market-based systems. It defines a set of primitive messages that can be used to implement complex negotiation protocols and provides transparent message routing among participants. The utilization of these market primitives allows the Market Exchange to accommodate different market models, even simultaneously and ensures that the infrastructure can apply rules for routing, validation and security. It also frees the participants from the need to validate each received message.

**Market Directory Service.** Provides a decentralized, market wide registry for participants of the market (providers, consumers) and the resources/services being traded. It offers a generic framework on which diverse specialized strategies can be plugged to adapt and optimize the discovery to the characteristics such as the density of resources and its distribution in the network [12], and support diverse query languages.

**Market Information Service.** Provides current aggregated information and historical statistics of market indicators, under publish/subscribe and query interfaces. Examples of such information are the level of activity in a market (indicated by the number of available products and the volume of traded products) and the current maximum, minimum or average price for a resource type. Trader agents will rely on this information to create or adapt their internal strategy like choosing the right market to negotiate for resources, finding the right time to enter or create markets, and to propose competitive bids.

**Logging Service.** Keeps a registry of the transactions occurred during a particular negotiation, and maintains the negotiation state across restarts of the Exchange Service. It can be used for accounting, dispute resolution and security purposes. To achieve these goals, it offers a secure and reliable storage of the messages that were exchanged during a negotiation. Transactions can be retrieved using the negotiation id or the specific transaction id as a key. More complex queries are not currently considered but can be implemented by indexes which can be stored internally in the DHT Layer (following a model similar to that of [9]) or in external repositories like relational databases.

**Currency Service.** Is a distributed banking service for the Grid which enables users to perform and receive payments for resource usage and sharing using a virtual currency (g-currency), without incurring in the cost of real payment mechanisms (fees and taxes). It can be used to control the behavior of participants, offering incentives for providers to share their resources and for clients to give a reliable valuation of their jobs. It also serves as an overall regulation system, by restricting users with a limited purchase power leading to price contention during peak demand periods

## 4.    Implementing Markets

The Market Exchange Service is organized around the basic concept of Exchange Sessions, which are a gathering mechanism that allow participants to engage in Negotiations to interchange Offers about the session's underlying subject (e.g. execution rights on a particular server) and potentially reach Agreements. An Offer represents the terms that the participant proposes for the negotiation. An Agreement is the confirmation that two parties agree on their mutual offers. Notice that session's subject are abstracts, and can refer to anything, from resources to be allocated to tasks to be executed.

The programming model for the Market Exchange Service is an asynchronous, event based model. It is based on two interfaces: the session handler and the negotiation handler. The combination of session and negotiation level handlers offers a versatile framework to implement diverse negotiation control policies. The participants obtain from an external source a reference to the session and join it specifying a negotiation handler that will handle this negotiations events.

In the next sections we show how this programming model can be used to implement two very different markets: a direct bargaining and an auction. These examples were chosen to show the flexibility of the model.

## 4.1    Implementing bargaining

This scenario (see figure 3(a)) is the simplest one: one of the participants starts a one-to-one negotiation with another participant creating a Session with an initial offer. The owner and the participant then exchange a series of offers until they both agree on the terms. The session handler can be used to implement an admission policy, to control, for example, that there is only one active negotiation at a time.

## 4.2    Implementing a double auction

In a double side auction (see figure 3(b)), the auctioneer doesn't make offers, but is just a facilitator that matches the offers sent by participants. These participants play complementary roles, such as sellers and buyers (as in the example below) or task requesters and task executors. This market is therefore a many-to-many negotiation. At the closing time, the auctioneer looks at all the offers and matches them according to an optimization criterion. When it finds a pair of matching offers, it exchanges the offers of the participants. For example, it sends the sellers offer to the buyer and vice versa. This causes two agreements to be formed between seller and buyer (one seller-buyer and the other buyer-seller), but those agreements are identical to any purpose.

## 5.    Related Work

There are, to our knowledge, few generic frameworks for developing grid markets. GridBus [3] is framework which provides a set of tools for the development, execution and management of grid applications using economic mechanisms. The main difference with GMM is that GridBus relies on the meta-scheduler model, on which users submits jobs (using a portal) to a economic scheduler which takes the allocation decisions based on the user supplied information, including budget. This model is more appealing for commodity markets. GMM, on the other hand, supports this model (even when it does

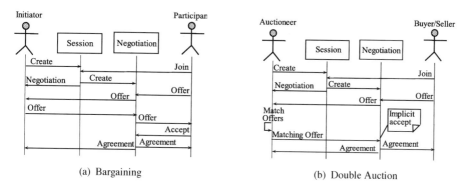

**Figure 3:** Implementation Markets

not provides a meta-scheduler) but also allows more open setups on which users submits jobs through agents that negotiate in one or more markets, better accommodating non commodity markets.

There has also been an important work in the development of market based agents in general [22] and for grid resource negotiation in particular [18–19]. However, these works generally focused on how to achieve desirable characteristics on individual agents (the strategies) or the negotiation protocols (the market mechanisms), but paid little attention to the infrastructure actually needed to run a market for grid resources. GMM is intended to provide such infrastructure and facilitate the transition from prototype to actual utilization in real grid environments of such agents.

With respect of the individual components of the GMM, we briefly summarize some relevant work below.

**Exchange.** OCEAN [15] is a software infrastructure to automated commercial resource exchange over the Internet. It offers an optimized P2P search protocol to find a set of potential sellers and the automatic negotiation of those resources based on rules defined in a XML format. The ability to define negotiation rules is a remarkable characteristic of OCEAN that allows the adaptation of the economic model to diverse applications. PeerMart [8] implements double auction over a P2P overlay network to distribute the auctioneer onto a clusters of peers, each being responsible for brokering several services. Its main limitation is the tightly integration of auction models in the framework.

**Directory.** The Grid Market Directory [25] is a SOAP based service which relies on a centralized repository and offers a simple matchmaking capability suited for undifferentiated commodities. The GMM's Market Directory, on the other hand, is fully decentralized and is designed to support non-commodity, specialized resources. DyMRA [14] considers a decentralized, DHT based,

Market Directory but it does not naturally supports complex multi-attribute and range queries needed in grid environments, even when those can be achieved extending its DHT's basic mechanisms [17].

**Information.** The Market Information Service integrates a publish-subscribe model with aggregation, filtering of routing messages, an important issue addressed in modern P2P systems. Systems like SDIMS [23] and Willow [16] uses DHTs specifically designed for this purpose. GMM's MIS, in the other hand, is built on top of a generic, unmodified DHT, which facilitate porting it to other DHT infrastructures. It also provides flexibility through a simple API that lets applications control propagation of queries and the aggregation of data.

**Logging.** [21] introduce publish/subscribe transactions for atomic production, delivery, and processing of asynchronous event notifications. As a general transaction management service, it incurs in a considerable overhead to maintain the atomicity of transactions. GMM's Logging, in the other hand, has been optimized to maintain a reliable log of activities under the control of a single Exchange Service instance. Distributed Log Service (DiLoS) [1] assigns log files within a given scope (for type of service, geography, hierarchy, etc.) to a service instance, which stores it and disseminate to other instances in other scopes for redundancy. Its main drawback is the static organization of the services in scopes, while the GMM's Logging Service uses DHT's intrinsic characteristics to fulfill this requirements transparently and dynamically.

**Currency.** In PeerMint [8] and Karma [20] the bank role is distributed among a set of untrusted peers which conform the whole system, using protocols to overcome malicious peer's interferences and achieve consistency. Both systems suffer of performance and scalability issues due to the overhead generated by their reliable protocols. GridBank [2] is a centralized bank extensible to whatever kind of payment deployed in e-commerce. It implements a resource usage mechanism by means of RURs (Resource Usage Record) which helps in the task of accounting what resources have been consumed by which users. Its scalability and efficiency is questionable due to its centralized architecture.

## 6.    Conclusions and Future Work

The Grid Market Middleware provides a number of core services for building sophisticate market mechanisms in Grids. Its main contribution is the simplification of the development of market based resource allocation mechanisms, without imposing restriction in the market models being used or the implementation of agent's strategies. In this paper we have shown how different market models such as bargaining and auctions can be implemented upon the GMM.

GMM's architecture takes advantage of overlay networks to support fully decentralized market models and achieve scalability and tolerance to failures and changes in the application level network topology. This way we address two main limitations of existing market based approaches: its centralization and inadequacy to open, continuously evolving environments.

We have implemented prototypes of various GMM services (exchange, currency, information, directory) and our initial experiences show that they greatly simplify the implementation of diverse market based resource allocation mechanisms. The prototypes were initially implemented separately, as part of the diverse projects we have been engaged. As we have learned more about both their particular traits and common ground, we have started to integrate them under the architecture shown in this paper, although there are several secondary issues to resolve such as the use of diverse overlays, each suited to the service's particular needs. As has also been noted in [6], one of the main challenges is how to implement the services using only a generic overlay infrastructure, without harming its performance.

Future work on the GMM also includes the development of high level programming models and abstractions to ease the development of participant agents, hiding most of the actions in the process of searching, ranking and negotiation with other agents, and making them policy based.

## Acknowledgments

This work was supported in part by the European Union under contracts Grid4All EU IST-FP6-034567 and SORMA EU IST-FP6-034286, and the the Ministry of Education and Science of Spain under Contract TIN2007-5614-C03-01 (P2P-GRID).

## References

[1] C. de Alfonso, M. Caballer, J. V. Carrin and V. Hernndez. Distributed General Logging Architecture for Grid Environments. *In High Performance Computing for Computational Science Conference: Selected and invited papers*, LNCS 4395, 2007.

[2] A. Barmouta and R. Buyya. Gridbank: a grid accounting services architecture for distributed systems sharing and integration. *In Parallel and Distributed Processing Symposium*, April 2003.

[3] R. Buyya and S. Venugopal. The Gridbus toolkit for service oriented grid and utility computing: an overview and status report. *1st IEEE International Workshop on Grid Economics and Business Models (CECOM)*, 2004

[4] Bai, X., Sivoncik, K., Turgut, D., Boloni, L. Grid Coordination with Marketmaker Agents. *International Journal of Computational Intelligence*, 3(2), 2006

[5] P. Chacin, F. Freitag, L. Navarro, I. Chao, O. Ardaiz. Integration of Decentralized Economic Models for Resource Self-Management in Application Layer Networks. *Second IFIP TC6 International Workshop on Autonomic Communications*, Athens, Greece, October 3-5, 2005

[6] Y. Chawathe, S. Ramabhadran, S. Ratnasamy, A. LaMarca, S. Shenker, J. Hellerstein. A case study in building layered DHT applications. *Proceedings of the 2005 Conference on Applications, technologies, Architectures, and Protocols for Computer Communications*, 2005

[7] F. Dabek, B. Zhao, P. Druschel, J. Kubiatowicz, I. Stoica. Towards a Common API for Structured Peer-to-Peer Overlays. *2nd International Workshop on Peer-to-Peer Systems*, LNCS 2735, 2003

[8] D. Hausheer, B. Stiller. PeerMart: The Technology for a Distributed Auction-based Market for Peer-to-Peer Services. *40th IEEE International Conference on Communications (ICC 2005)*, Seoul, Korea, May 2005.

[9] R. Huebsch, J.M. Hellerstein, N. Lanham, B.T. Loo, S. Shenker and I. Stoica. Querying the internet with PIER. *Proceedings of the 29th international conference on Very large data bases*, 2003

[10] B. A. Huberman and T. Hogg. Distributed Computation as an Economic System. *Journal of Economic Perspectives*, 9(1):141-152, 1995.

[11] Hurwicz, L. The Design of Mechanisms for Resource Allocation. *The American Economic Review*, 63(2), 1973

[12] A. Iamnitchi, I. T. Foster On Fully Decentralized Resource Discovery in Grid Environments. *Proceedings of the Second International Workshop on Grid Computing*, p.51-62, 2001

[13] L. Joita, O.F.Rana, P. Chacin, I. Chao, F. Freitag, L. Navarro, O. Ardaiz. Application Deployment on Catallactic Grid Middleware. *IEEE Distributed Systems Online* 7(12), Dec. 2006

[14] D. Lzaro, X.Vilajosana and J. M. Marqués. DyMRA: Dynamic Market Deployment for Decentralized Resource Allocation. *On the Move to Meaningful Internet Systems Workshops*, LNCS vol 4805, 2007

[15] P. Padala, C. Harrison, N. Pelfort, E. Jansen, M. P Frank and C. Chokkareddy. OCEAN: The Open Computation Exchange and Arbitration Network, A Market Approach to Meta computing. *In proceedings of the International Symposium on Parallel and Distributed Computing (ISPDC'03)*, Oct 2003

[16] R. van Renesse and A. Bozdog. Willow: Dht, aggregation, and publish/subscribe in one protocol. *In Proceedings Third International Workshop on Peer-To-Peer Systems*, LNCS 3279, 2004.

[17] J. Risson and T. Moors. Survey of research towards robust peer-to-peer networks: search methods. *Computer Networks: The International Journal of Computer and Telecommunications Networking*, Vol 50(17). 2006.

[18] Kwang Mong Sim. From market-driven agents to market-oriented grids (position paper). *ACM SIGecom Exchanges, Vol. 5(2)*. 2004.

[19] H. Tianfield. Towards agent based grid resource management. *Proceedings of Fifth IEEE International Symposium on Cluster Computing and the Grid (CCGrid'05)*. 2005

[20] V. Vishnumurthy, S. Chandrakumar, and E. Sirer.Karma: A secure economic framework. *In Proceedings of the Workshop on the Economics of Peer-to-Peer Systems*, June 2003.

[21] L. Vargas, L.I. W. Pesonen, E. Gudes, J.Bacon. Transactions in Content-Based Publish/-Subscribe Middleware. *27th International Conference on Distributed Computing Systems Workshops*, 2007

[22] . M.P. Wellman.Market-Aware Agents for a Multiagent World. *Proceedings of the 8th European Workshop on Modelling Autonomous Agents in a Multi-Agent World. LNCS* Vol. 1237. Springer, 1997.

[23] P. Yalagandula and M. Dahlin. A scalable distributed information management system. *SIGCOMM Computer Communications Review*, 34(4):379-390, 2004.

[24] C. S. Yeo and R. Buyya. A Taxonomy of Market-based Resource Management Systems for Utility-driven Cluster Computing. *Software: Practice and Experience (SPE)*, 36(13):1381-1419, Wiley Press, New York, USA, Nov. 2006.

[25] J. Yu, S. Venugopal and R. Buyya. A Market-Oriented Grid Directory Service for Publication and Discovery of Grid Service Providers and their Services. *The Journal of Supercomputing*, 36(1), Springer, 2006.

# MINING@HOME: PUBLIC RESOURCE COMPUTING FOR DISTRIBUTED DATA MINING

D. Barbalace, C. Lucchese, C. Mastroianni, S. Orlando, D. Talia

*DEIS, University of Calabria, Rende, Italy*
*ISTI, C.N.R., Pisa, Italy*
*ICAR, C.N.R., Rende, Italy*
*Department of Computer Science, University of Venice, Italy*

barbalace@si.deis.unical.it, c.lucchese@isti.cnr.it, mastroianni@icar.cnr.it, orlando@dsi.unive.it, talia@deis.unical.it

**Abstract**    Several kinds of scientific and commercial applications require the execution of a large number of independent tasks. One highly successful and low cost mechanism for acquiring the necessary compute power for these applications is the "public-resource computing", or "desktop Grid" paradigm, which exploits the computational power of private computers. So far, this paradigm has not been applied to data mining applications for two main reasons. First, it is not trivial to decompose a data mining algorithm into truly independent sub-tasks. Second, the large volume of data involved makes it difficult to handle the communication costs of a parallel paradigm. In this paper, we focus on one of the main data mining problem: the extraction of *closed frequent itemsets* from transactional databases. We show that is possible to decompose this problem into independent tasks, which however need to share a large volume of data. We thus introduce a *data-intensive computing network*, which adopts a P2P topology based on super peers with caching capabilities, aiming to support the dissemination of large amounts of information. Finally, we evaluate the execution of our data mining job on such network.

**Keywords:**    Public Resource Computing, Desktop grids, Data Mining, Closed Frequent Itemsets, Peer-to-Peer Computing

## 1.    Introduction

In this work we aim to explore the opportunities offered by the volunteer computing paradigm for making feasible the execution of compute-intensive data mining jobs that have to explore very huge data sets.

On the one hand, during recent years, volunteer computing has become a success history for many scientific applications. In fact, Desktop Grids, in the form of volunteer computing systems, have become extremely popular as a mean to garnish many resources for a low cost in terms of both hardware and manpower. Two of the popular volunteer computing platforms available today are BOINC and XtremWeb.

BOINC [2] is by far the most popular volunteer computing platform available today, and to date, over 5 million participants have joined various BOINC projects. The core BOINC infrastructure is composed of a scheduling server and a number of clients installed on users' machines. The client software periodically contacts a centralized scheduling server to receive instructions for downloading and executing a job. After a client completes the given task, it then uploads resulting output files to the scheduling server and requests more work. The BOINC middleware is especially well suited for CPU-intensive applications but is somewhat inappropriate for data-intensive tasks due to its centralized nature that currently requires all data to be served by a group of centrally maintained servers. BOINC was successfully used in projects such as Seti@home, Folding@home, and Einstein@home.

XtremWeb [4][7] is another Desktop Grid project that, like BOINC, works well with "embarrassingly parallel" applications that can be broken into many independent and autonomous tasks. XtremWeb follows a centralized architecture and uses a three-tier design consisting of a worker, a coordinator, and a client. The XtremWeb software allows multiple clients to submit task requests to the system. When these requests are dispensed to workers for execution, the workers will retrieve both the necessarily data and executable to perform the analysis. The role of the third tier, called the coordinator, is to decouple clients from workers and to coordinate tasks execution on workers.

On the other hand, due to the exponential growth of the information society, data mining applications need to deal with larger and larger amounts of data, so that, in the future, they will likely become large scale and expensive data analysis activities. However, the nature of data mining applications is very different from usual "@home" applications. First, they are not easily decomposable into a set of small independent tasks. Second, they are data-intensive, that is any sub-task needs to work an a large portion of data. These two issues make it very challenging to distribute sub-tasks to volunteer clients. In fact, neither BOINC or XtremWeb does utilize ad hoc algorithms for the propagation of large amounts of data. Nevertheless, we believe that data mining may take advantage of a volunteer computing framework in order to accomplish complex tasks that would be otherwise intractable.

In this paper we focus on the *closed frequent itemsets mining problem* (CFIM). This requires to extract a set of significant patterns from a transactional dataset, among the ones occurring not less than a user defined threshold.

We also introduce a novel *data-intensive computing network*, which is able to efficiently carry out our mining task by adopting a volunteer computing paradigm. The network exploits caching techniques across a super-peer network to leverage the cost of spreading large amounts of data to all the computing peers.

Some previous efforts aimed at exploiting Grid functionalities and services to support distributed data mining algorithms. Grid Weka [8] and Weka4WS [10] extend the Weka toolkit to enable the use of multiple computational resources when performing data analysis. In those systems, a set of data mining tasks can be distributed across several machines in an ad-hoc environment. However, they do not use any decentralized or peer-to-peer technique to improve scalability and fault-tolerance characteristics.

We used an ad hoc simulator, fed with statistics concerning a real CFIM application, in order to evaluate our data-intensive computing network. To the best of our knowledge, this is the first time that the deployment of a complex data mining task over a large distributed peer-to-peer network is shown to be effective.

## 2.     Parallel Mining of Closed Frequent Itemset

Frequent Itemsets Mining (FIM) is a demanding task common to several important data mining applications that look for interesting patterns within databases (e.g., association rules, correlations, sequences, episodes, classifiers, clusters). The problem can be stated as follows. Let $\mathcal{I} = \{a_1, ..., a_M\}$ be a finite set of *items* or *singletons*, and let $\mathcal{D} = \{t_1, ..., t_N\}$ be a dataset containing a finite set of *transactions*, where each transaction $t$ is a subset of $\mathcal{I}$. We call $k$-itemset a set of $k$ items $I = \{i_1, ..., i_k \mid i_j \in \mathcal{I}\}$. Given a $k$-itemset $I$, let $\sigma(I)$ be its *support*, defined as the number of transactions in $\mathcal{D}$ that include $I$. Mining all the frequent itemsets from $\mathcal{D}$ requires to discover all the itemsets having a support greater or equal to a given minimum support threshold $\overline{\sigma}$. We denote with $\mathcal{L}$ the collection of frequent itemsets, which is indeed a subset of the huge search space given by the power set of $\mathcal{I}$.

State-of-the-art FIM algorithms visit a lexicographical tree spanning over such search space, by alternating *candidate generation*, and *support counting* steps. In the candidate generation step, given a frequent itemset $X$ of $|X|$ elements, new candidate $(|X| + 1)$-itemsets $Y$ are generated as supersets of $X$ that follow $X$ in the lexicographical order. During the counting step, the support

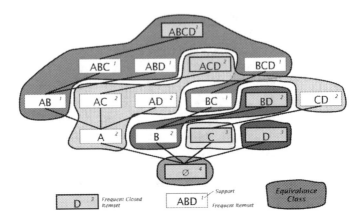

**Figure 1:** Lexicographic spanning tree of the frequent itemsets, with closed itemsets and their equivalence classes, mined with $\overline{\sigma} = 1$ from the dataset $\mathcal{D} = \{\{B, D\}, \{A, B, C, D\}, \{A, C, D\}, \{D\}\}$.

of such candidate itemsets is evaluated on the dataset, and if some of those are found to be frequent, they are used to re-iterate the algorithm recursively.

The collection of frequent itemsets $\mathcal{L}$ extracted from a dataset is usually very large. This makes the task of the analyst hard, since he has to extract useful knowledge from a huge amount of patterns, especially when very low minimum support thresholds are used. The set $\mathcal{C}$ of closed itemsets [11] is a concise and lossless representation of frequent itemsets that has replaced traditional patterns in all the other mining tasks, e.g. sequences and graphs.

DEFINITION 1 *An itemset $I$ is said to be* closed *iff*
$$c(I) = f(g(I)) = f \circ g(I) = I$$
*where the composite function $c = f \circ g$ is called* Galois operator *or* closure operator, *and the two functions $f$,$g$ are defined as follows:*
$$f(T) = \{i \in \mathcal{I} \mid \forall t \in T, i \in t\}, \qquad g(I) = \{t \in \mathcal{D} \mid I \subseteq t\}$$

The closure operator defines a set of equivalence classes over the lattice of frequent itemsets: two itemsets belong to the same equivalence class *iff* they have the same closure, i.e. they are supported by the same set of transactions. Closed itemsets are the maximal elements of these equivalence classes (see Fig. 2).

It comes from Definition 1 that it is not easy to find the closure of a pattern: either we need a global knowledge of the dataset or a global knowledge of the collection of frequent itemsets and their equivalence classes. For this reason, it is not easy to desing a parallel CFIM algorithm.

The first algorithm for mining closed itemsets in parallel, MT-CLOSED [9], was proposed very recently. Analogously to other CFIM algorithms, MT-

CLOSED executes two scans of the dataset in order to initialize its internal data structures. A first scan is needed to discover frequent single items, denoted with $\mathcal{L}^1$. During a second scan, a vertical bitmap representing the dataset is built by considering frequent items only. The resulting bitmap has size $|\mathcal{L}^1| \times |\mathcal{D}|$ bits, where the $i$-th row is a bit-vector representation of the tid-list $g(i)$ of the $i$-th frequent item.

The kernel of the algorithm consists in a recursive procedure that exhaustively explores a subtree of the search space given its root. The input of this procedure is a seed closed itemset $X$, and its tid-list $g(X)$[1]. Initially, $X = c(\emptyset)$, and $g(X) = \mathcal{D}$. Similarly to other CFIM algorithms, given a closed itemset $X$, new candidates $Y = X \cup i$ are created according to the lexicographic order. If a candidate $Y$ is found to be frequent, then its clusure is computed and $c(Y)$ is used to continue the recursive traversal of the search space.

Every single closed itemset $X$ can be thought as the root of a sub-tree of the search space which can be mined independently from any other (non overlapping) portion of the search space. Note that this is a peculiarity of MT-CLOSED. We refer to $J = \langle X, g(X), \mathcal{D} \rangle$ as a *job description*, since it identifies a given sub-task of the mining process.

Thus, it is possible to partition the whole mining task into independent regions, i.e. sub-trees of the search space, each of them described by a distinct job descriptor $J$. One easy strategy would be to partition the search space according to frequent singletons. We would obtain $|\mathcal{L}_1|$ independent jobs. Unfortunately, especially with dense datasets, it is very likely that one among such jobs has a computational cost that is much higher than all the others.

Among the many approaches to solve this problem, an interesting one is [5]. First the costs of the jobs associated with the frequent singletons are estimated by running a mining algorithm on significant samples of the dataset. Then, the most expensive jobs are split on the basis of the 2-itemsets they contain.

In our setting, we are willing to address very large datasets. In this case, the large number of resulting samplings to be performed and their costs make the above strategy not suitable. Therefore, our choice is to avoid any expensive pre-processing.

First, in order to obtain a fine-grained partitioning of the search space, we will materialize jobs on the basis of the 2-itemsets in the cartesian product $\mathcal{L}^1 \times \mathcal{L}^1$. This produces a large number of jobs and sufficient degrees of freedom to evenly balance the load among workers.

Second, we will consider the opportunity to group together jobs, when their number is too large. Notice that a set of 1,000 frequent singletons results in about 500,000 jobs. Since such a large number of jobs will introduce a large

---

[1]The input should also include the set of items used to calculate closures, which is not described here because of space constraints. Please refer to [9].

overhead, we will group together $k$ consecutive jobs, where $k$ is a system-wide configuration parameter. We group together two consecutive jobs only if they share the same prefix. For instance, $\{ab\}$ and $\{ac\}$ may be grouped together, while $\{az\}$ and $\{bc\}$ may not.

The reason for this constraint is given by the *partitioning optimizations* usually adopted in mining algorithm that we want to use in our caching strategies. Suppose that a job corresponds to the mining of all the itemsets beginning with the a given item $i$: then any transaction that does not contain $i$ can safely be disregarded. This technique significantly reduces the amount of data to be processed by a single job. This also explains why we only group 2-itemsets having the same prefix: we group jobs together only if the share the same projection of the data.

This data projection approach is very important in our framework. We can reduce the amount of data needed to accomplish a given job, and therefore the amount of data to be sent through the netowork.

## 3.     A Data-Intensive Computing Network

We already proposed a preliminary framework for data dissemination suitable scenarios (e.g., processing of astronomical waveforms, analysis of audio files [1]) in which the partition of an application into independent jobs is trivial and the input dataset is the same for all the tasks. Here, the algorithm is adapted for the CFIM data mining problem, in which the specification of independent jobs is obtained through the MT-CLOSED algorithm and the input dataset may be different for different jobs.

Our algorithm exploits the presence of a super-peer network for the assignment and execution of jobs, and adopts caching strategies to make the data distribution more efficient. Specifically, it exploits the presence of different types of nodes that are available within a super-peer topology, as detailed in the following:

- the *Data Source* is the node that stores the entire data set that must be analyzed and mined.

- the *Job Manager* is the node in charge of decomposing the overall data mining application in a set of independent tasks, according to the MT-CLOSED algorithm. This node produces a *job advert* document for every task, which describes its characteristics and specifies the portion of the data needed to complete the task. This node is also responsible for the collection of output results.

- the *Miners* are the nodes that are available for job execution. A miner first issues a *job query* and a *data query* to retrieve the a job and the corresponding data.

- *Data-Cachers* are super-peers having the additional ability to cache data and the associated data adverts. Data cachers can retrieve data from the data source or other data cachers, and later provide such data to Miners.
- *Super-Peers* nodes constitute the backbone of the network. Miners connect directly to a Super-Peer, and Super-Peers are connected with one another through a high level P2P network. Super-peers play the role of *rendezvous nodes*, i.e. meeting places for job or data providers and consumers. They match Miners' queries with *job* and *data adverts*.

In order to execute our data mining algorithm, the network works as follows (see Fig. 2). A set of *job adverts* are generated by the *Job Manager* node. A job advert corresponds to the job descriptor discussed in the previous section. An available miner $M$ issues a *job query* (step 1), that travels across the super-peer interconnections, to the Job Manager. A matching *job advert* is sent back to $M$ (setp 2). Thanks to the *job advert*, the miner is also informed of the data necessary to complete its job. Thus, it issues a *data query* to discover a Data-Cacher (step 3). Since multiple Data-Cachers may answer (step 4), the miner selects the nearest one and gives it the responsibility to retrieve the required input data. In our example, the selected Data-Cacher $DC_1$ (step 5) does not hold the data neede by $M$, and issues a query to the data source $DS$ or to the other Data-Cachers (step 6). Eventually, $DC_1$ retrieves the data from $DS$ (step 7), stores it and provides it to the miner $M$ (step 8). In the future, $DC_1$ will be able to provide the same data to other miners or to other Data-Cachers. Finally, the miner $M$ executes the job.

Our implementation includes a number of techniques that can speed up the execution, depending on the state of the network and the dissemination of data. For example, in the case that the cacher $DC_1$ has already downloaded data, steps

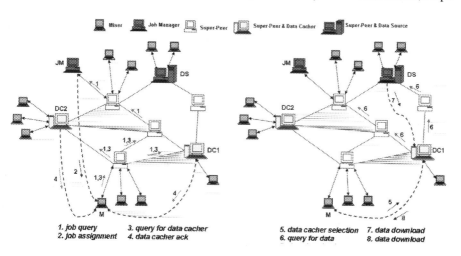

**Figure 2:** Caching algorithm in a sample super-peer network.

6 and 7 are unnecessary. Also, once a Miner has discovered the Job Manager or a Data-cacher, it could decide to contact them directly without paying the cost of sending a message across the Super-Peers network. More interestingly, a miner may have the ability to store some data. In the following, we discuss this aspect and introduce two possible caching scenarios on the miner side.

The presence of data cachers helps the dissemination of data and can improve the performance of the network. It is also useful to verify if miners themselves could give a contribution to speed up computation, in the case that they have the ability and they are willing to store some input data (in general, the public resource computing paradigm does not require hosts to store data after the execution of a job). In fact, it often happens that the input data of a job overlaps, completely or partially, with the input data of another job executed previously. Therefore, the miner could retrieve the whole data set when executing the first job, and avoid to issue a data query for the subsequent job. On the other hand, if miners have no storage capabilities, they have to download the associated input data for each job they have to execute. Therefore, two different caching strategies have been analyzed and compared:

- **Strategy #1: miners cannot store data.** The miner downloads from the data cacher only the portion of the data set that it strictly needs for job execution, and discards this data after the execution.
- **Strategy #2: miners can store data.** The miner downloads from the data cacher the entire data set the first time that it has to execute a job. Even though the miner will only use a portion of this data set, data will be stored locally and can be used for successive job executions.

Depending on the application, these simple strategies may be significantly improved. One possible approach could be to use the information present in the job adverts, in order to retrieve only those transactions of the dataset that the miner does not already store. Indeed, a wide range of opportunities is open.

## 4.    Performance Evaluation

We used an event-based simulation framework (similar to that used in [1]) to analyze the performance of our super-peer protocol. In the simulation, the running times of the jobs were obtained by actually executing the serial algorithm MT-CLOSED on specific data, and measuring the elapsed times. To model a network topology that approximates a real P2P network as much as possible, we exploited the well known power-law algorithm defined by Albert and Barabasi [3]. The bandwidth and latency between two adjacent super-peers were set to 1 Mbps and 100 ms, respectively, whereas the analogous values for the connections among a super-peer and a local miner were set to 10 Mbps and 10 ms. If during the simulation a node (e.g., a data source or a data cacher) needs to simultaneously serve multiple communications (with different miners),

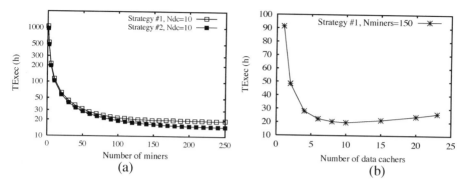

**Figure 3:** (a) Running time vs. number of mining peers (10 data cachers). (b) Running time vs. number of of data cachers (150 mining peers).

the bandwidth of each communication is obtained by dividing the downstream bandwidth of the server by the number of simultaneous connections.

The input dataset used to measure the running times of the various MT-CLOSED jobs is Synth2GB, which has about 1.3 millions transactions and 2.5 thousands distinct items, for a total size of 2 GB. It was produced by using the IBM dataset generator. By running the algorithm with a minimum absolute support threshold of 50,000, we obtained the info about 469,200 jobs, that were later grouped by 100 to reduce the total number of jobs. The time needed to complete the mining on a single machine was about ten hours. In order to simulate a very expensive mining task, we multiplied the running time of each job by a factor of 100. This is perfectly reasonable, since the time needed to execute a job increases exponentially when decreasing the minimum support threshold.

Figure 3(a) shows the overall running time on varying the number of mining peers by using strategies #1 and #2, in case of 10 data cachers. It is worth noting that, by using multiple distributed miners, the execution time decreases from over 1000 hours to about 20 hours when exploiting strategy #1. With strategy #2, according to which miners can store data in their own cache, the execution time is further reduced. Each miner downloads the entire data set to execute before executing the first job, and then reuses the data for all the following jobs.

The plot of Figure 3(a) also shows that when strategy #1 is adopted, an appropriate number of miners is 150, since the overall time does not decrease if additional miners are available. Of course, the "optimal" number of miners strictly depends on the problem, which impact on data sizes and job processing times.

Also the number of available data cachers has an important influence on the overall execution time. To analyze this issue, in Figure 3(b) we report the execution time obtained with strategy #1 and 150 active miners, on varying the number of data cachers. The execution time decreases as the number of data cachers increases from 1 to 10, since miners can concurrently retrieve data from different data cachers, thus decreasing the length of single download operations. However, the execution time increases again as more than 10 data cachers are made available. The main reason is that many of these data cachers retrieve data directly from the data source, so that the downstream bandwidth of the data source is shared among a large number of connections. Results show that the time needed to distribute data to more than 10 data cachers is not compensated by the time saved in data transfers from data cachers to miners. Therefore an "optimum" number of data cachers can be estimated. This number is 10 in this case, but in general depends on the application scenario, for example on the number and length of the jobs to execute.

## 5.  Conclusions

In order to test our volunteer network, we chose a very tough data mining task. In particular, the extraction, in a reasonable time, of all the (closed) frequent patterns from a huge database, with low minimum support. This is only feasible if we can exploit a multitude of computing nodes, like those made available by our volunteer network. Due to the features of the embarrassingly parallel tasks obtained, which require to effectively distribute large sets of similar data to the miner peers, we tested an efficient data distribution technique based on cooperating super-peers with caching capabilities. The first simulated tests of our network, for which we used parameters obtained from real runs of our data mining application, are very promising.

Our approach for distributing large amounts of data across a P2P data mining network, opens up a wide spectrum of opportunities. In fact P2P data mining a recently gained lots of interest. Not only because of the computing power made available by volunteer computing, but also because of new emerging scenarios, such as sensor networks, where data are naturally distributed, and nodes of the network are not reliable. Even if many P2P data mining algorithms, such as clustering [6] and feature extraction [12], have been developed, still they suffer the cost of data dissemination. Not only our approach alleviates this cost, but it can easily deal with failure and load balancing problems. For these reasons we believe that our proposed data-intensive computing network may be a bridge towards P2P computing for other data mining applications dealing with large amounts of data, e.g. web documents clustering, or dealing with a distributed environment, e.g. analysis sensor data.

Many directions for future works are open. Among them, we can mention: (i) the adoption of more advanced strategies to disseminate and cache data in the P2P network, (ii) the use of the volunteer computing paradigm to solve even more challenging data mining problems and (iii) the testing of the presented approach on a real distributed platform.

# References

[1] Al-Shakarchi, E., Cozza, P., Harrison, A., Mastroianni, C., Shields, M., Talia, D., and Taylor, I. (2007). Distributing workflows over a ubiquitous p2p network. *Scientific Programming*, 15(4):269–281.

[2] Anderson, D. P. (2004). Boinc: A system for public-resource computing and storage. In *GRID '04: Proceedings of the Fifth IEEE/ACM International Workshop on Grid Computing (GRID'04)*, pages 4–10.

[3] Barabási, A.-L. and Albert, R. (1999). Emergence of scaling in random networks. *Science*, 286(5439):509–512.

[4] Cappello, F., Djilali, S., Fedak, G., Herault, T., Magniette, F., Neri, V., and Lodygensky, O. (2005). Computing on large-scale distributed systems: Xtrem web architecture, programming models, security, tests and convergence with grid. *Future Generation Computer Systems*, 21(3):417–437.

[5] Cong, S., Han, J., and Padua, D. A. (2005). Parallel mining of closed sequential patterns. In *KDD '05: Proceedings of the eleventh ACM SIGKDD international conference on Knowledge discovery in data mining*, pages 562–567.

[6] Datta, S., Bhaduri, K., Giannella, C., Wolff, R., and Kargupta, H. (2006). Distributed data mining in peer-to-peer networks. *IEEE Internet Computing*, 10(4):18–26.

[7] Fedak, G., Germain, C., Neri, V., and Cappello, F. (2001). Xtremweb: A generic global computing system. In *Proceedings of the IEEE Int. Symp. on Cluster Computing and the Grid*, Brisbane, Australia.

[8] Khoussainov, R., Zuo, X., and Kushmerick, N. (2004). A toolkit for machine learning on the grid. ERCIM News No. 59.

[9] Lucchese, C., Orlando, S., and Perego, R. (2007). Parallel mining of frequent closed patterns: Harnessing modern computer architectures. In *ICDM '07: Proceedings of the Fourth IEEE International Conference on Data Mining*.

[10] Talia, D., Trunfio, P., and Verta, O. (2005). Weka4ws: A wsrf-enabled weka toolkit for distributed data mining on grids. In *Proc. of the 9th European Conference on Principles and Practice of Knowledge Discovery in Databases (PKDD 2005)*, Porto, Portugal.

[11] Wille, R. (1982). Restructuring lattice theory: an approach based on hierarchies of concepts. In Rival, I., editor, *Ordered sets*, pages 445–470, Dordrecht–Boston. Reidel.

[12] Wurst, M. and Morik, K. (2007). Distributed feature extraction in a p2p setting: a case study. *Future Gener. Comput. Syst.*, 23(1):69–75.

# HLA COMPONENT BASED ENVIRONMENT FOR DISTRIBUTED MULTISCALE SIMULATIONS

Katarzyna Rycerz
*Institute of Computer Science, AGH, al. Mickiewicza 30,30-059 Kraków, Poland*
kzajac@agh.edu.pl


Marian Bubak
*Institute of Computer Science, AGH, al. Mickiewicza 30,30-059 Kraków, Poland*
*Academic Computer Centre – CYFRONET, Nawojki 11,30-950 Kraków, Poland*
bubak@agh.edu.pl


Peter M.A. Sloot
*Faculty of Sciences, Section of Computational Science, University of Amsterdam*
*Kruislaan 403, 1098 SJ Amsterdam, The Netherlands*
sloot@science.uva.nl

**Abstract**    In this paper we present the Grid environment that supports application building basing on a High Level Architecture (HLA) component model. The proposed model is particularly suitable for distributed multiscale simulations. Original HLA partly supports interoperability and composability of simulation models, where interactions between modules (federates) in a simulation system (federation) are defined and set by federates themselves. On the contrary, in the proposed component model the particular behavior of component and it's interactions with others are defined and set by an external module (e.g. builder) on the user request which is more flexible and increases reusability of components. We also propose to integrate our HLA component solution with the Grid which will allow users working on distributed simulations to more easily exchange the models already created. The focus of this paper is on design of the HLA component. We show how to insert simulation logic into a component and make possible to steer from outside its interactions with other components. Its functionality is shown on the example of multiscale simulation of a stellar system.

**Keywords:**    Components, Grid computing, HLA, distributed simulation

## 1. Introduction

Environments supporting application building from existing software components on the Grid are an interesting topic of research. In this paper we would like to propose such environment oriented towards distributed simulations consisting of modules of different time and space scale (multiscale). The paper describes a High Level Architecture (HLA) component model that defines software modules comprising application to be build.

We have choosen HLA [5] as it is a standard for large scale distributed interactive simulations. and offers many advanced features specific for such applications (like time, data and ownership management). There is an ongoing research of making solutions provided by HLA more scalable and efficient in distributed environments. One worth to be mentioned is a service oriented HLA RTI (SOHR) framework [11], which provides the functionalities of an RTI as Grid services and enables large scale distributed simulations to be conducted on a heterogeneous Grid.

HLA also offers the ability of plugging and unplugging various simulation models ( also with different internal types of time management) to/from a complex simulation system. Additionally, HLA introduces a uniform way of description of events and objects being exchanged between federates. Also, HLA separates communication runtime infrastructure (RTI) from actual simulation. All these features can be used to create HLA-based component model, where components are independent simulation modules that can be dynamically joined into a coherent whole. The difference between the component view proposed in this paper and an original HLA approach is that the behavior of component and it's interactions are defined and set by an external module on the user request. In original HLA, the interactions between federates in a federation are defined and set by federates themselves. The proposed approach is more flexible and increases reusability of components as it separates component developers from the users wanting to set up particular distributed simulation system from existing components. It also differs from other popular component models (e.g. CCA [1]), as the federates are not using direct connections. Instead, all federates within federation are connected together using HLA tuple space, which they can use for interaction (e.g. subscribing and publishing events and data objects). The federates can also make use of advanced time management provided by HLA, which is particularly useful for multiscale simulations.

In this paper we propose to build the Grid environment that will support HLA component model. We are using Grid technology [7, 18], as it is oriented towards joining geographically distributed communities of scientists working on similar problems - this will allow users working on distributed simulations to more easily exchange the models already created. Therefore, the attempt to integrate HLA with new possibilities given by both Grid and component technologies is a promising approach. As a Grid platform hosting HLA components we have chosen H2O environment [7].

In this paper we focus on the design of HLA component itself. We show how to insert simulation logic into a component and how to make it possible to steer its interactions with other components from outside. The functionality of the system is shown on the example of multiscale simulation of a dense stellar system.

The approach described in this paper is directed to the users that want to create new multiscale simulation systems from existing components or join their own new component to the multiscale system. For the users that have they own HLA application and want to run it almost unaltered efficiently using the Grid, we suggest to apply the solution elaborated in our previous work [14], where we have focused on execution management of existing legacy HLA applications and the best usage of available Grid resources, which can be achieved by using provided migration and monitoring services.

This paper is organized as follows: in Section 2 we outline related work, in Section 3 we describe the HLA component model. Section 4 presents the idea of the Grid support system for such model and the design and implementation of a HLA component - the element of the designed system responsible for storing simulation logic and enabling steering its interactions with others from outside of it. Section 5 presents experiment with example multiscale simulation of a dense stellar system. Summary and future plans are described in Section 6.

## 2. Related Work

Building application from existing software modules is a wide range topic. This issue includes defining interoperable and reusable pieces of software – services and component technologies. The most popular services standards include Web Services [17] and its extension with stateful resources [18]. The most important component standards are: Common Component Architecture (CCA)[1] (with its implementations like XCAT[6] or MOCCA [8]), Fractal [2] and its extension - Grid Component Model [10] (with its implementation ProActive [13]). However, none of this models provides advanced features for distributed multiscale simulations. In particular they do not support advanced time management mechanism, which in our model is achieved by integrating mechanism provided by HLA with component solutions. An important approach to using services and component technology to distributed simulations is described in [3]. However, the proposed solution is addressed in general to distributed simulations, without special focus on multiscale simulations systems. Another worth to be mentioned component framework for simulations [12] is specifically designed for partial differential equations.

## 3.    HLA Component Model

As already mentioned in the previous Section, one of the important features of HLA is the ability of plugging and unplugging pieces of functionality to/from a complex application. In that sense it is possible to create a HLA–based component model. Unlike popular component models (e.g. CCA [1]), the federates are not using direct connections (e.g. in CCA one component is connected with other component, when its *uses port* is connected with partner's *provides port*). Instead, all federates within federation are connected together using tuple space, which takes care of sending the appropriate data from the publisher to the subscriber. HLA also includes advanced time management mechanism that allows to connect federates with different internal time management together. It is possible for federates to dynamically subscribe/unsubscribe and publish/unpublish their data as well as dynamically change their use of time management. Additionally, these decisions can not only be taken by the actual federate itself, but also by other federate that can steer subscription/publication mechanism of others.

All these features allow to think about a HLA component as about an entity that can be joined to a set of other components (the set represents a federation) and interact with them by publish/subscribe mechanism of exchanging data and using HLA time management if necessary. If needed, each component can also be executed independently of others. The presented model will be especially useful for the applications that would benefit from HLA (mainly distributed simulations). Because of advanced HLA time management facility that enables to join components of different internal time management and scale, it would be particularly useful for multiscale simulations, on which we would like to focus.

The difference between a component view proposed in this paper and an original HLA approach is that the particular behavior of component and it's interactions with others are defined and set by an external module on the user request. This enables the user to create federations from federates developed by others without changing their implementation. The particular federation, in which a federate is going to take part, does not need to be defined by a federate developer, but can be created later – from outside – in the process of setting up distributed simulation system. Therefore the presented approach increases reusability and composability of simulations.

## 4.    Grid system supporting HLA components

In this paper we would like to propose a solution that would support the HLA component model on the Grid. The user will be able to decide how components will interact with each other (e.g. by setting up appropriate subscription/publication and time management mechanism). The user also will be

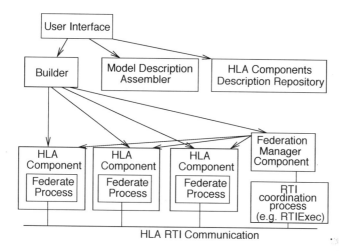

**Figure 1:** Grid system supporting HLA–based component model.

able to plug/unplug components and change nature of their interactions during simulation runtime. Fig.1 shows the proposed support for HLA component model (CompoHLA). Apart from the actual HLA communication level, there is a Grid level consisting of following elements:

**Builder** – sets up a simulation system on behalf of the user. It uses Federation Management Component to create federation and instructs HLA Components to join it. It also can instruct chosen components to set appropriate time management mechanism and subscribe or publish chosen data objects or events.

**HLA Component Description Repository** – stores description of components - including information about data objects and interactions that the component can exchange with others (which is called Simulation Object Model), the type of time management that makes sense for this component and additional information that may be useful for the user that wants to set up multiscale system (e.g. units of produced data, scale of simulation time, if rollback is possible, how subscription for particular data affects simulation, average execution time etc.).

**Model Description Assembler** - produces Federation Object Model needed to start federation from given Simulation Object Models of components that will comprise simulation system.

**Federation Manager Component** - manages whole federation on the component level and sets up connection with coordination process for federations.

**HLA Components** – wrap actual functionality of federates into components (described later in this section)

The relations between system elements is shown in the Fig.1. A user can use the HLA Components Description Repository and the Model Description As-

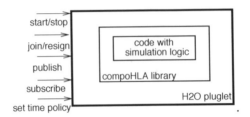

**Figure 2:** Relationship between component's developer code (simulation logic), HLA RTI implementation and compoHLA library.

sembler to build a federation description and pass it to the Builder that sets up the federation from appropriate HLA Components. The user than can dynamically change nature of interactions between components using the Builder.

**HLA Component in CompoHLA.** As described in Section 3, a HLA component should be able to be joined to/resigned from federation as well as be able to react on user requests to subscribe/publish appropriate data and use time management mechanism if necessary. In this paper, we present HLA component prototype that is designed as entity that can be requested to join the federation and then to resign from it during component lifetime. Independently from being joined/disjoined each component can be started and stopped during its lifetime. In [16] we described how the user can change interactions (subscription/publication and time management) between components during lifetime. As a Grid framework we have chosen the H2O [7] platform as it is lightweight and enables for dynamic remote deployment. A HLA component is implemented as a H2O pluglet having requests to start, stop, join, resign (described in this paper) and requests to change publications, subscriptions as well as type of time management (described in [16]). The component developer has to provide a simulation logic code which is connected with a pluglet by interfacing the compoHLA library as shown in the Fig.2. The purpose of compoHLA library is to simplify use of HLA time management and data exchange mechanisms for component developers. It also allows HLA component to be steered from outside (by external requests as described above).

The more detailed relations in the form of a simplified class diagram between HLA RTI, the compoHLA library and a developer code (simulation logic) are shown in the Fig.3. The CompoHLA library introduces two classes with abstract methods that should be overridden by component developer. One is a `CompoHLASimulator` class, from which the developer has to inherit and point to the main function starting a simulation. There is also a `CompoHLADataObject` class that has to be inherited for each data object that is going to be published/- subscribed by the federate and be visible outside for an external user (who is going to chose this component to be connected to his simulation system).

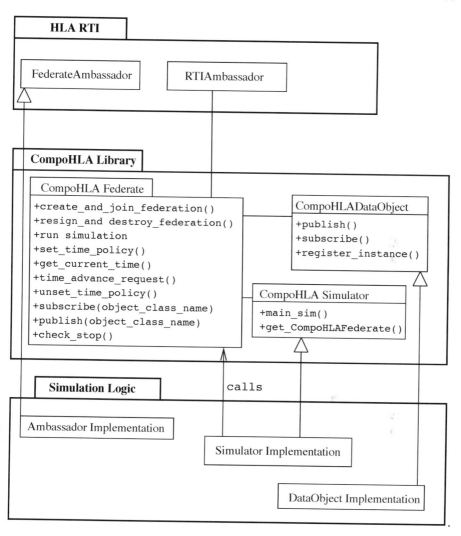

**Figure 3:** Simplified class diagram illustrating relations between crucial classes of HLA RTI, compoHLA library and component developer code (simulation logic).

The developer has to specify how the actual simulation data fits into HLA data objects that could possibly be exchanged with other federates.

The simulation developer can also call methods of a CompoHLAFederate class which, in turn, uses HLA a RTIambassador class (main class providing HLA services). The methods include getting info about federate time and requests of time advance as well as checking if stop request came (in order to perform final operations before the simulation exit).

A developer has also to override `FederateAmbassador` class callbacks (there are used by RTI to communicate with a developer code e.g. when receiving data from other federates) as in an original RTI federate. The use of the compoHLA library does not free the developer from understanding HLA time management and data exchange mechanisms, but simplifies use of them and allows a HLA component to be steered from outside (by external requests as described above).

## 5. Experiments with MUSE

For the purposes of this research we have used simulation modules of different time scale taken from Multiscale Multiphysics Scientific Environment (MUSE)[9] for simulating dense stellar systems like globular clusters and galactic nuclei. The original MUSE consists of the Python scheduler and three simulation modules of different time scale: stellar evolution (in macro scale), stellar dynamics (nbody simulation - in meso scale) and hydro dynamics (simulation of collisions - in micro scale). Also, there are plans to add additional modules. For the purposes of this paper, we have chosen to make components from two MUSE modules: evolution (macro scale) and dynamics (meso scale) that run concurrently. The simulation system has to make sure that dynamics will get update from evolution before it actually passes the appropriate point in time. The HLA time management mechanism [5] of *regulating* federate (evolution) that controls time flow in *constrained* federate (dynamics) could be there very useful.

In [15] we have compared sequential execution of chosen MUSE modules with their distributed execution using HLA on the Grid. We have shown that the such distribution can be beneficial for described application. In particular, we have shown the usefulness of HLA advanced time management for this kind of simulations. In this paper we would like to test mechanism that allows HLA Components to be accessible to the external user wanting to set up the simulation system from existing dynamics and evolution components created by someone else.

**Performance Results.** We have created two prototype HLA components for dynamics and evolution simulations and measured execution time of requests to them. In our implementation we have used H2O v2.1 and HLA Certi implementation v3.2.4. Experiments were done on Dutch Grid DAS3 [4]. The RTI control process was run on Grid node at the Amsterdam Free University the dynamics component at University of Amsterdam, the evolution component at Delft, and the client was run at Leiden University. The bandwidth between Grid sites is 10Gbps and latency (measured by ping) is around 2 ms.

We have tested following scenario: start dynamics – start evolution – join dynamics to federation – join evolution to federation – resign dynamics – resign

| Request | avr time, sec | $\sigma$ |
|---|---|---|
| start dynamics | 0.008 | 0.001 |
| start evolution | 0.009 | 0.001 |
| join dynamics | 0.181 | 0.003 |
| join evolution | 0.52 | 0.08 |
| resign dynamics | 0.006 | 0.0004 |
| resign evolution | 0.007 | 0.0003 |
| stop dynamics | 0.3 | 0.2 |
| stop evolution | 0.2 | 0.2 |

**Table 1:** Time of HLA Component request execution for evolution and dynamics components taken from MUSE [9]

evolution – stop dynamics – stop evolution. In [16] one can find results of experiments with changing interactions – subscription/publication and time management – between components during lifetime.

Tab.1 shows results of this experiment (average of 10 runs). $\sigma$ indicates standard deviation. In general, execution time of all requests are small. The start, stop and resign requests are similar for both modules. However, as we can see, realization of join request by second component is longer then by first component. This can be explained by the fact that joining to the federation that already have some members requires to make connections to these members. These overhead depends on the HLA implementation, not the design of the HLA component. Also performance of stop request requires explanation. The request does not stop the simulation immediately, but sends requests to the simulation and waits for it to check if that request came (we would like to give the control to the component developer and let him to save the results of a simulation, if necessary). Therefore, the execution time of stop request can vary depending on this waiting time. This is illustrated by quite large standard deviation. To summarize, execution times of all requests are promising and show that component layer does not introduce much overhead, but we have to have in mind factors independent on the HLA Component design (overhead of particular HLA implementation and the frequency of checking if the stop request came in the component developer code).

# 6. Summary and Future Plans

Our previous work [14] was directed to the users that want to run their own legacy multiscale simulation that uses HLA on the Grid. In this paper we have presented the idea of a HLA component model, which enables the user to dynamically compose/decompose distributed simulations from multiscale elements residing on the Grid. We have also shown the architecture of the system supporting such model and build preliminary prototype of a HLA component that stores simulation logic and makes possible to steer from outside its interactions with other components. This approach differs from that in original HLA, where all decisions about actual interactions are made by federates themselves. The functionality of the prototype is shown on the example of multiscale simulation of a dense stellar system – MUSE environment [9]. The results of the experiment show that that component layer does not introduce much overhead. In the future we plan to fully design and implement other modules of the presented support system.

## Acknowledgments

The authors wish to thank Maciej Malawski for discussions on component models and Simon Portegies Zwart for valuable discussions on MUSE. This research was also partly funded EU IST Project CoreGRID and the Polish State Committee for Scientific Research SPUB-M.

## References

[1] R. Armstrong, G. Kumfert, L. C. McInnes, S. Parker, B. Allan, M. Sottile, T. Epperly, and T. Dahlgren. The CCA component model for high-performance scientific computing. *Concurr. Comput. : Pract. Exper.*, 18(2):215–229, 2006.

[2] E. Bruneton, T. Coupaye, and J.-B. Stefani. Recursive and dynamic software composition with sharing. In *Proceedings of Seventh International Workshop on Component-Oriented Programming*, June 2002.

[3] X. Chen, W. Cai, S. J. Turner, Y. Wang: SOAr-DSGrid: Service-Oriented Architecture for Distributed Simulation on the Grid. Principles of Advanced and Distributed Simulation (PADS) 2006: 65-73

[4] The Distributed ASCI Supercomputer 3 web page http://www.cs.vu.nl/das3

[5] IEEE Standard for Modeling and Simulation (M&S) High Level Architecture (HLA), 2004. http://standards.ieee.org/catalog/olis/compsim.html.

[6] S. Krishnan and D. Gannon. XCAT3: A Framework for CCA Components as OGSA Services. In *Proc. Int. Workshop on High-Level Parallel Progr. Models and Supportive Environments (HIPS)*, pp. 90–97, Santa Fe, NM, USA, 2004.

[7] D. Kurzyniec, T. Wrzosek, D. Drzewiecki, and V. S. Sunderam. Towards Self-Organizing Distributed Computing Frameworks: The H2O Approach. *Parallel Processing Letters*, 13(2):273–290, 2003.

[8] M. Malawski, D. Kurzyniec, and V. S. Sunderam. MOCCA - Towards a Distributed CCA Framework for Metacomputing. In *19th International Parallel and Distributed Processing Symposium (IPDPS 2005), CD-ROM / Abstracts Proceedings, 4-8 April 2005, Denver, CA, USA*, 2005.

[9] MUSE Web page http://muse.li/

[10] OASIS team: Proposals for a Grid Component Model CoreGRID project Technical report, 2004. http://www.coregrid.net

[11] K. Pan, S.J. Turner, W. Cai and Z. Li: A Service Oriented HLA RTI on the Grid in: Proceedings of IEEE International Conference on Web Services, 2007 - ICWS 2007, 9-13 July 2007, Salt Lake City, UT, pp. 984-992

[12] S.G. Parker. A Component-Based Architecture for Parallel Multi-physics PDE Sim ula-tion. Future Generation Computer Systems, 22(1-2):204–216, 2006.

[13] ProActive project homepage. http://www-sop.inria.fr/oasis/ProActive/.

[14] K. Rycerz, M. Bubak, P.M.A. Sloot, V. Getov: Problem Solving Environment for Dis-tributed Interactive Simulations in: S. Gorlatch, M. Bubak, and T. Priol (Eds). Achieve-ments in European Reseach on Grid Systems. CoreGRID Integration Workshop 2006 Springer, 2008, pp 55 - 66.

[15] K.Rycerz, M. Bubak, P.M.A. Sloot Using HLA and Grid for Distributed Multiscale Simu-lations Proceedings of International Conference of Parallel Processing and Applied Math-ematics (PPAM'07), Gdansk, September 2007, LNCS (to appear).

[16] K.Rycerz, M. Bubak, P.M.A. Sloot Dynamic Interactions in HLA Component Model for Multiscale Simulations. Proccedings of International Conference on Computational Science, ICCS 2008. (to appear)

[17] Web Services. http://www.w3.org/2002/ws/.

[18] Web Services Resource Framework. http://www.globus.org/wsrf.

# Author Index